celebrating artistic vision

SPLASH 12

THE BEST OF WATERCOLOR

edited by
Rachel Rubin Wolf

NORTH LIGHT BOOKS
CINCINNATI, OHIO
www.artistsnetwork.com

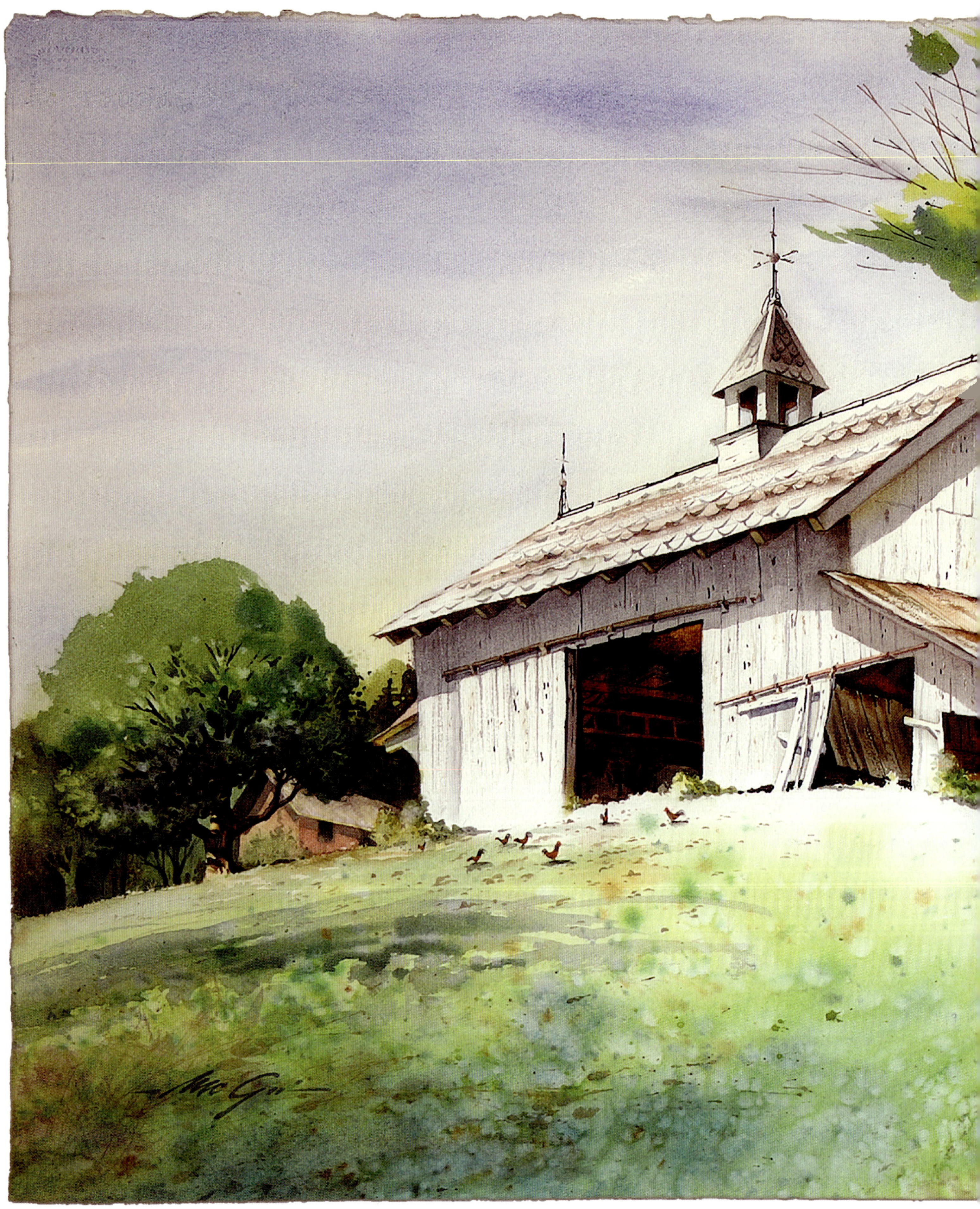

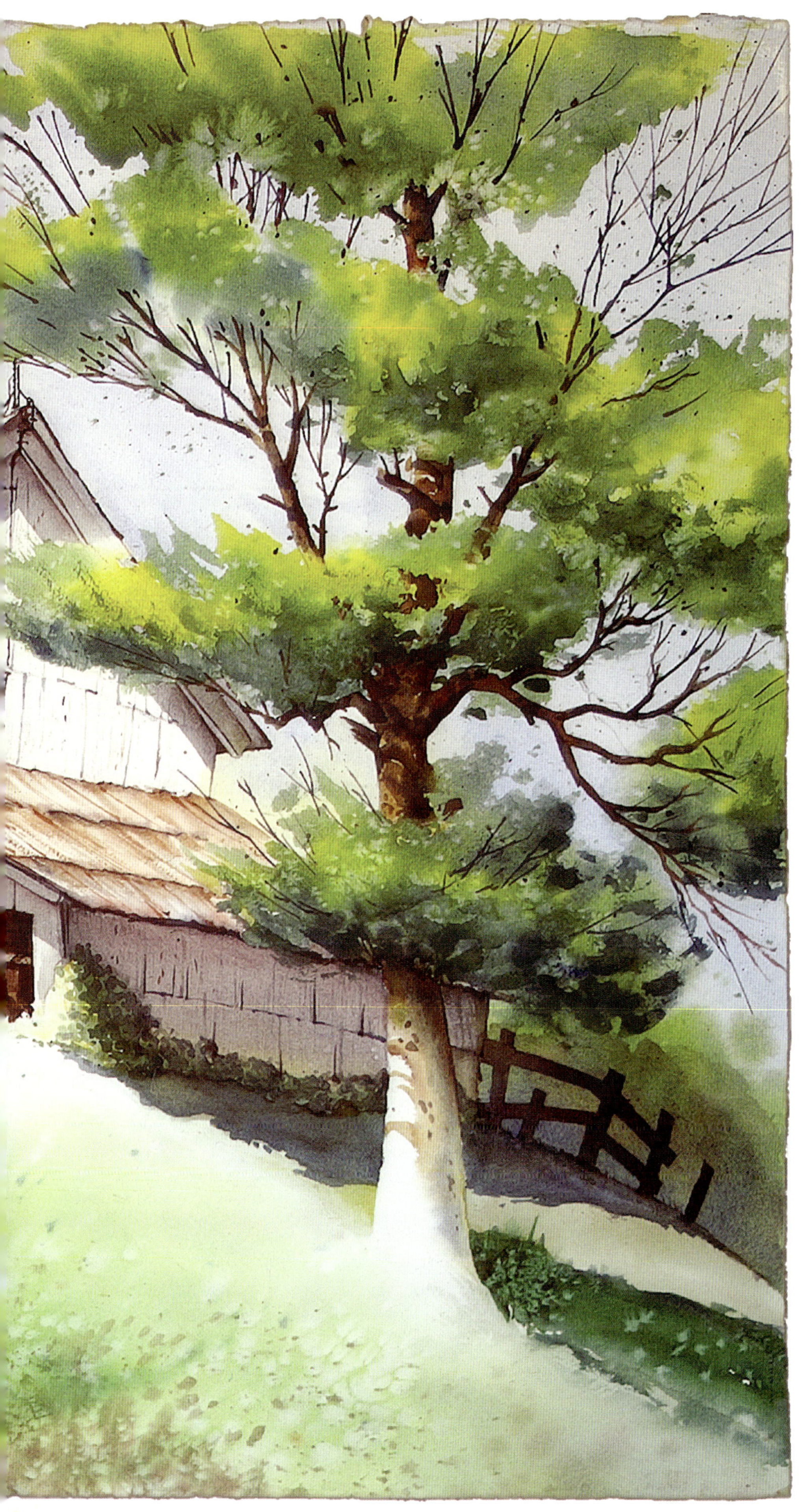

THE HENS ARE IN THE HEN HOUSE
MICHAEL ALLEN MCGUIRE
Transparent watercolor on 140-lb. (300gsm) Arches, 22" × 30" (56cm × 76cm)

This watercolor was done from a black-and-white felt-pen drawing I created on site in rural Ohio. The actual drawing for this watercolor is featured in North Light Books' *Strokes of Genius 2*. I grew up around these charming farm relics, working and playing within their cavernous walls, always in awe of their magnificence yet wary of what could lurk in the dark and mysterious corners. When I happened upon this gem, I was struck by how stately it stood atop this private hillside presenting such powerful perspective. So with quick permission, I captured what has become one of my favorites of all the barns I've been privileged to study. I continue to delight in sketching these vanishing monarchs.

CONTENTS

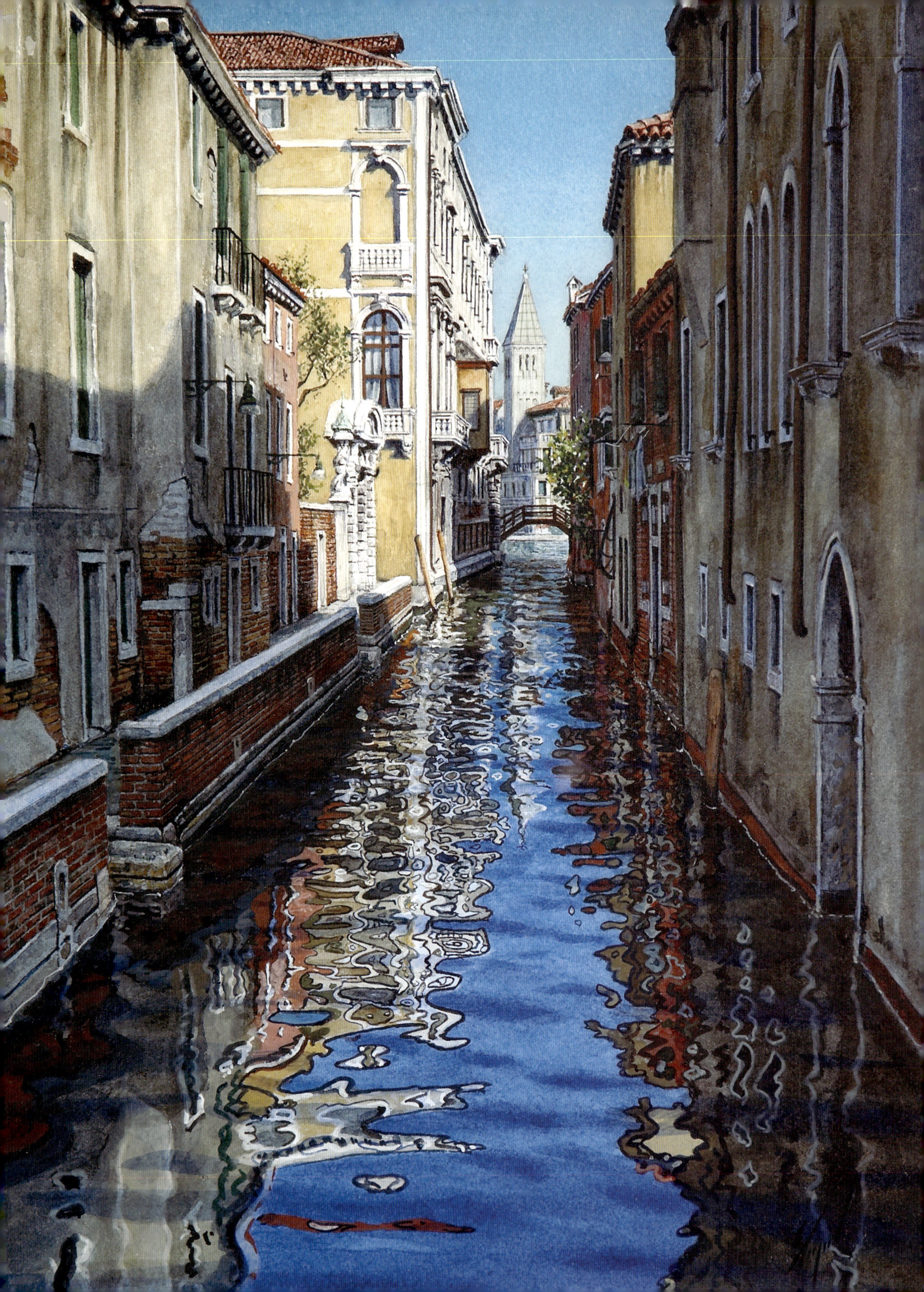

INTRODUCTION

Though we travel the world over to find the beautiful, we must carry it with us or we find it not.

Ralph Waldo Emerson

In this edition of *Splash* we are celebrating artistic vision—that undefinable gift of the artist—the ability to make visual that which exists in the mind's eye, or perhaps only in the heart. Some inspiration comes from the beauty around us, yet each artist still exercises the "beauty receptors" he or she carries within—each different, each unique.

Sandra Blair submitted a quote from Vincent van Gogh: "It is not the language of painters but the language of nature which one should listen to. The feeling for the things themselves, for reality, is more important than the feeling for pictures."

Then again, Nancy Fortunato finds that she was inspired directly from the language of painters—in fact that of van Gogh himself! Several others found vision in old family photographs, melding interesting images with deep connections and emotions. Still-life artists find inspirational vision in placing meaningful, or perhaps even humorous, objects together, thereby creating a small personal cosmos and bringing it to life.

Many artists exercise their vision in observing people and expressing the emotion of a fleeting moment in a facial expression or a bodily gesture. Others find their inspiration in the timeless moments of nature and in things that will far outlast our lifetimes. But in all of these cases each artist carries within them the beauty that is just waiting to be energized by an inspirational moment or idea.

And, oh yes, we are reminded by Bev Jozwiak that there is also some hard work involved. Having one's "beauty receptors" in place is the first step but, as Bev says, "To be able to fulfill your artistic vision, you must first put in the hard work of learning to paint. Tenacity wins out over talent every time."

This is why we are celebrating the vision of the artists in this book. They not only admired the beauty they saw or imagined, they put in the time to learn how to translate it into paint and paper so that we can share their vision. For that we are all richer.

Rachel

RIO DI SAN BARNABA (CA' REZZONICO) | JAMES TOOGOOD

Watercolor on paper, 14" × 11" (36cm × 28cm)

The Ca' Rezzonico, on the left, is a splendid 17th century palazzo (palace) that faces the Grand Canal in the Dorsoduro section of Venice. I took several liberties including giving the back wall of the palazzo more color, and exaggerating atmospheric perspective to the far buildings. I made architectural changes to the buildings on both sides of *Rio di San Barnaba*, and changed the patterns of light so that shadows would climb up a portion of the wall on the left. Finally I used the work of Jean Dubuffet as inspiration to simply make up abstract patterns of reflections in the water, all to give the painting more visual interest.

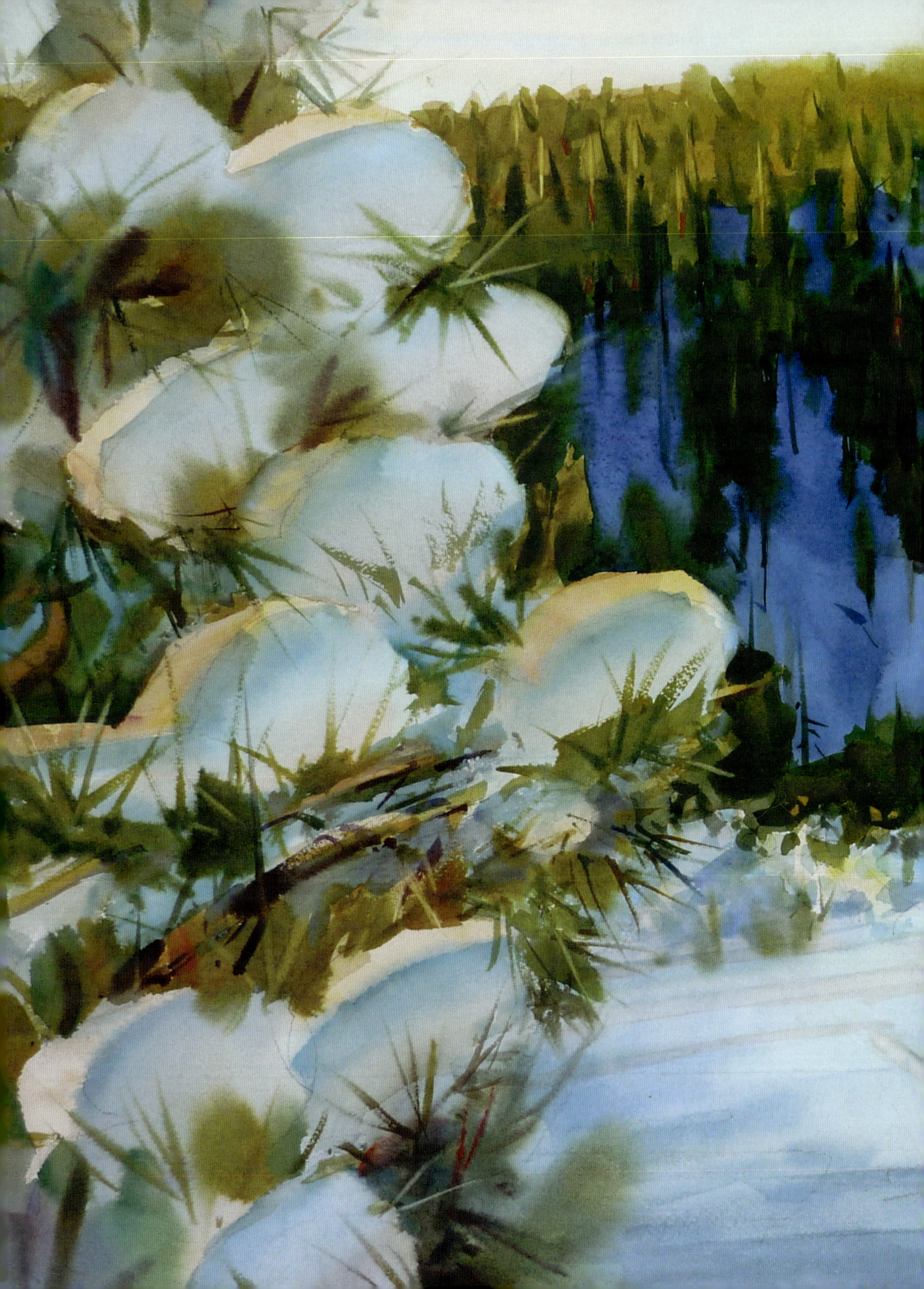

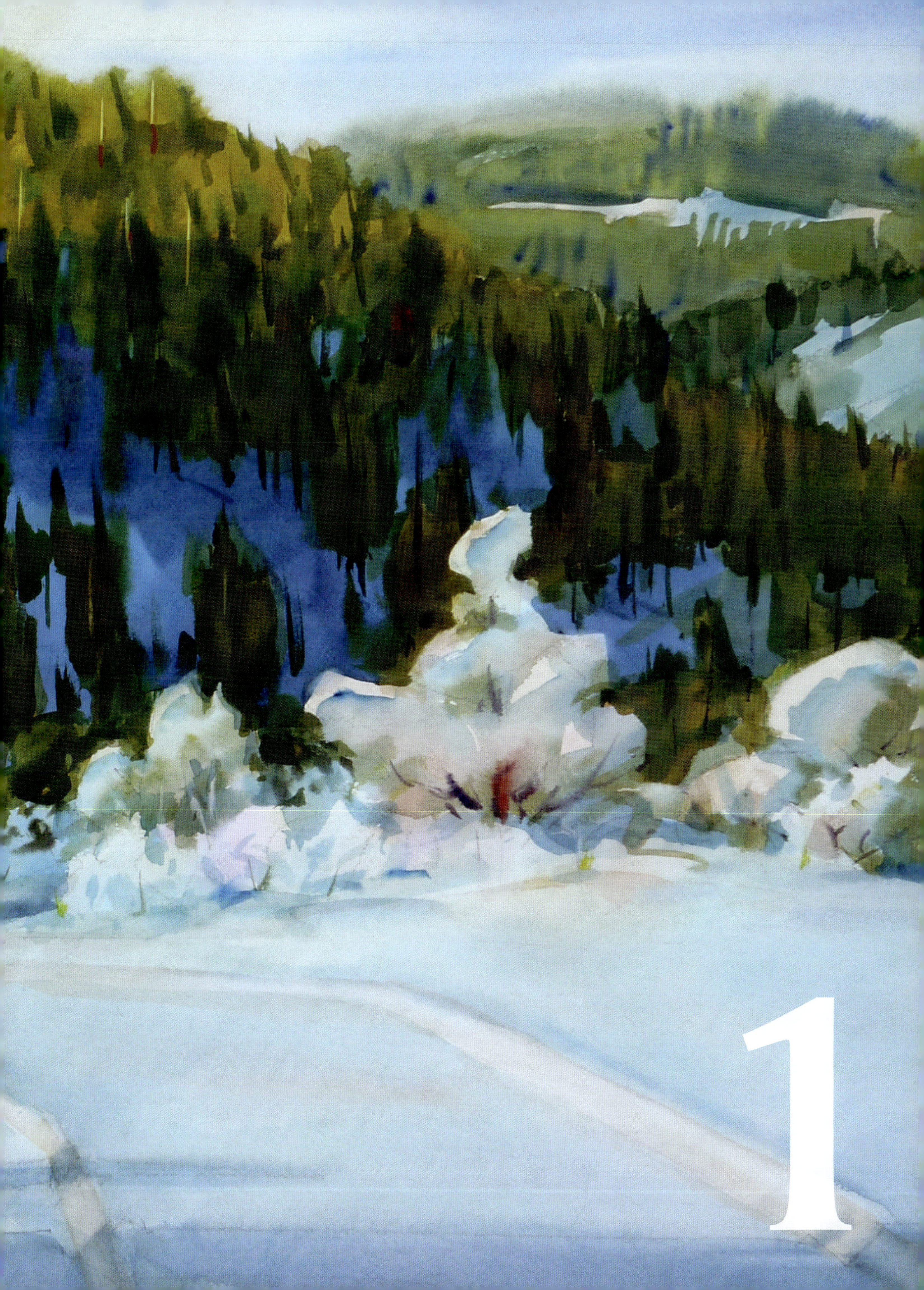

1

1 | NATURE

One of the great epiphanies on the artistic road is the realization that we are painting light, not things. If you can paint light, you can paint anything under the sun.

Frank LaLumia

{ art on previous spread }

SNOW IN THE FOOTHILLS | FRANK LALUMIA

Transparent watercolor on cold-pressed Arches, 22" × 30" (56cm × 76cm)

Snow in the Foothills is our road home, the foothills of the Sangre de Cristo Mountains just west of Trinidad, Colorado. Whether we're driving or walking through the hills with our dog Naya, it is a landscape to which I feel deeply connected. I've painted it in all seasons, both plein air and in the studio. Drawing inspiration from the world around us is a big part of being an artist. Your body of work is your autobiography.

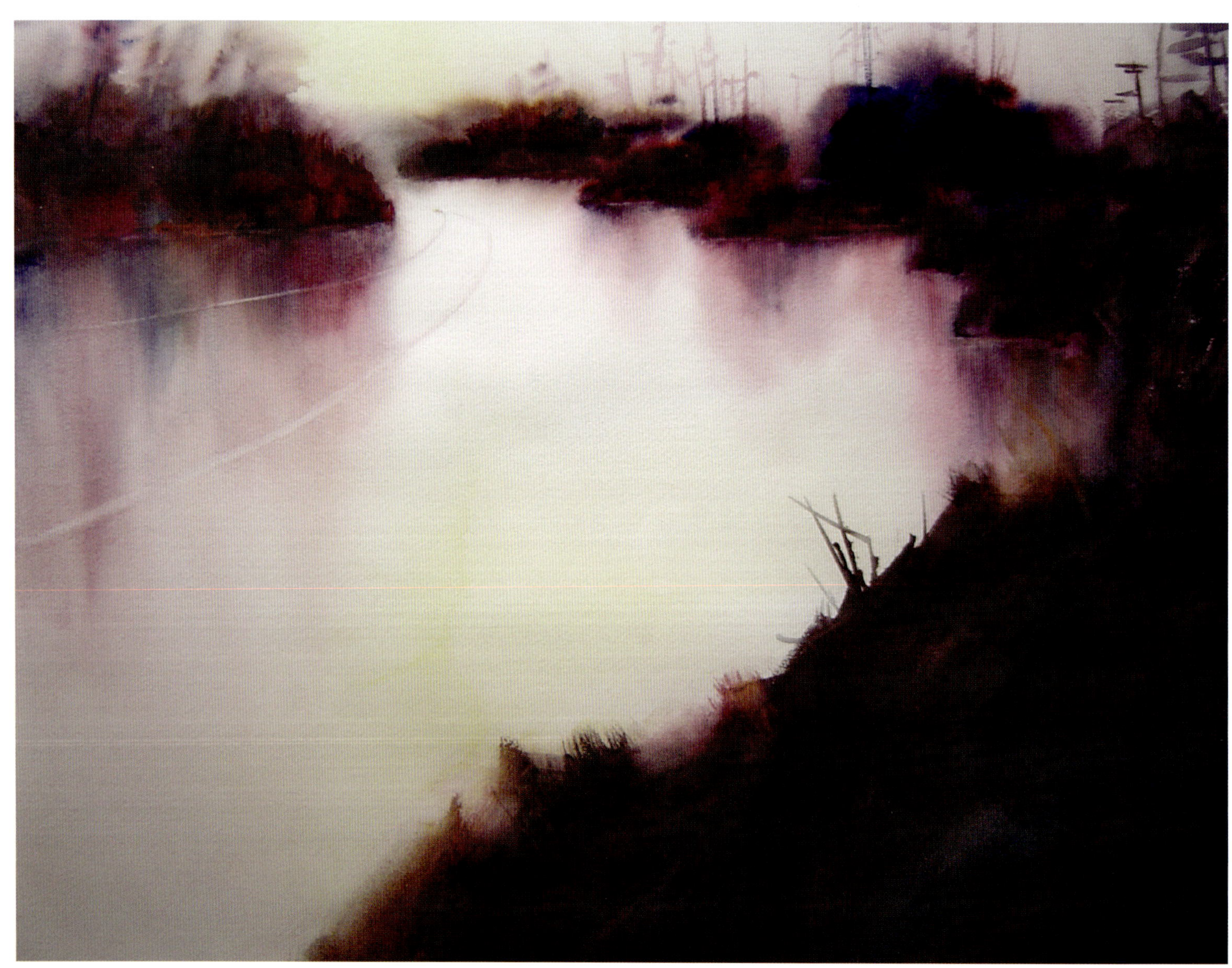

AT THE CENTER | KATHY COLLINS

Watercolor on paper, 22" × 30" (56cm × 76cm)

If in doubt, fade it out!

Kathy Collins

Bicycling by a river in early evening, I witnessed shimmering light on the water contrasted with the dark wooded riverbanks. Pulling a sketchbook from my backpack, I penned a quick line drawing. Just then, a motorboat rounded the river's curve, leaving a wake in the form of an arabesque—a perfect focus for the composition! In the studio I splashed watercolor onto a full sheet of paper, trying to recreate my impression of the dramatic value contrast, while retaining the softness of the fading light.

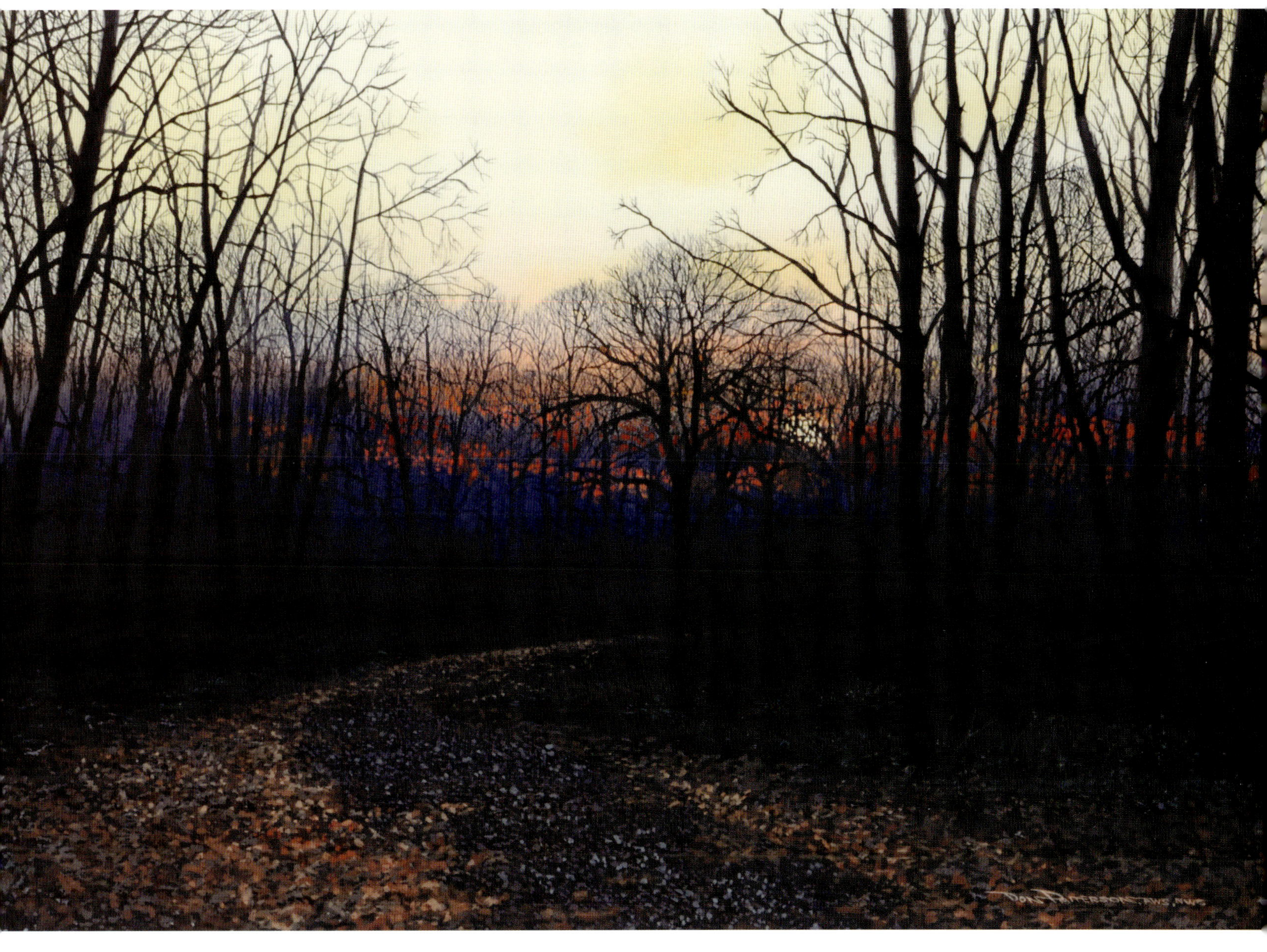

DUSK | DONALD W. PATTERSON
Transparent watercolor with gouache on 300-lb. (640gsm) cold-pressed Arches, 14¾" × 22" (37cm × 56cm)

I first painted this location from a photo taken in early winter. The gravel path you see was a snow-covered winding railroad track. The first painting was competently executed but did not touch me emotionally. Months later I revisited the same location and was captivated by the warm rosy glow as it filtered through the lacy tree branches. However, the glistening tracks disrupted the quiet mood of evening. Replacing the tracks with a more appealing gravel path was the perfect solution. I enhanced the sunset by carefully inserting a few gouache highlights into the negative spaces between the branches.

Artistic vision comes from seeing with your eyes and feeling with your heart.

Donald W. Patterson

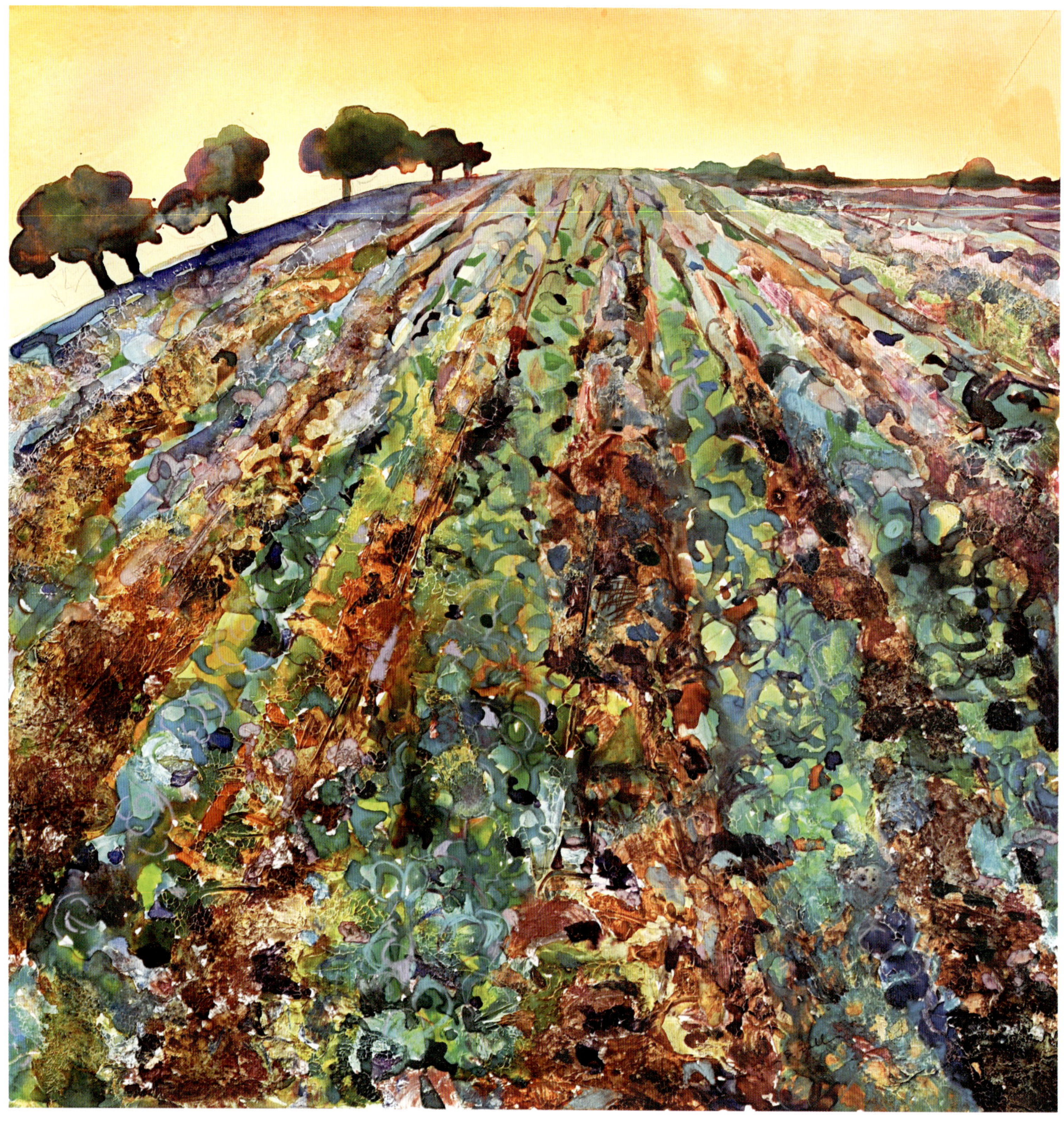

UP THE HILL | DEENA S. BALL
Transparent watercolor and watercolor pencils on Strathmore 500 Series plate bristol with a ground of acrylic gesso and gel, 15" × 15" (38cm × 38cm)

Emerging from the low dense valley, the ground rose and directly ahead were stripes of blue, aqua and purple cabbages against the red earth. The lines of the cabbages and earth pointed into the setting sun. *Up the Hill* is based on a sketch and photograph of this experience. I added a textured base to bristol paper. When paint is applied to the textured surface it runs into the gullies creating unanticipated pools of color. Once painted, I find the contrast between the textured and smooth areas interesting and beautiful.

Painting is a dance between controlled and anticipated marks, and random surprises.

Deena S. Ball

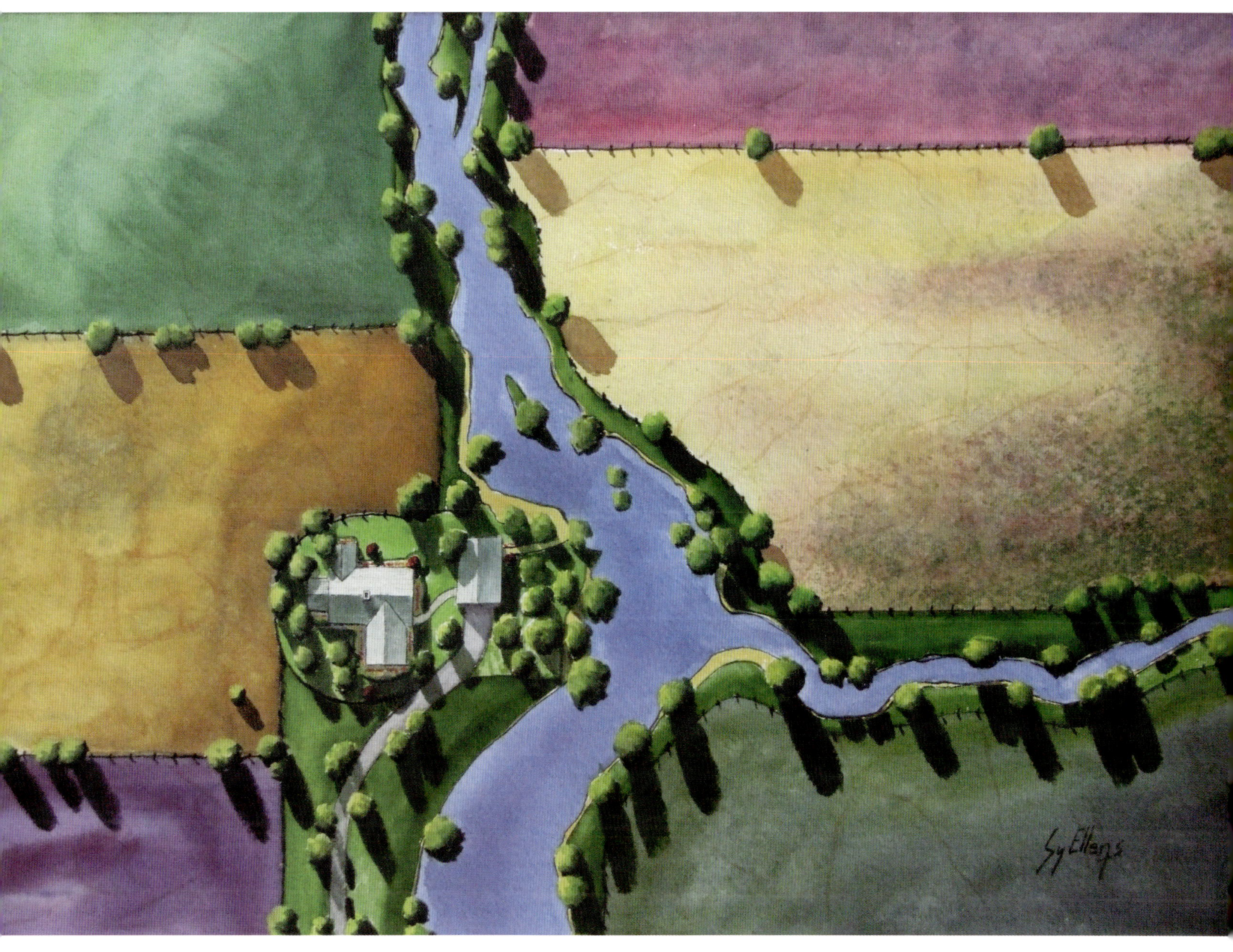

SERENITY | SY ELLENS
Transparent watercolor on 300-lb. (640gsm) cold-pressed paper, 20" × 28" (51cm × 71cm)

There are many ways to view the world. We can use a microscope and marvel at what a cell looks like. We can look at things at ground level, from normal eye level, from the top of a high building, or from a hot air balloon or an airplane. Some have even viewed the earth from a space station or the moon. After experiencing the land close up, growing up on a farm, and later from a distance in a plane, I had the vision of bringing the two together. While in my studio, using watercolor and working from memory, I chose a view directly above my subject to create field patterns and textures that I knew so well from my early experience.

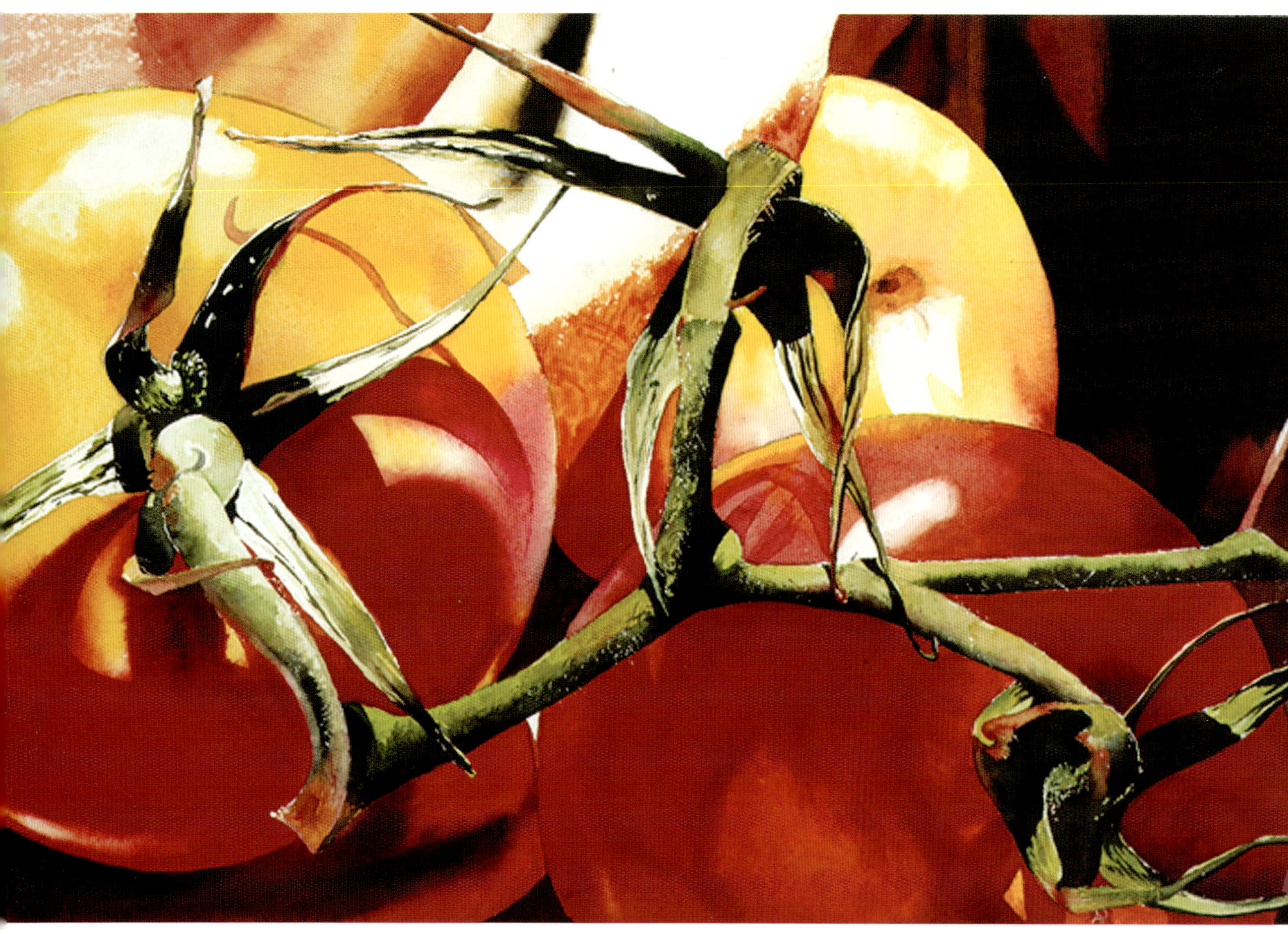

SUNCLUSTER | A. CHADDOCK

Watercolor on 300-lb. (640gsm) cold-pressed watercolor paper, 15" × 22" (38cm × 56cm)

This subject required working with very strong primary colors. I have found that lightening primaries often produces dull color. To prevent this, I darken negative space so I can present the saturated primaries as my lights, maintaining clean color. I often use very dark color that requires a long value scale. I placed these tomatoes in very strong light to get their glow and very hard cast shadows. I brushed on saturated color so I would not have to go back and layer. Charging the pigment onto the paper, I could wash it out a bit to lighten without losing the character of the color.

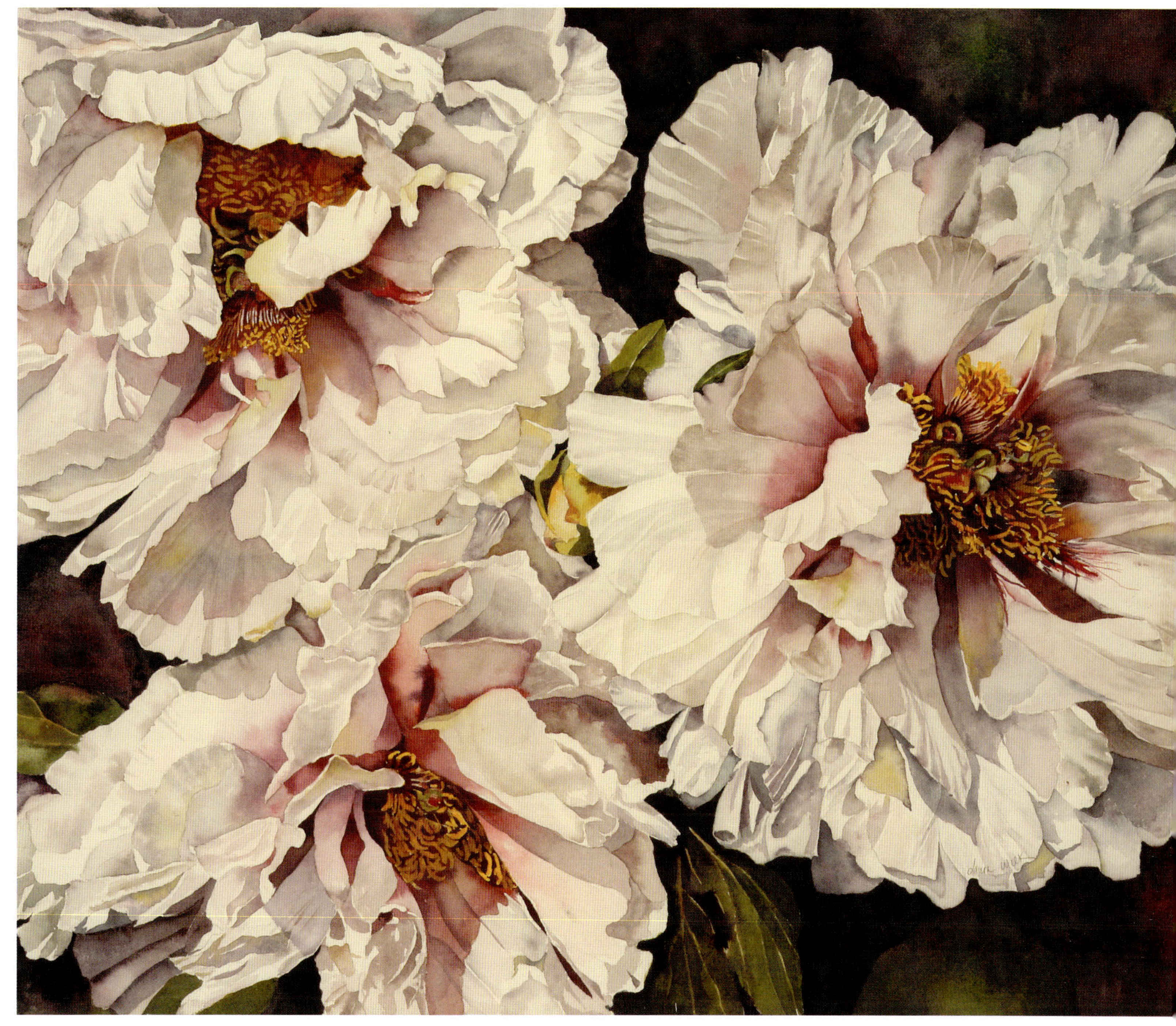

PURPLE-HEARTED PEONIES | LAURA WILK
Transparent watercolor on 140-lb. (300gsm) cold-pressed Arches, 21" × 25" (53cm × 64cm)

I used to paint on silk and loved to watch the vivid dyes flow and mingle on the silk's surface. Thirty years ago, I discovered that the same luminosity could be achieved on paper with transparent watercolor. I am particularly enamored by the gorgeous colors and graceful shapes of flowers. But their delicate beauty can be surprisingly hard to capture. Tree peonies flaunt many-layered, pink-tinged outer petals that contrast dramatically with their complex, deeply hued interiors. I work from photographs and life in my studio. Masking the lighter details in the centers, I then go in with as many as thirty layers of transparent color to achieve luminosity. The edges are then blended and softened, to help the viewer glide over the neutral-tinged outer petals, alight on the golden stamens, admire the greenish carpeled crown, then plunge into the purpled magenta depths.

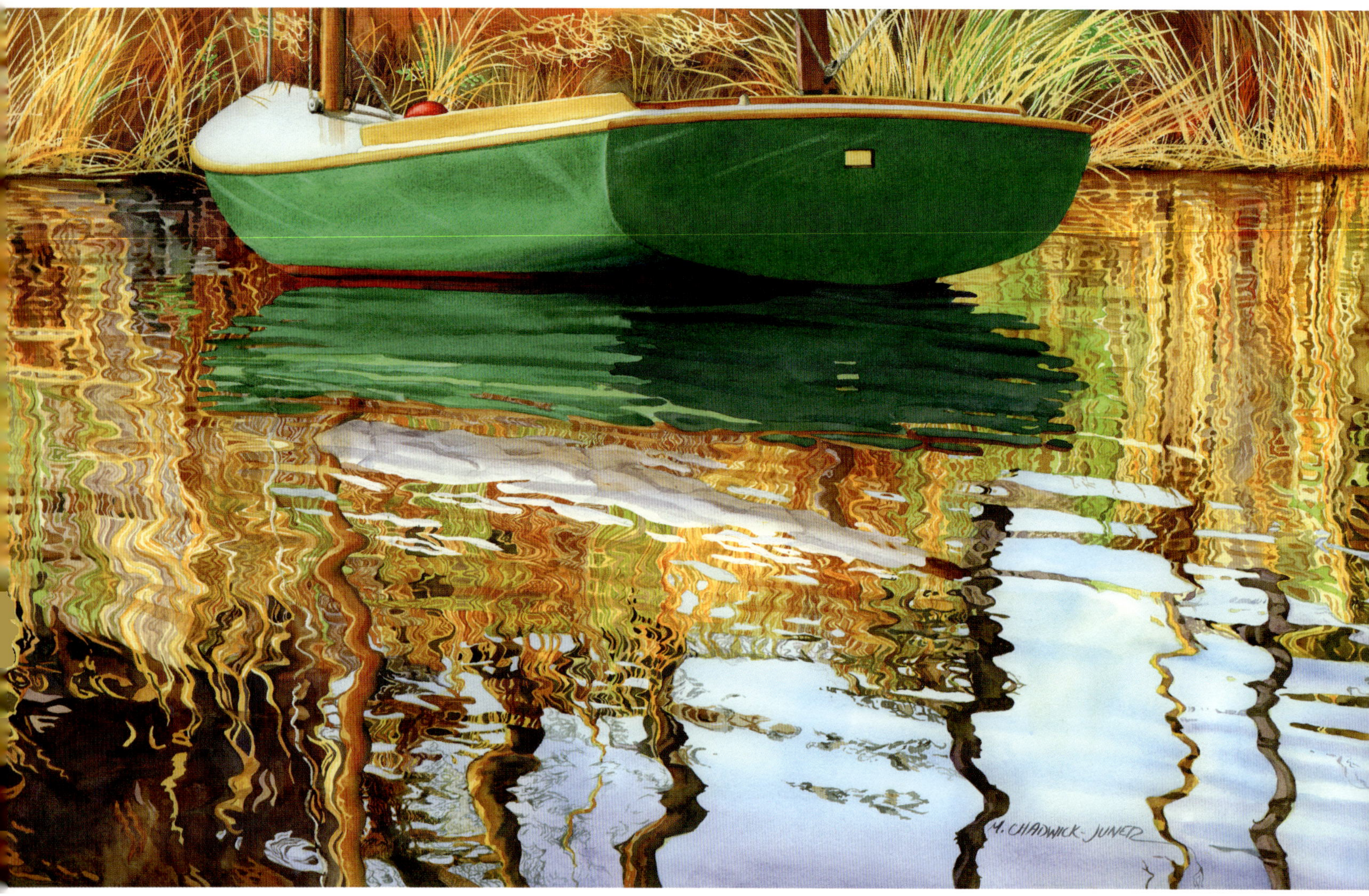

MOMENT OF REFLECTION XI | MARGUERITE CHADWICK-JUNER
Transparent watercolor on 140-lb. (300gsm) cold-pressed Arches, 15¾" × 27" (40cm × 69cm)

This is the "imagineering" of several photographs into one image. I love the abstraction of objects in gently disturbed, almost still water, and have a file of photographs of marsh grasses and vegetation taken in the fall. The orange and golden colors are the perfect complement to the reflected blue sky. The boat is from a completely different setting. The high horizon line focuses attention on the abstractions in the water while giving a frame of reference. This was painted in a very straightforward manner with the exception of the use of masking fluid on the marsh grasses.

GOING FOR GRAPENESS | DIANE FUJIMOTO
Transparent watercolor on 140-lb. (300gsm) paper, 28" × 20½" (71cm × 52cm)

We all have a unique voice—a language that celebrates our artistic vision.

Diane Fujimoto

This was a top-ten, picture-perfect day of bike-riding with my husband through the vineyards of the Burgundy region of France. Our camera caught the late afternoon sun on the bursting grapes; I couldn't wait to get home and paint them. My goal was to make the viewer want to reach out and pluck one of the grapes. Glazing played an important role in capturing the various shades and the feeling of sunlight. Iridescent watercolors helped create texture as well as depth of color.

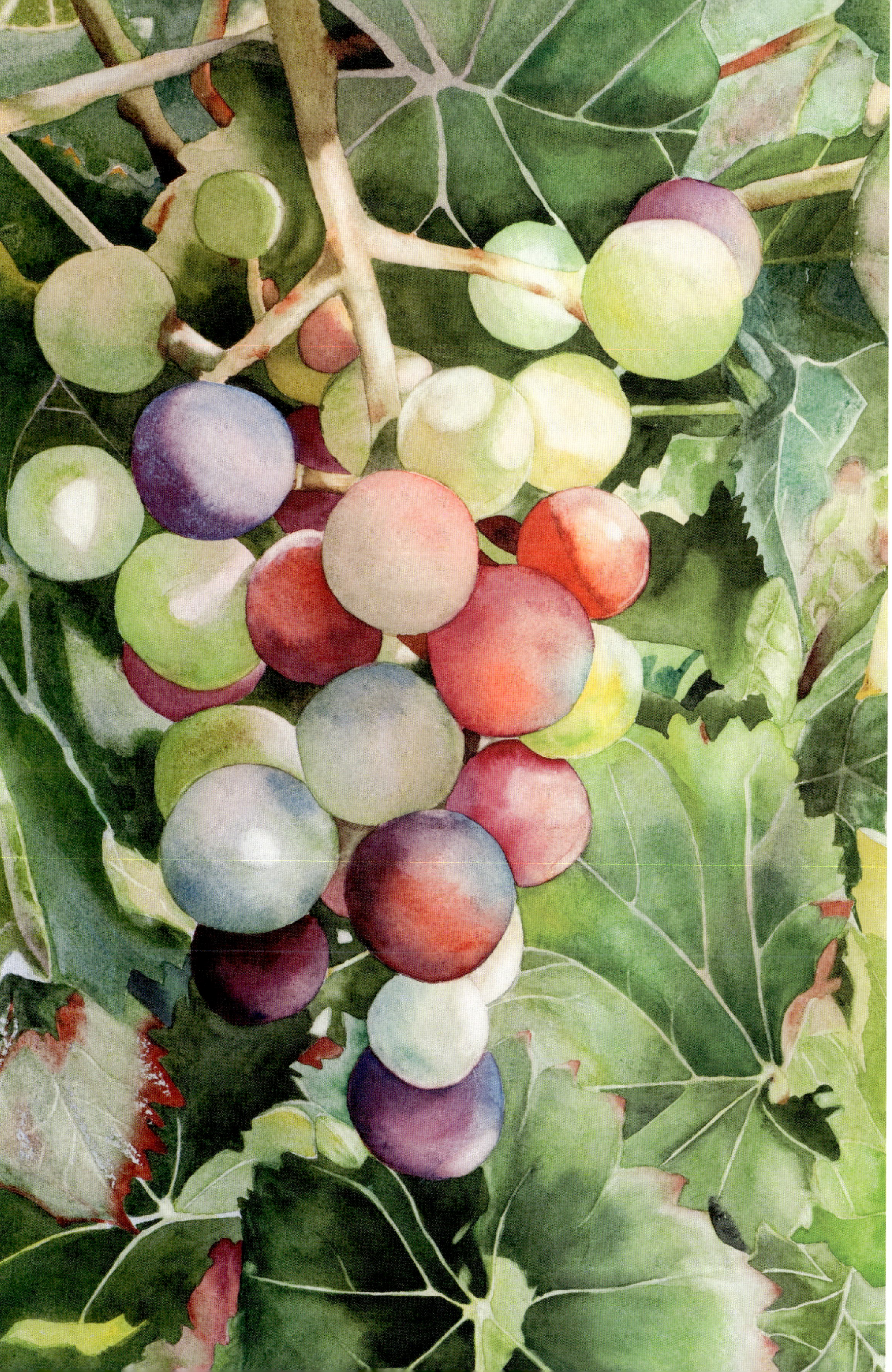

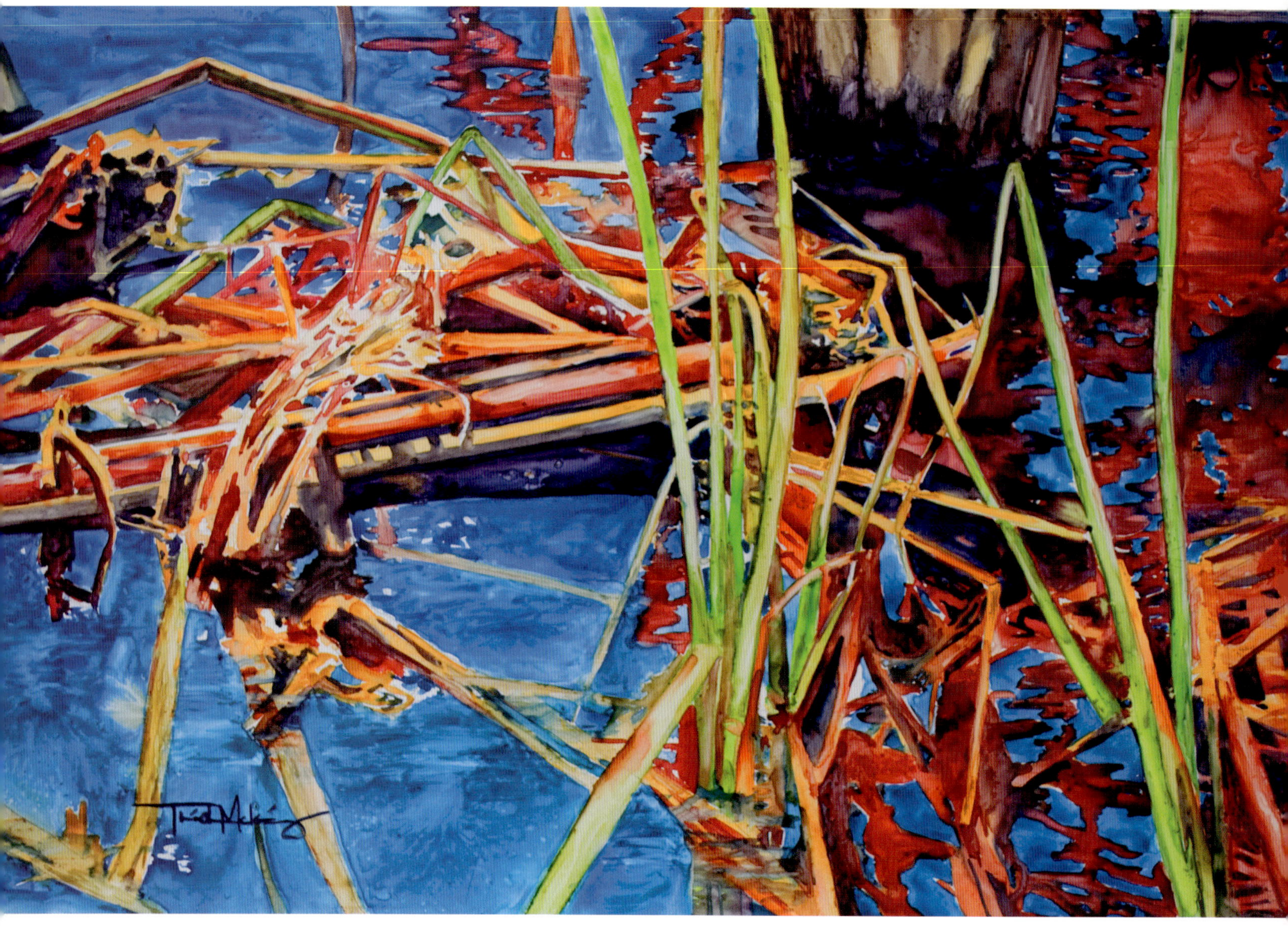

WATER FIREWORKS | TRISH MCKINNEY
Transparent watercolor on Yupo, 26" × 39" (66cm × 99cm)

I shut my eyes in order to see.

— *Paul Gauguin*

Water and fire are opposing forces; the challenge was to harmonize them. While walking with my artist friend down a quiet road in Charleston, South Carolina, a vision of imaginary fireworks in the lush marsh grasses inspired me. We each took reference photos of the area. It is exciting to see the vision of another artist! Yupo paper helped make the water "wet" and I created the feeling of fire through the choice of color. This painting celebrates my community of artists who inspire my vision.

BACK TO THE SEA | SANDY O'CONNOR
Transparent watercolor on 300-lb. (640gsm) cold-pressed Arches , 22½" × 16" (57cm × 41cm)

As the day dawned over Nantucket Sound, the gentle early morning tide advanced and receded, again and again, leaving traces of delicately sculpted passages in the golden sand. I found the cadence of millennia framed within my vision. Back in my studio, I tried to communicate the same sensations of a blazing sun on my face and cool sand underfoot. The light sparkling through the grass and off the sand and water was masked, sandpapered and picked out to reveal the pure white of the paper.

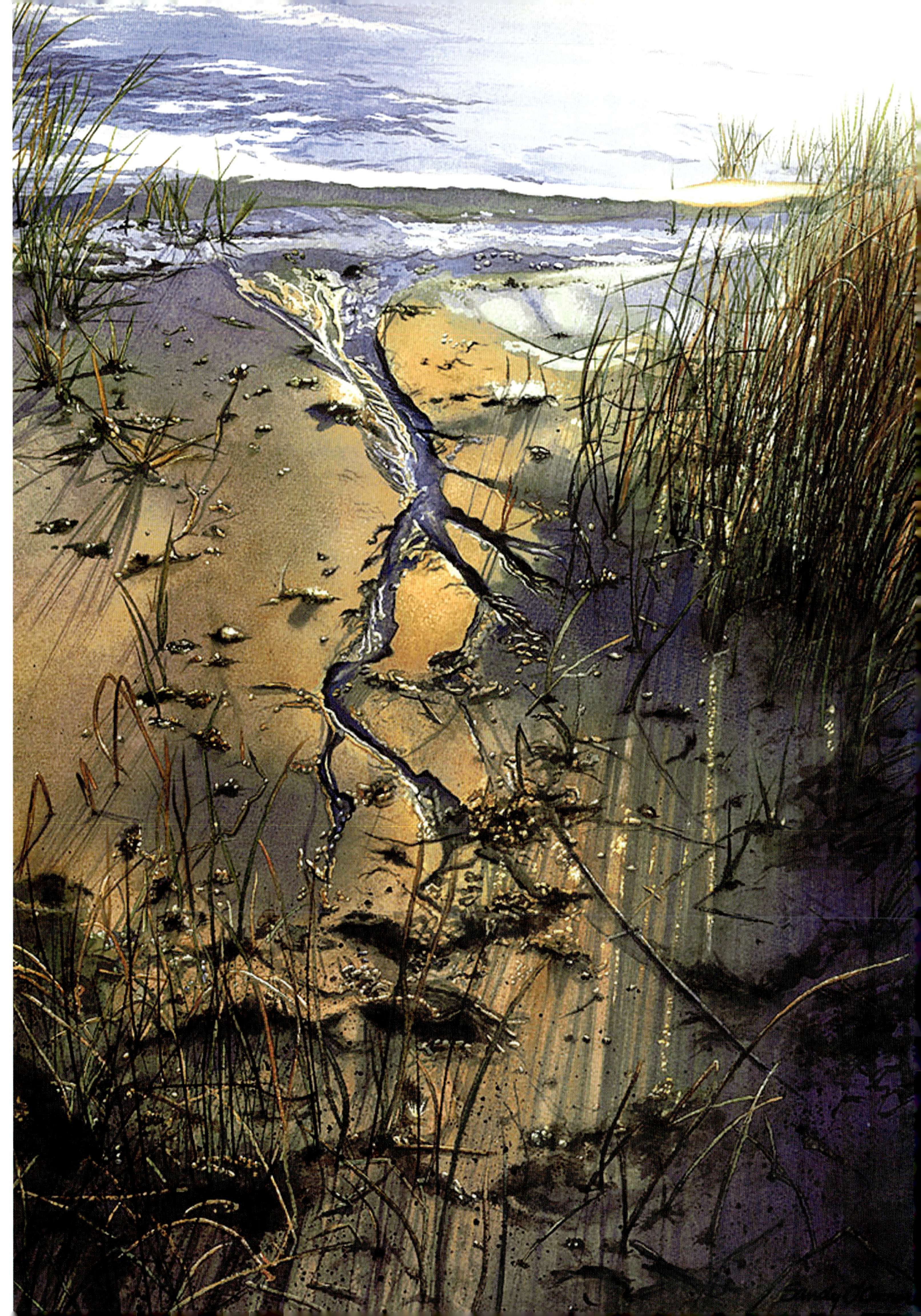

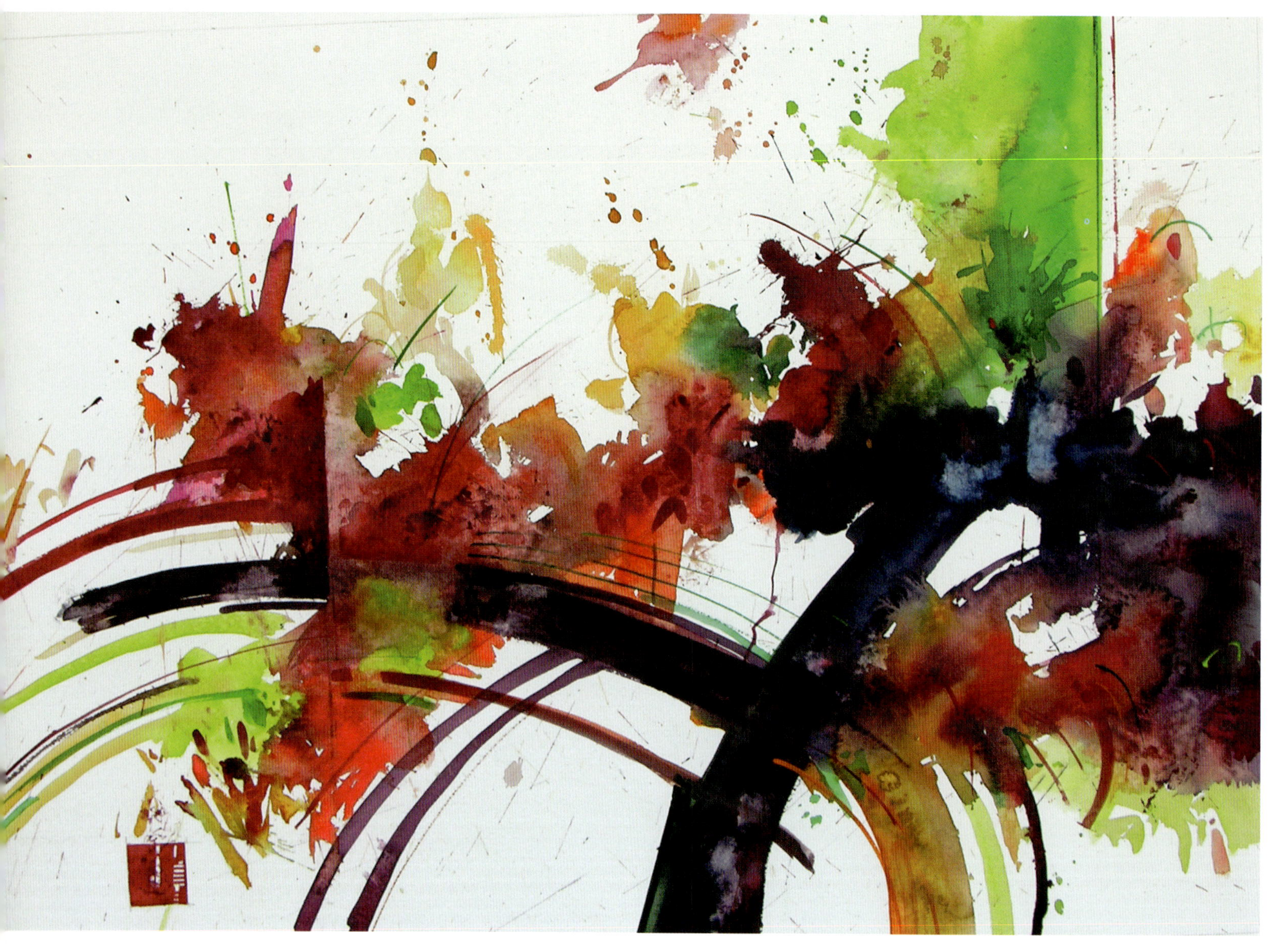

SEASONS 2 | RICHARD H. DUTTON

Transparent watercolor on 140-lb. (300gsm) cold-pressed Arches, 20" × 28" (51cm × 71cm)

The conceptualization of the seasons has existed in many art forms throughout history. *Seasons 2* is from a series of watercolors that represents my own fascination with the different times of year. The painterly fluid strokes express the dynamic poetry of the seasons, while the large brushwork and brilliant colors capture the energy and vibrancy of nature—in this case, summer. Seeing the formal gardens and art of China, Europe and the U.S. has helped form my artistic vision, as has spending the formative part of my life on a farm.

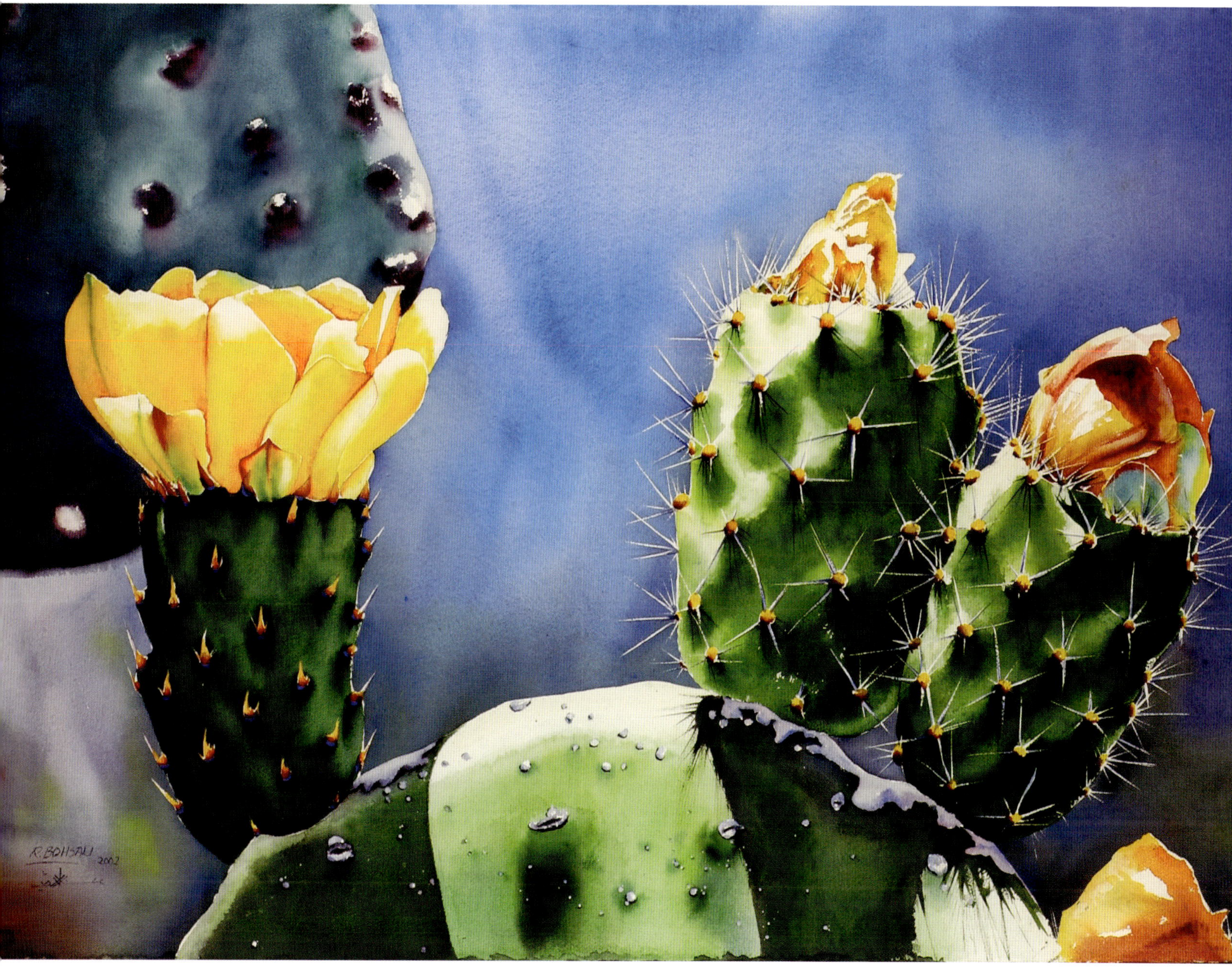

SELF ... PORTRAIT | RACHED K. BOHSALI
Transparent watercolor on 100 percent Aquarelle (Perrigot) Arches, 30" × 42" (76cm × 107cm)

Masking the white areas helps me make speedy directional brushstrokes without hesitation in the large areas of the background. This enhances the vibration of the sparkling white gaps on the rough paper surface after removing the mask. The wet-into-wet does the rest of the job. I compare myself to a cactus plant because the cactus widely opens its welcoming hands, but the thorns in its palms defend against intruders. If you can get through it ... its prickly pears have a sweet taste. Moreover, its leaves are laid out chaotically, yet the systematic pattern of the thorns is tidy and organized.

Why watercolor? It is transparent and sensitive, yet direct and bold; every brushstroke is improvised and unpredictable—like jazz!

Rached K. Bohsali

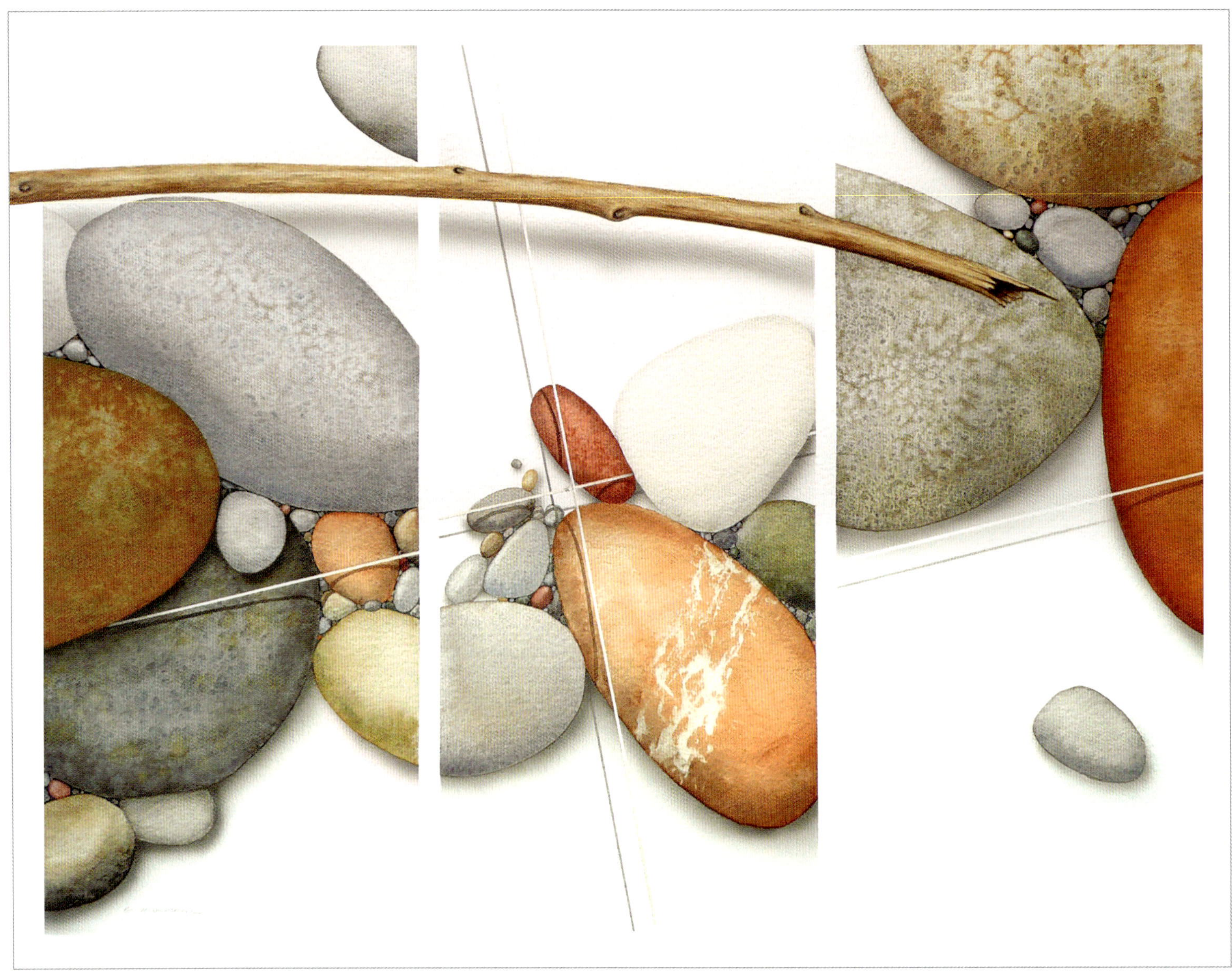

THREE RIVER SERIES: THE ROGUE | GEOFFREY MCCORMACK
Watercolor on 300-lb. (640gm) cold-pressed Arches, 22" × 30" (56cm × 76cm)

While printing an archival copy of my earlier *Greek Stones Speak* series, there were multiple printer errors resulting in the look of a rough triptych. I liked the accidental output and pinned it to my studio wall. Several months later, I began thinking about a new series. I liked the rocks, sticks, string and shallow space of the *Greek* paintings, and decided to combine those aspects with the triptych format from the accidental prints on my wall.

The Rogue was the first painting in my new series, which refers to the rivers of western Oregon. I draw and design directly on 300-lb. (640gsm) cold-pressed Arches and paint with transparent watercolor. The cold-pressed paper takes advantage of the granulating quality of some pigments to create realistic textures and enhanced salt lifts. I used tape in a variety of widths to save the white of the strings and control the edges of the triptych panels. My hope is that the many ambiguous connections in the painting, both visual and conceptual, engage the viewer in conversation.

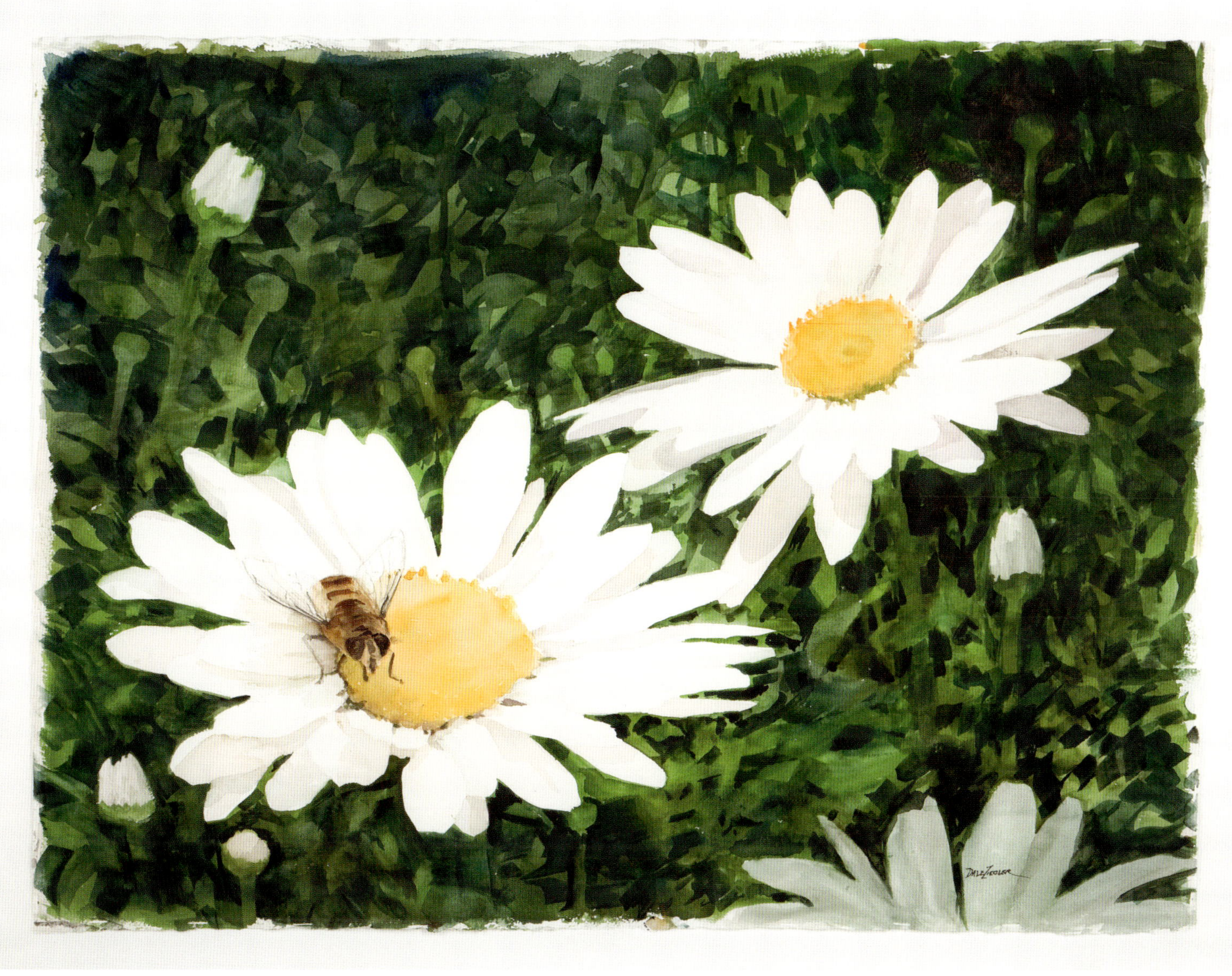

NECTAR FOR BREAKFAST | DALE ZIEGLER

Transparent watercolor with no masking on 300-lb. (640gsm) cold-pressed watercolor paper, 20" × 28" (51cm × 71cm)

Nothing compares with on-site painting, but at 86 I now work from my reference photos and memory. I never just copy a photo and often combine elements from two or three. In the corner of one of my daisy reference shots I noticed a bee gathering nectar. It was out of focus, but enough to get me started. I found better flower photos and arranged my composition. I laid a pale gray wash over the less important daisies before laying a dark green wash over the whole background, carefully cutting around the white flowers. I did further modeling on the daisy, added the bee and painted darker green to suggest foliage in the background. I avoid masking whenever possible. To me, it looks a little too mechanical.

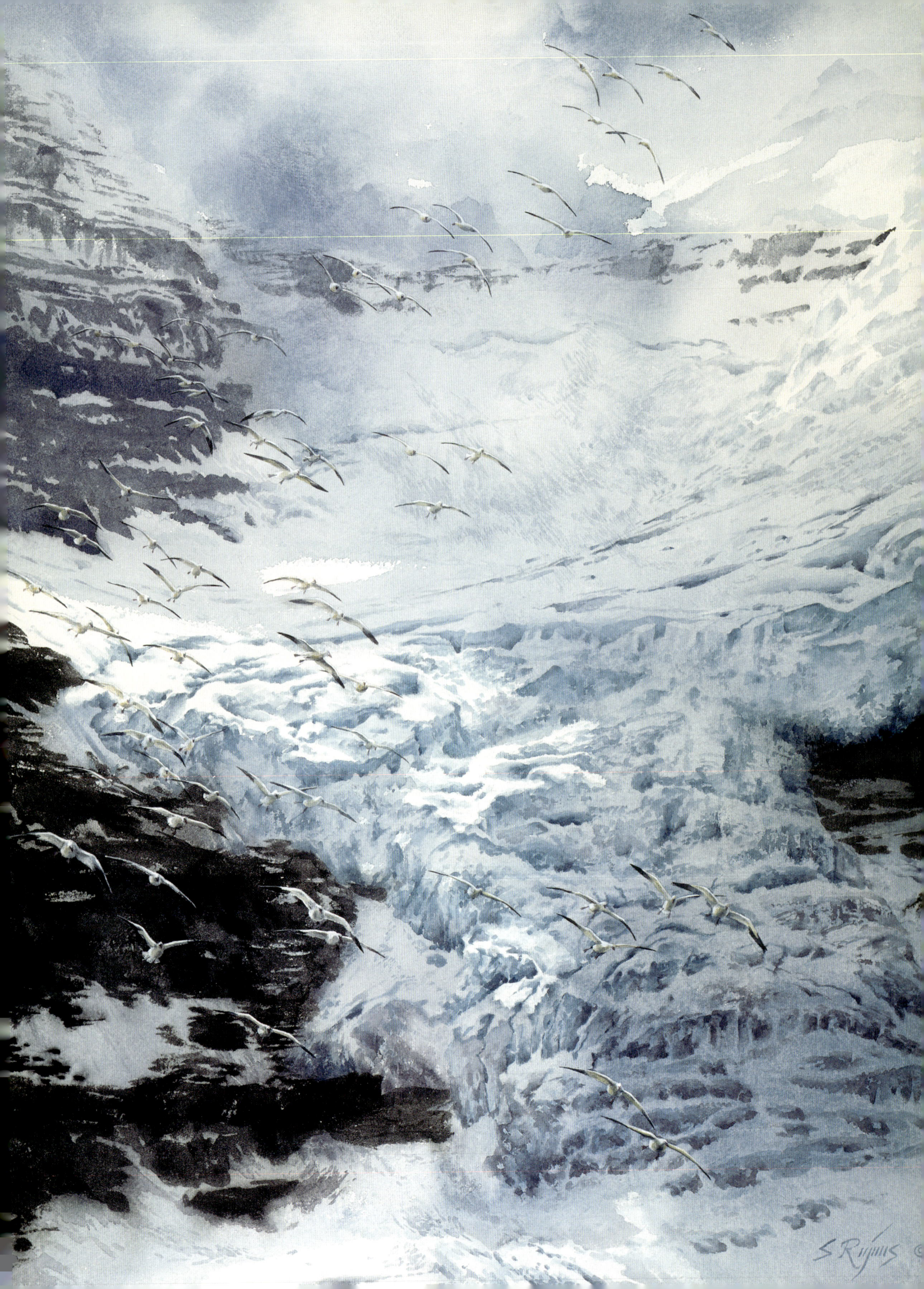

CASCADING SNOWS | SHARON RAJNUS

Watercolor on 300-lb. (640gm) cold-pressed Arches, 30" × 22" (76cm × 56cm)

Spectacular aerial views are the norm from the small planes my husband and I flew over Canada and Alaska. The North is a place of annual return and breeding grounds for the many species of geese of North America. This series celebrates the genesis or beginning of the birds and their trek. Using sketches and photos, numerous thumbnails led to the full-size drawing on 300-lb. (640gsm) cold-pressed Arches. The placement of the birds is as important as the shape of cliffs and ice floes. Technique ranges from soft-edged wash to hard-edged detail.

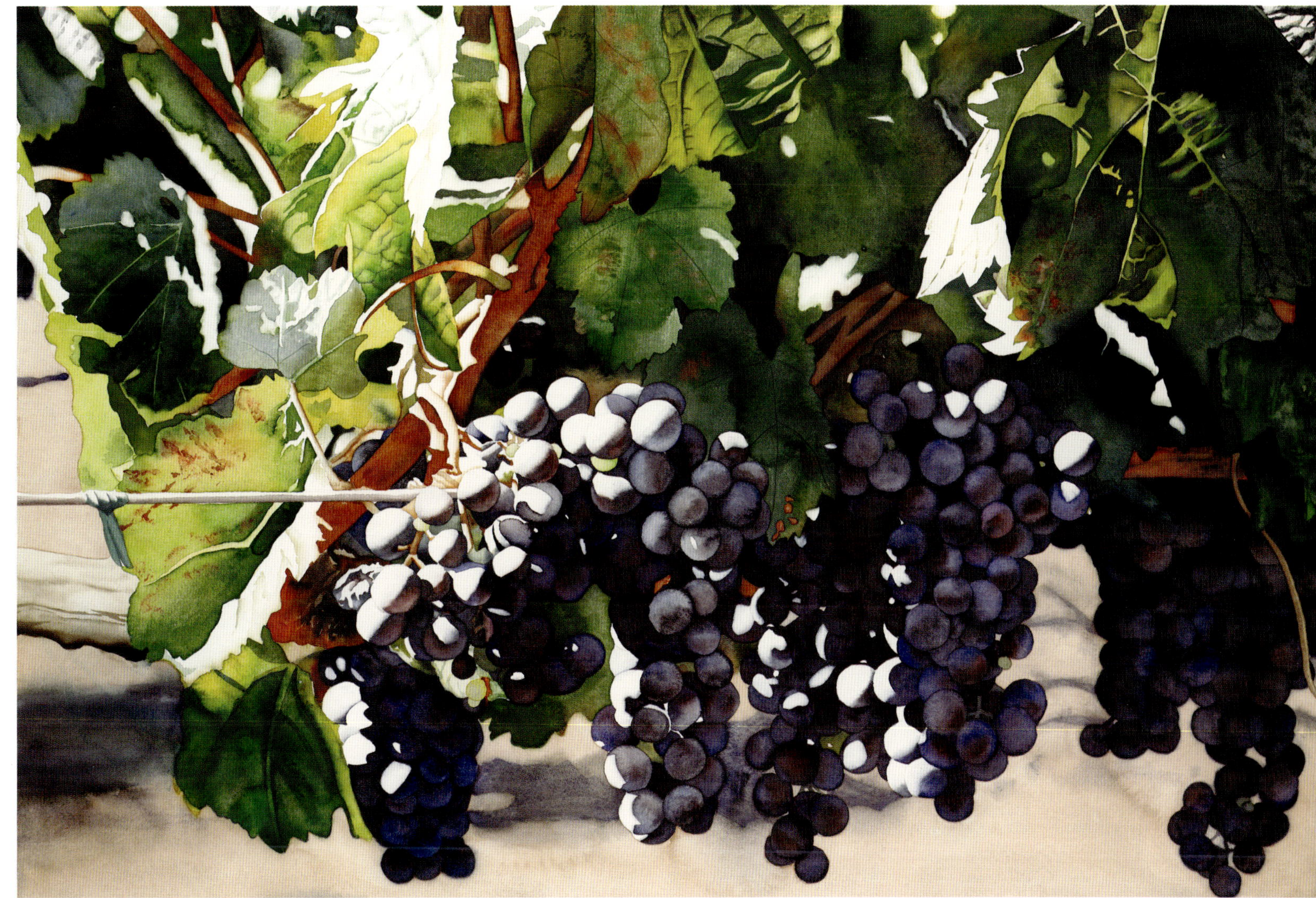

SONOMA VINES | KATHLEEN ALEXANDER

Transparent watercolor, 25" × 38" (64cm × 97cm)

> Don't be afraid to use more paint!
>
> *Kathleen Alexander*

I had been pursuing a tropical theme for several years when I had the opportunity for an autumn-inspired show. In my stockpile of photos was a reference photo I'd taken at the Kenwood Vineyards in Sonoma County, California. All the experience from painting tropical flowers and foliage translated perfectly into this new subject. I established the structure of the leaves with an Indigo underpainting, then glazed with varied greens, dropping in Burnt Sienna. The grapes were painted with Indigo, Cobalt Blue and Perylene Violet. The extreme contrast between the sunlit portions and the shadows makes the painting very dynamic. This began a new *California* series.

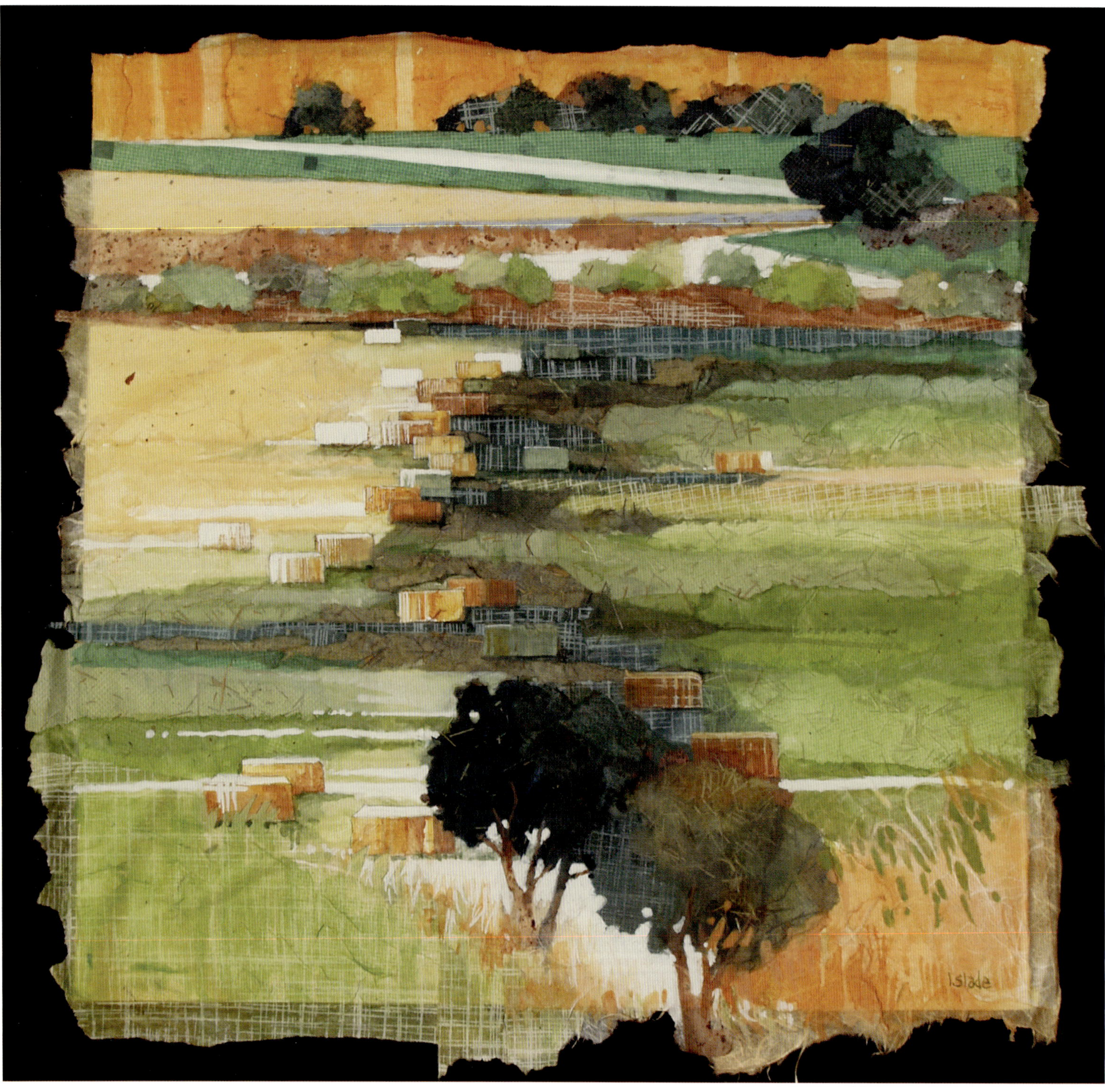

BALE PATTERNS | LYNN SLADE

Watercolor and rice paper collage on 300-lb. (640gsm) Fabriano, 14" × 14" (36cm × 36cm)

Bale Patterns was created from photos of the endless farmland—its repetitive patterns and colors—near Hailey, Idaho. I begin painting by designing the light and dark values and preparing a full-size overlay on tracing paper of the final value study; this becomes the "map" for the painting. Instead of blending color with liquid paint, I blend my colors with layers of hand-painted rice papers. The resulting color and texture combinations—some expected, some not—take the painting forward. Once the paper is down, I paint into the image, blending areas, enhancing shapes and adding detail.

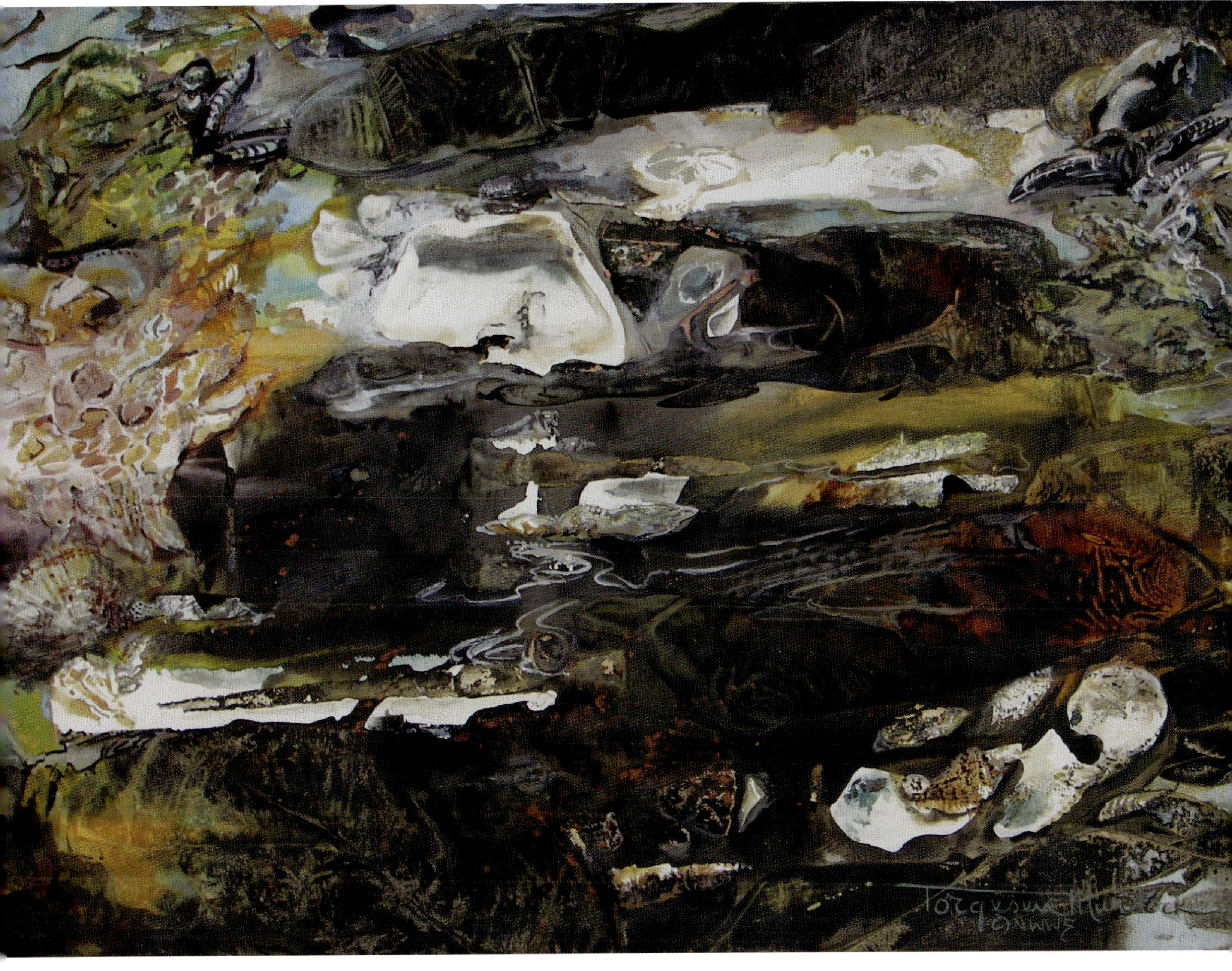

STREWN JEWELS | TORGESEN MURDOCK
Transparent watercolor and inks on Strathmore double-sided illustration board, 22" × 30" (56cm × 76cm)

The artist tells a lie to get at the truth.

— *Edgar Degas*

Strewn Jewels began its life as one of a dozen or more pours done in the studio using liquid transparent watercolor and inks. Wax paper, plastic wrap, coffee filters, string, skewers et al are used to create textures which I allow to "cook" for a week or so under pressure before the unveiling. The watermedia mixes and runs—has a life of its own. It creates fabulous shapes and textures that the brush could never duplicate. I am a certified scuba diver and have taken my inspiration for years from the ocean, rocks and tide pools, with their half-submerged shells, sand and mosses. My huge collection of shells and coral from both the Pacific and Atlantic beaches, supplies the models for the finish work done with a brush on the tide-pool paintings.

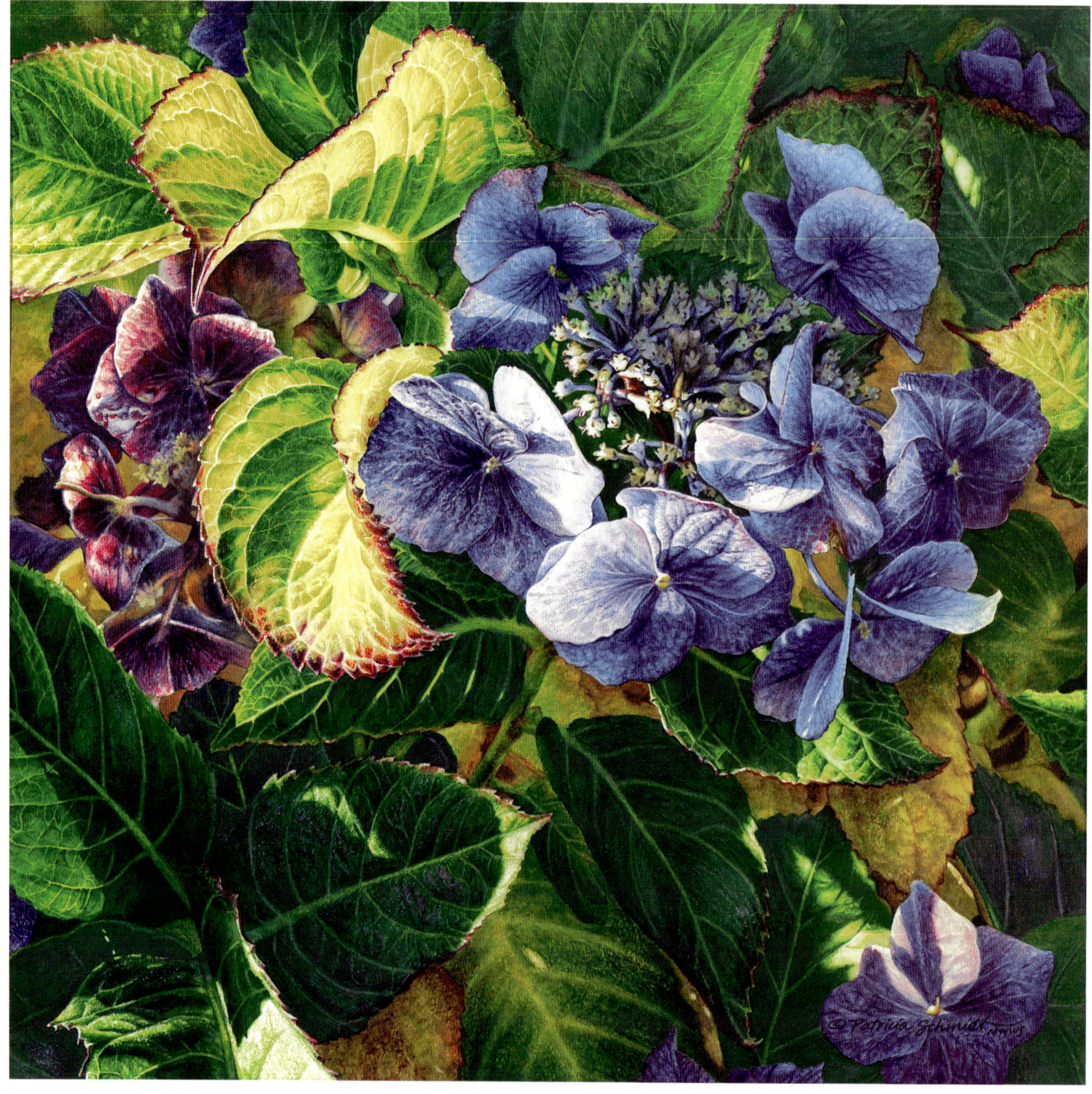

SILETZ BAY HYDRANGEA | PATRICIA SCHMIDT
Transparent watercolor on 300-lb. (640gsm) cold-pressed Arches, 20" × 21" (51cm × 53cm)

Siletz Bay Hydrangea was inspired by the evening light glowing through the blossoms and leaves. The complexity of the patterns and color intrigued me. Composing from photographs, the largest blossom filled the upper-right sweet spot; a few leaves were rearranged for a better composition. On scrap paper, I tested to see which watercolor layers would achieve glowing or muted colors. With the white areas masked, the entire paper was washed with a light Winsor Yellow. Many glazes of various colors developed the rich, glowing color. What a wonderful hydrangea adventure!

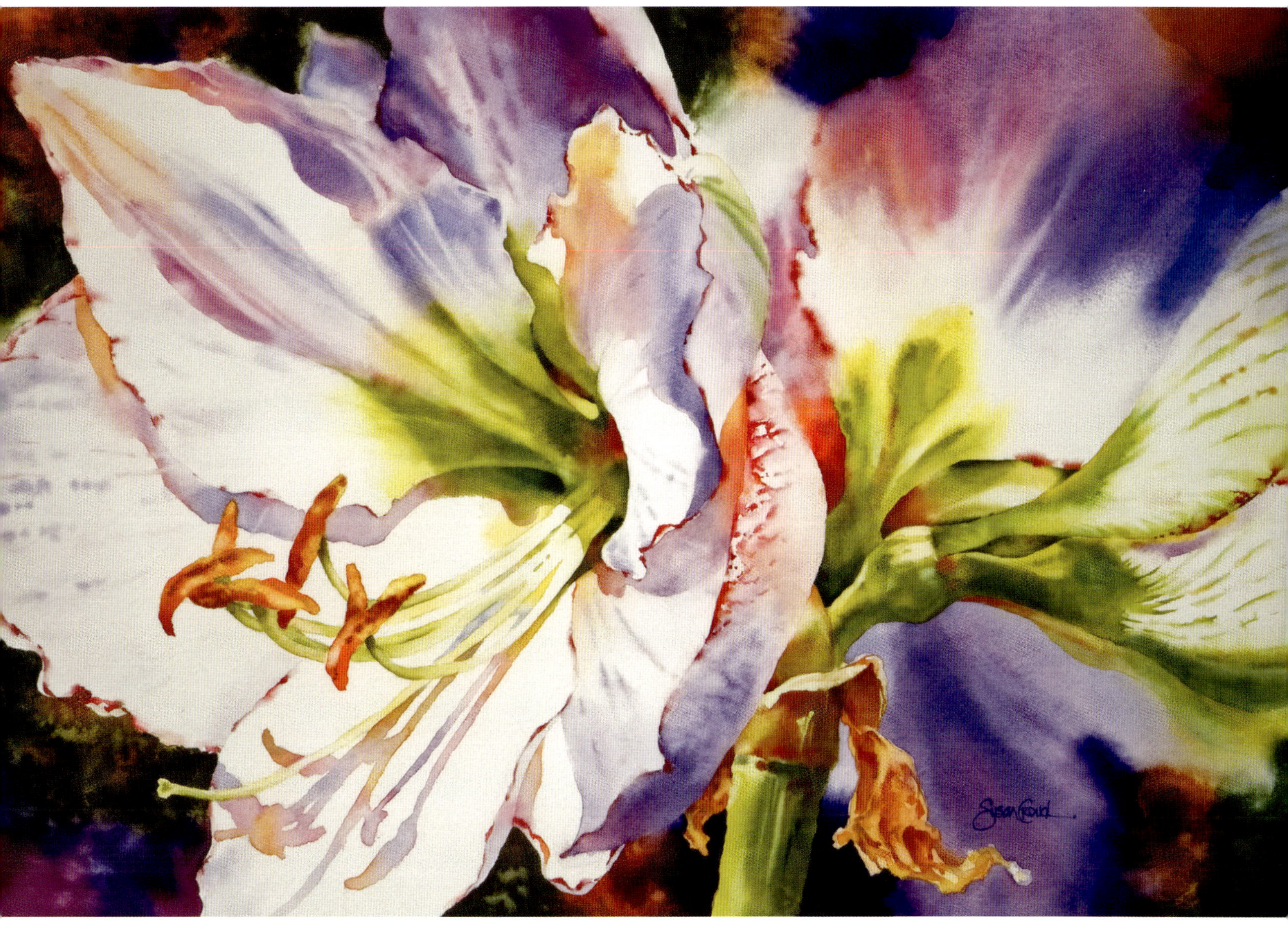

PURE HEART | SUSAN CROUCH

Transparent watercolor on 300-lb. (640gsm) cold-pressed Arches, 18" × 28" (46cm × 71cm)

Three photographs from my files were used to compose this painting. I was drawn to the delicate tangle of stamens and their shadows. The primary technique was a wet-into-wet application of transparent watercolor. Paint was allowed to mingle on the wet paper producing a soft transition of color, and I chose a close-focus perspective to communicate intimacy. This white amaryllis was painted during a season of personal reflection. It represents the concept of an undivided heart, which is referred to in Ezekiel 11:19. The undivided heart suggests a singleness of purpose, and the purity of the white amaryllis is a visual reminder to me of that intention.

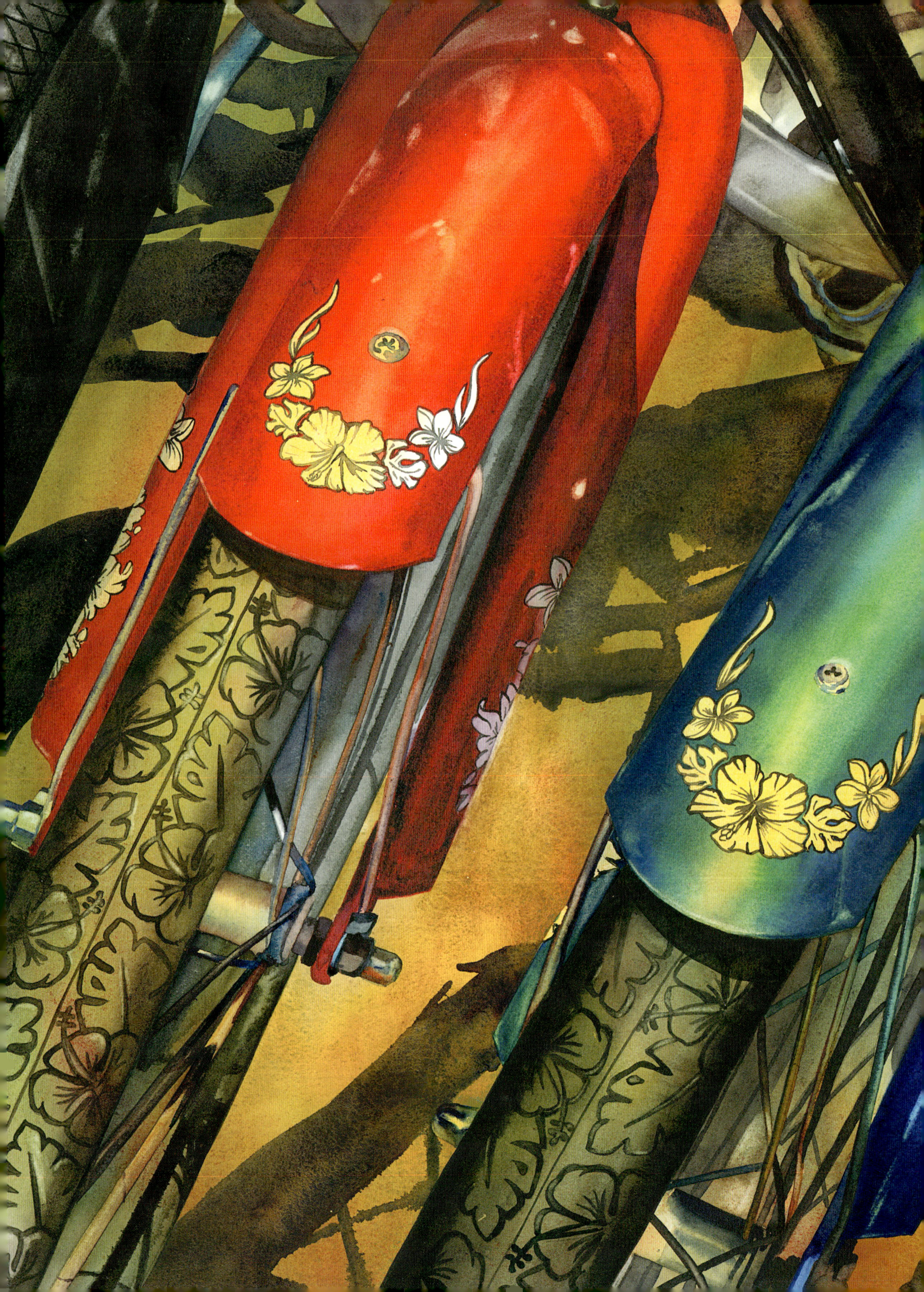

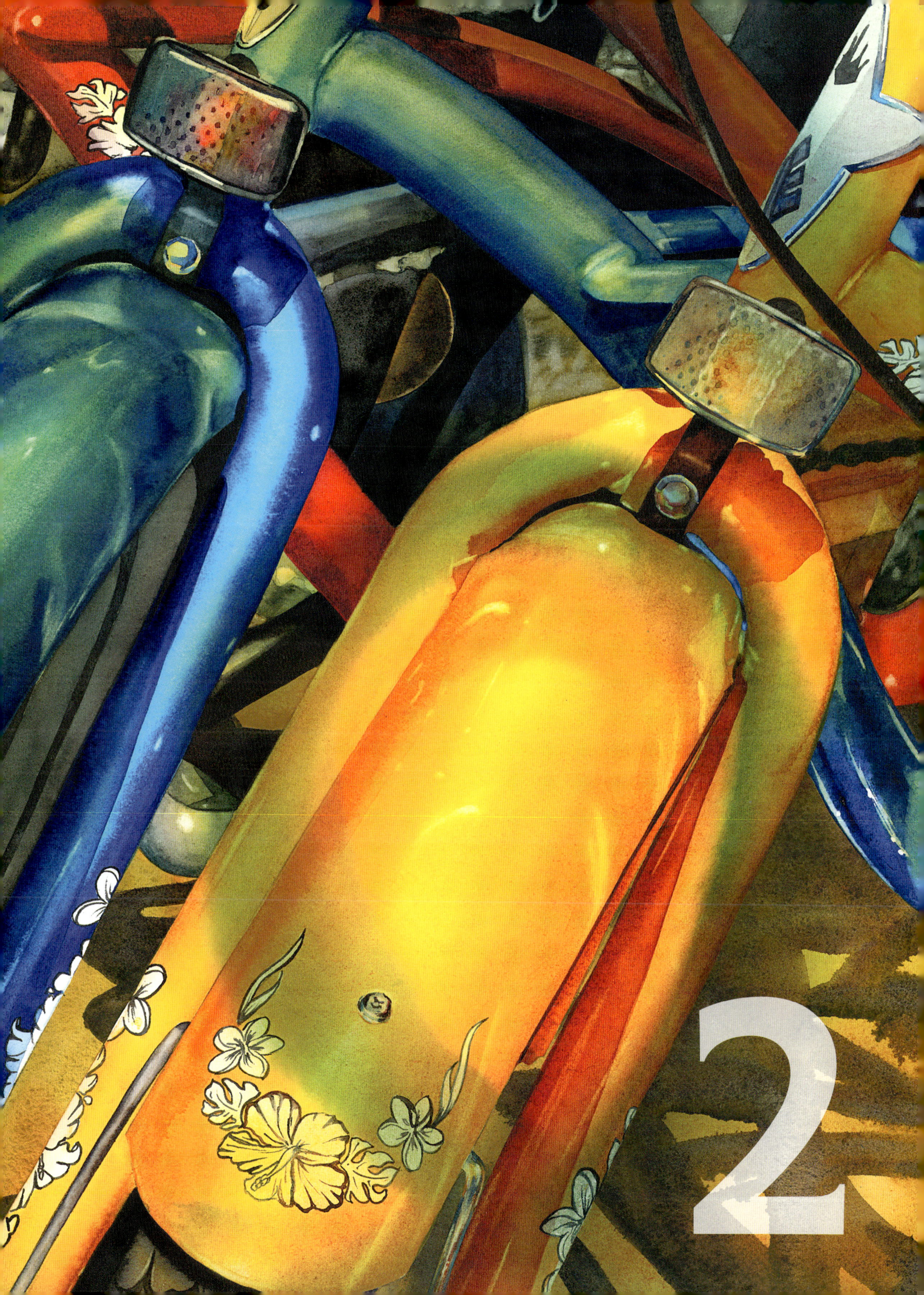
2

2 | WHEELS AND WHATSITS

{ art on previous spread }

PEDAL POWER | TERRI HILL

Transparent watercolor on 300-lb. (640gsm) Arches , 22" × 29" (56cm × 74cm)

Coming home from the coast with my group of artists, I saw these bikes for sale on the street. I hopped out of the van and fired away a couple shots, wondering if I could paint the colorful and beachy atmosphere. I love pumping in color, and this subject accepted it with vigor. How can one not smile with the happy tire treads smiling right back?

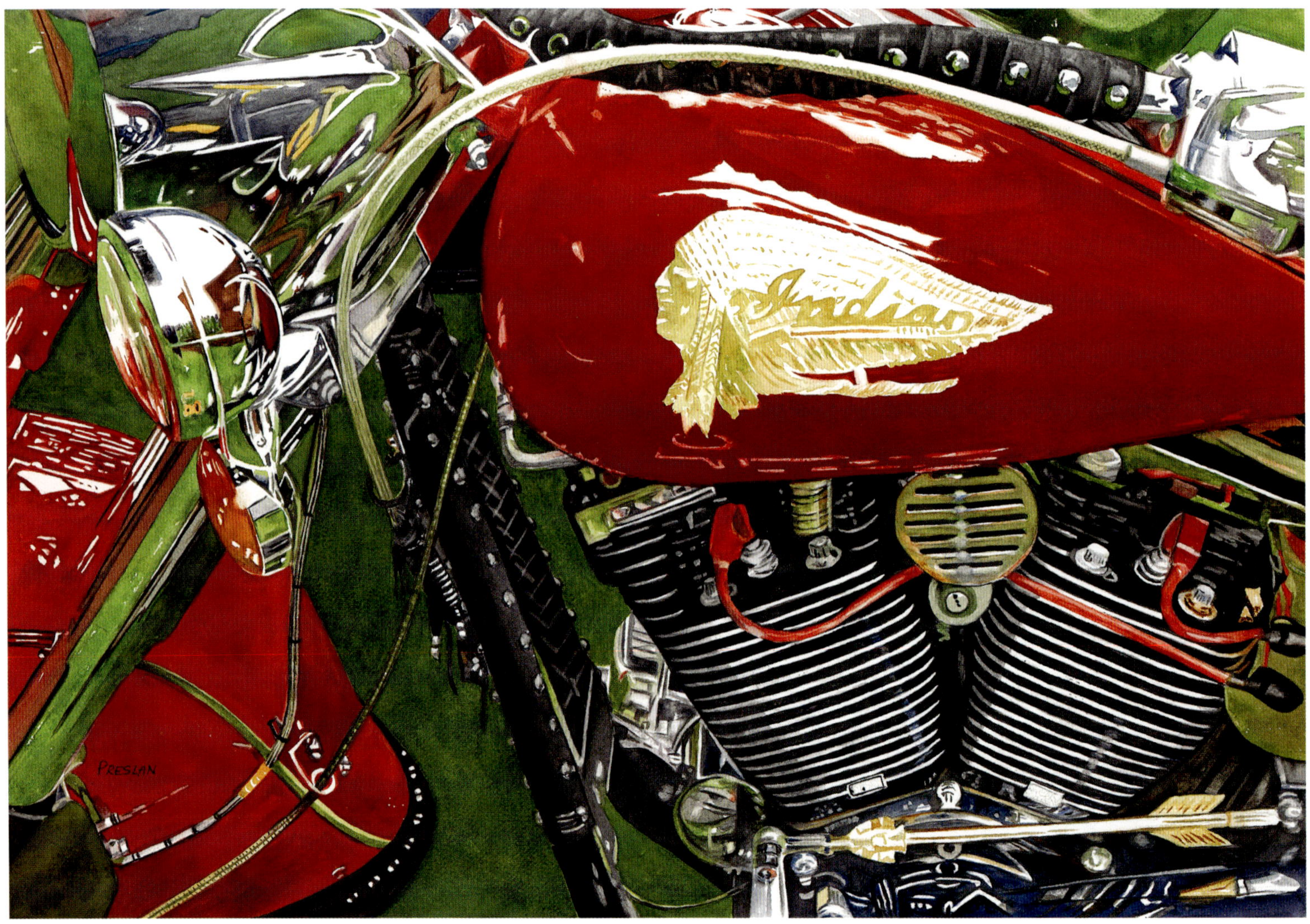

THE OLD INDIAN | KRIS PRESLAN

Transparent watercolor, 14½" × 21" (37cm × 53cm)

A vintage Citroën, parked on the village streets of Monpazier, France, sparked my interest in painting reflections and chrome. I was mesmerized by the quaint shops reflected in its polished metal. This new interest, and a visit to the Pebble Beach Concours d'Elegance, led to my watercolor painting series called *Cars I'll Never Own. Next*, my attention was drawn to a motorcycle sitting on a green lawn. I had no idea what all the parts were for, but they were beautiful shiny shapes I knew I had to paint. I never leave my house without my camera. I never know what new inspiration might be found ... even a red motorcycle.

We can do this … it's just shapes.

Kris Preslan

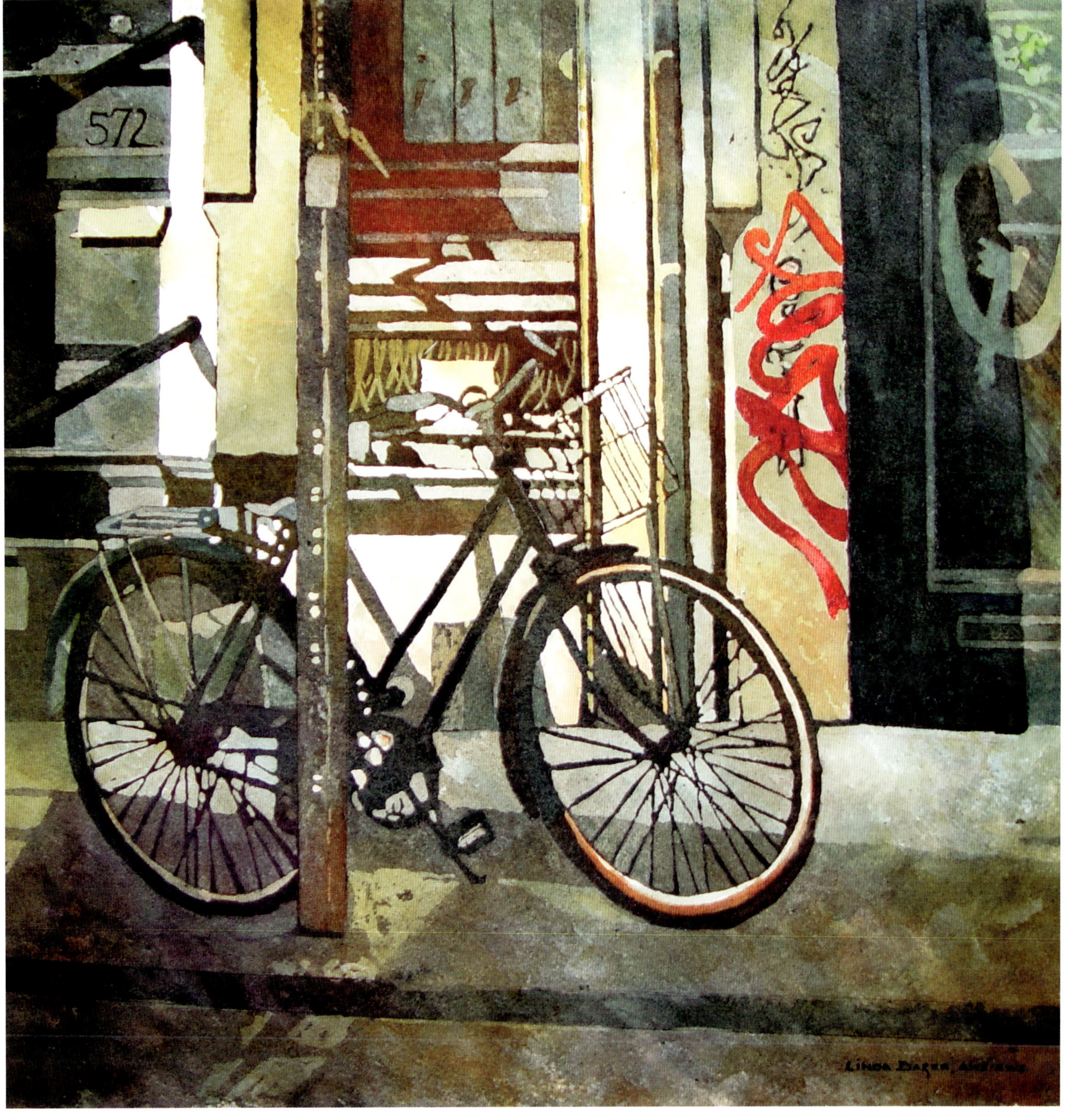

BACK IN FIVE: LIFE CYCLE SERIES | LINDA BAKER
Transparent watercolor, 16" ×16" (41cm × 41cm)

Artistic vision is the artist's ability to view a scene and interpret it into a story for the viewer.

— *Linda Baker*

Back in Five was created from a city scene in the SoHo neighborhood in New York City. I was particularly drawn to the vacant bicycle leaning against the pole with the graffiti in the background. I intentionally made the graffiti red to bring this element forward. My process is to layer paint with resist repeatedly until all the light areas in the scene are protected. Depending on the complexity of the scene, a painting could have as many as twenty layers. The combination of the everyday bicycle with the urban sophistication of SoHo tells the viewer a story of conflicting life styles.

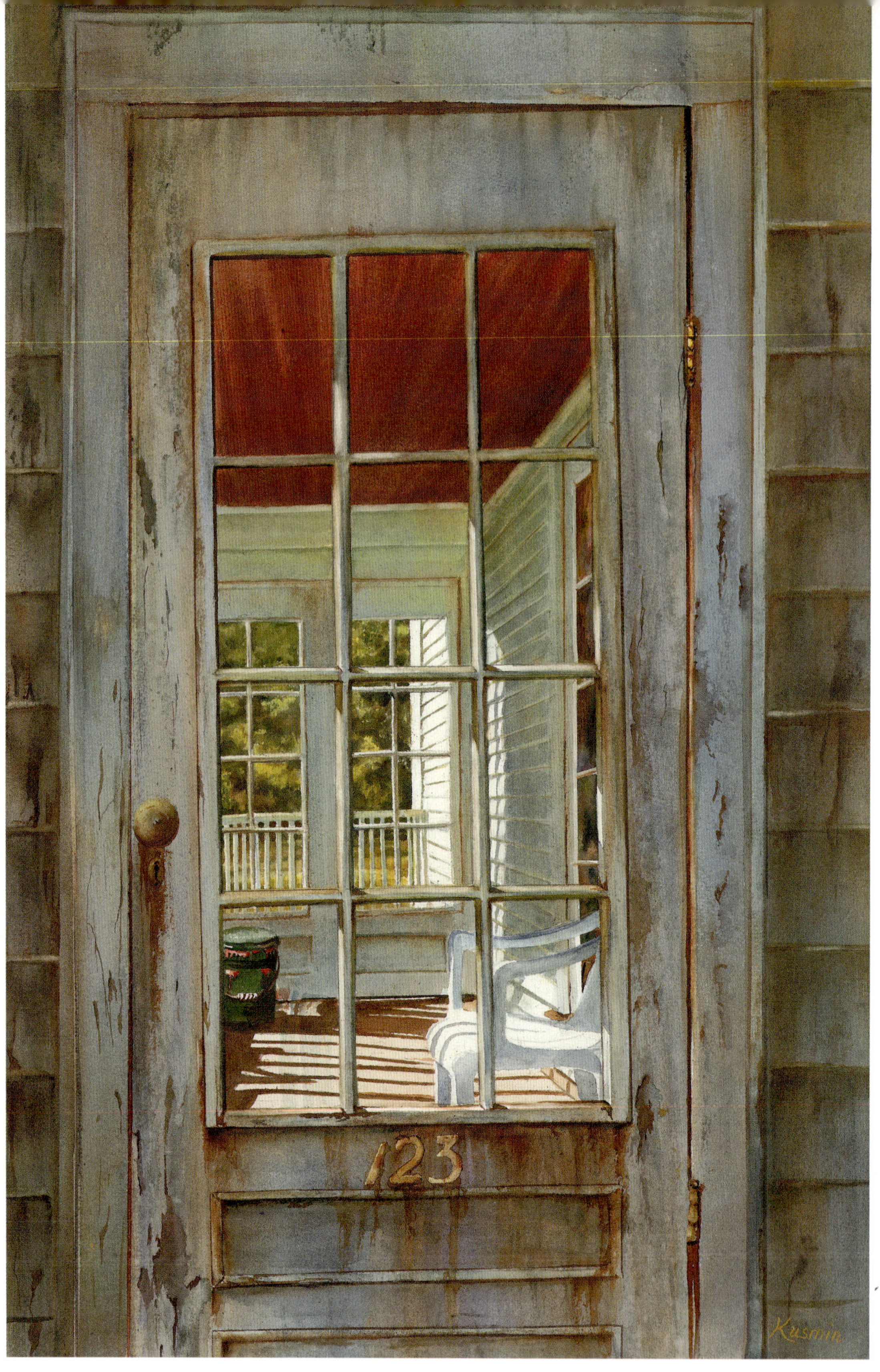

DOOR TO DOOR | ANDREW KUSMIN
Transparent watercolor on 300-lb. (640gsm) cold-pressed Arches, 29" × 17" (74cm × 43cm)

CARDIAC ARREST | ANDREW KUSMIN
Transparent watercolor on 300-lb. (640gsm) cold-pressed Arches, 29" × 22" (74cm × 56cm)

At first glance the objects in both *Door to Door* and *Cardiac Arrest* spark instant nostalgia in most viewers. Inspired by real locations, but created in the studio from photos taken at many different angles, I downplayed location specifics to enhance the universal connection. My primary tools are thought and patience. My best work is often developed years after the initial inspiration (in this case, four years). Specific details of the structures were minimized and faded—I did not want the technical architecture or the strokes to distract the viewer from an emotional response. Touched by man, worn by time, the human presence, with a bit of mystery, remains in these abandoned structures.

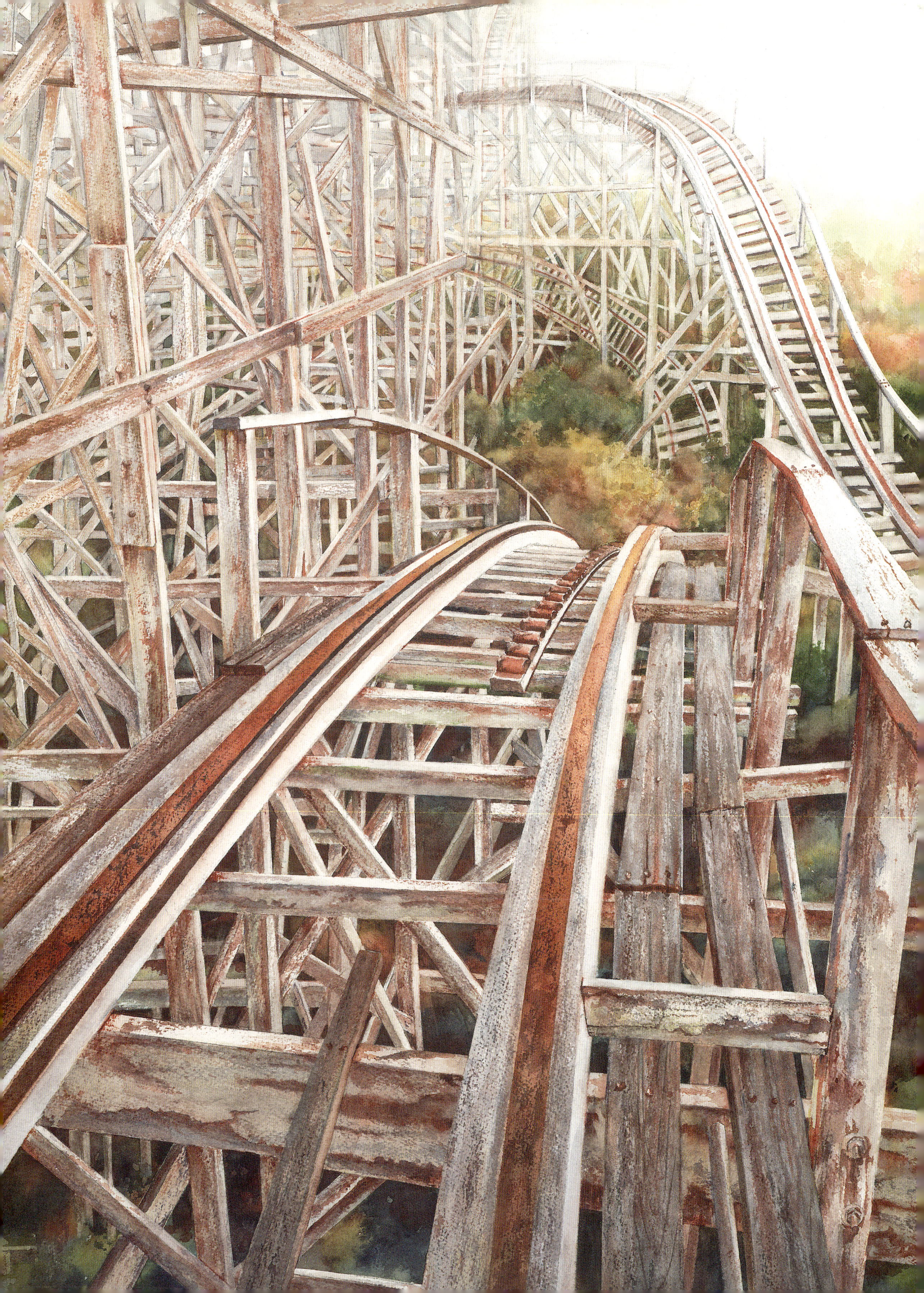

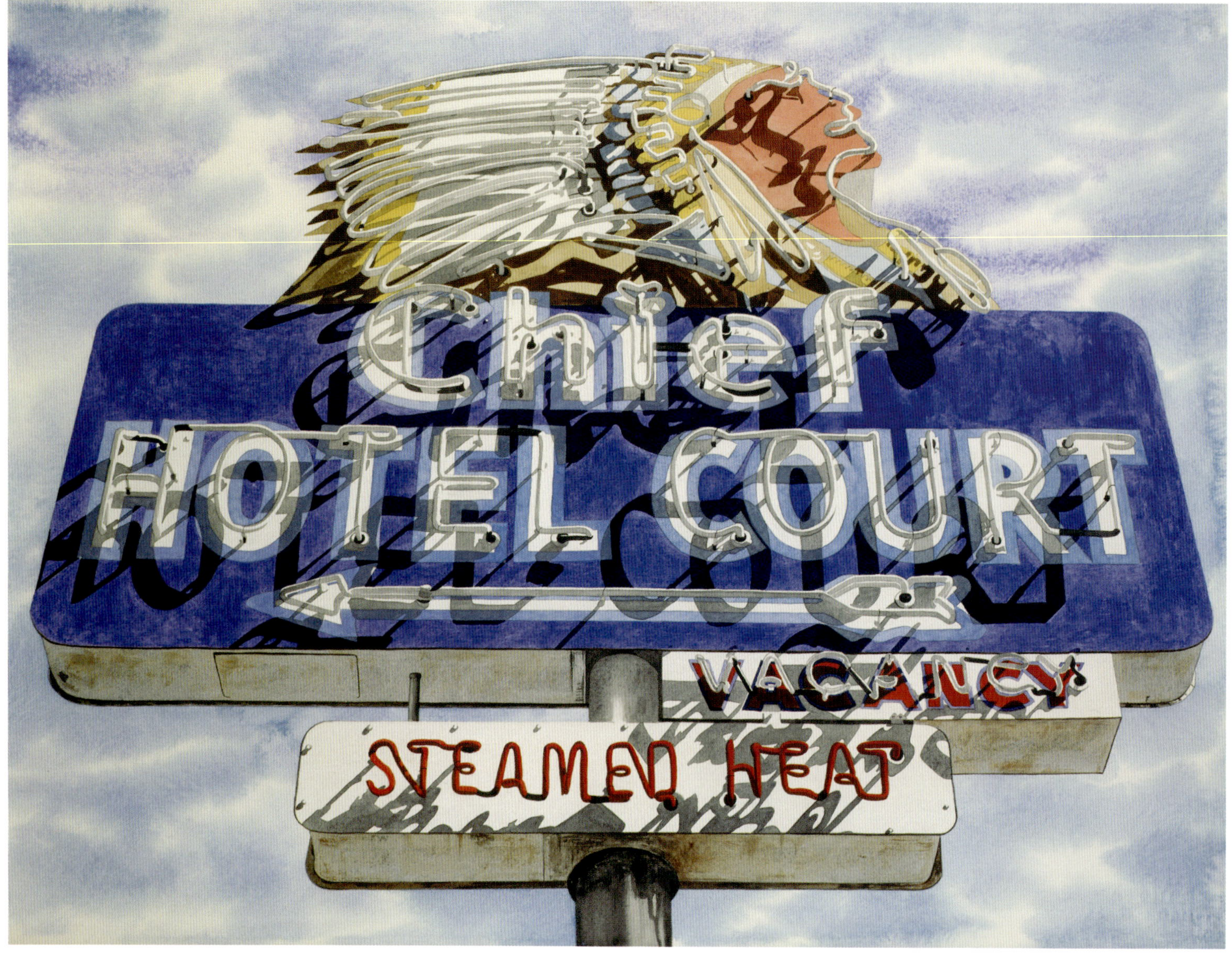

CHIEF HOTEL COURT | DAVID MILTON
Transparent watercolor on 300-lb. (640gsm) Arches, 22" × 30" (56cm × 76cm)

This wonderful old neon sign, Chief Hotel Court (circa 1940s) was a Las Vegas icon. It was taken down with the building but saved for restoration. It was put back on public display on Fremont Street in the original downtown. I found the subject and waited until the lighting was perfect for long shadows and interesting shapes. The piece fits nicely in my series of Americana that I have been developing for more than thirty years.

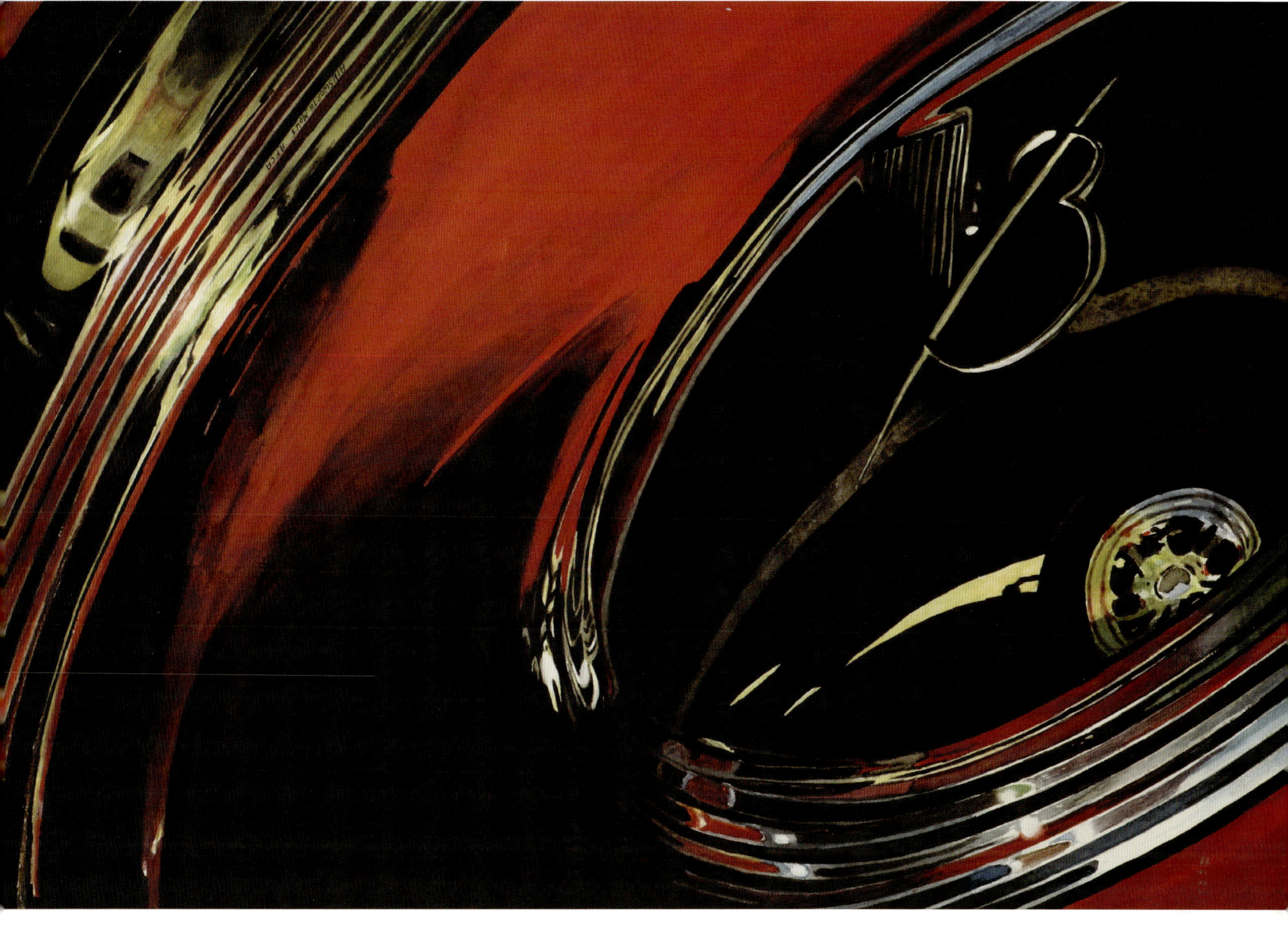

RED WHEEL: REFLECTIONS SERIES | GLORIA AINSWORTH MOUT
Watercolor on 140-lb. (300gsm) cold-pressed Arches, 14" × 21" (36cm × 53cm)

This painting is one of a current series called *Reflections*, often done after visits to outdoor auto shows. I am inspired when I see the often-abstract reflections that are usually totally missed by those around me. On this day, I knew I had hit the jackpot when I came upon a vehicle with a great set of chrome wheels right next to one with a luscious red paint job. Auto shows usually have large crowds, so getting a good photo is sometimes a challenge. That, with the complicated nature of the subject, dictates that I paint back in my studio. Once there, I select the best photos and then crop until I have what I believe will be a tight and interesting composition. I paint in a straightforward manner, always making sure that I "punch up" the lights and the darks to make a more dramatic painting.

Paint that which inspires you. It will show in your work!

— *Gloria Ainsworth Mout*

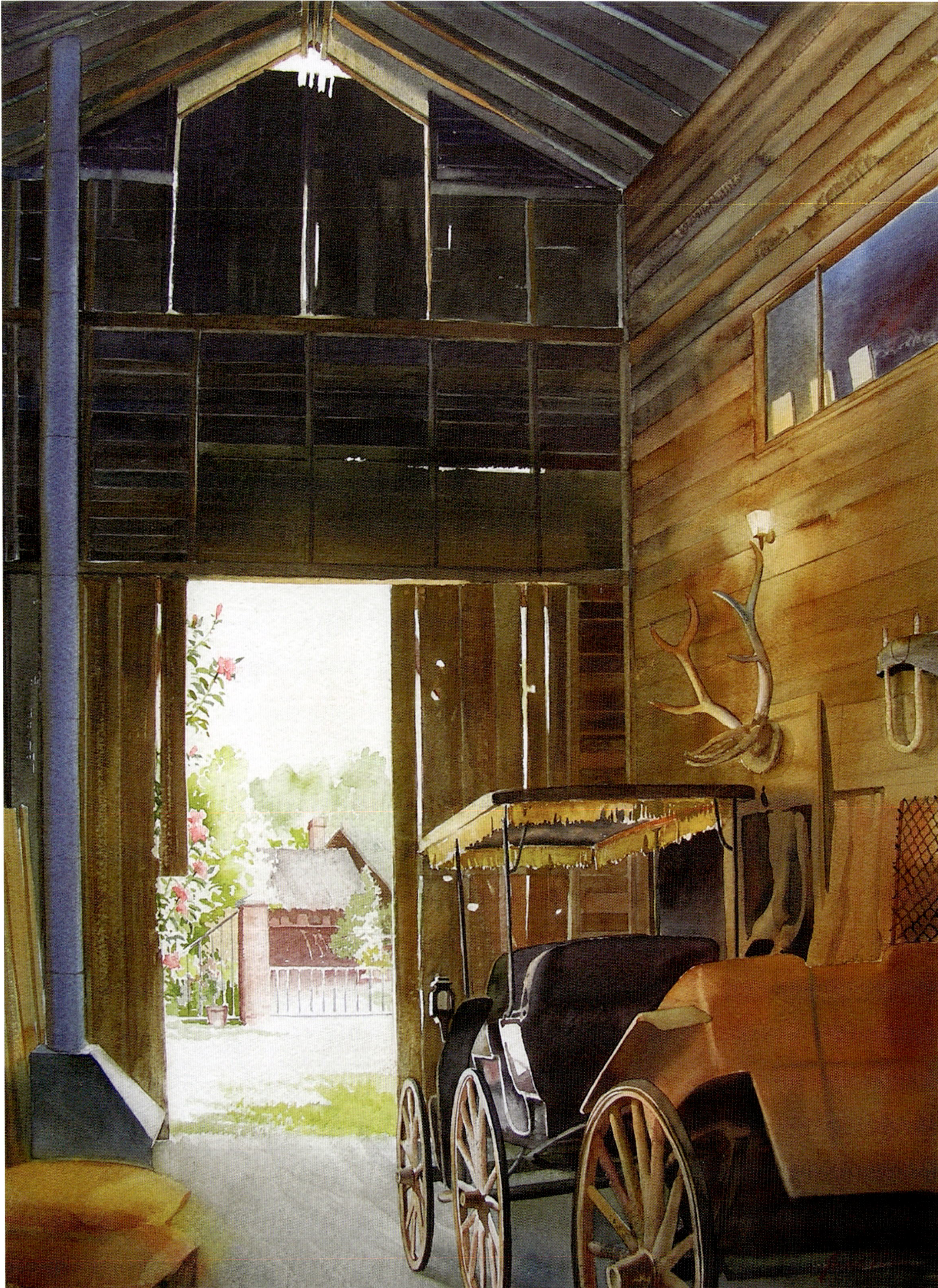

LET THE SUNSHINE IN | JUAN PEÑA

Transparent watercolor on paper, 29" × 21" (74cm × 63cm)

Throughout America you can find old barns that have intriguing little treasures tucked away. This is the 150-year-old Jack Tone Barn and Mr. Tone's personal museum in Lodi, California. Inside this barn, one feels the ghosts of the past. The light through the doorway contrasted with the 150-year-old darkness filling the unusual cathedral ceiling. I always tell my students, "You're grown-ups. Don't be afraid of the dark."

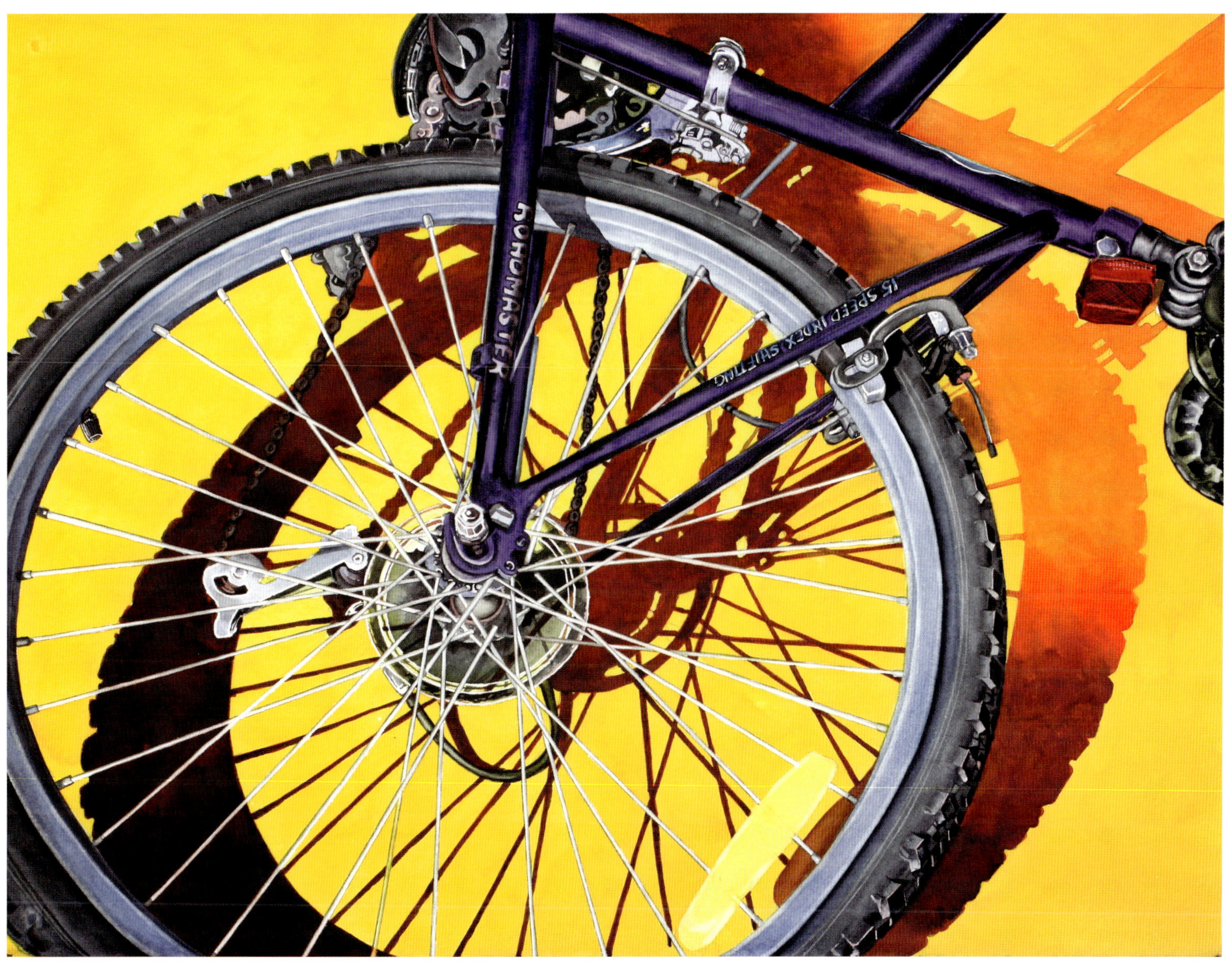

CIRCLE OF WHEEL | SOON Y. WARREN

Transparent watercolor on cold-pressed paper, 22" × 30" (56cm × 76cm)

The bicycle lying on the driveway was drenched by early afternoon sun. Working from my photo, I did a tight drawing. After applying masking fluid to details, I applied a creamy mixture of Cadmium Yellow Medium over the entire surface of the background, then glazed over it with Scarlet Lake to achieve the orange color on the shadow area. To the darker shadow areas I added a mixture of Sepia and Permanent Alizarin Crimson. After the background was set, I removed the masking fluid and defined the subject. The bold strong background complements the detailed bike tire.

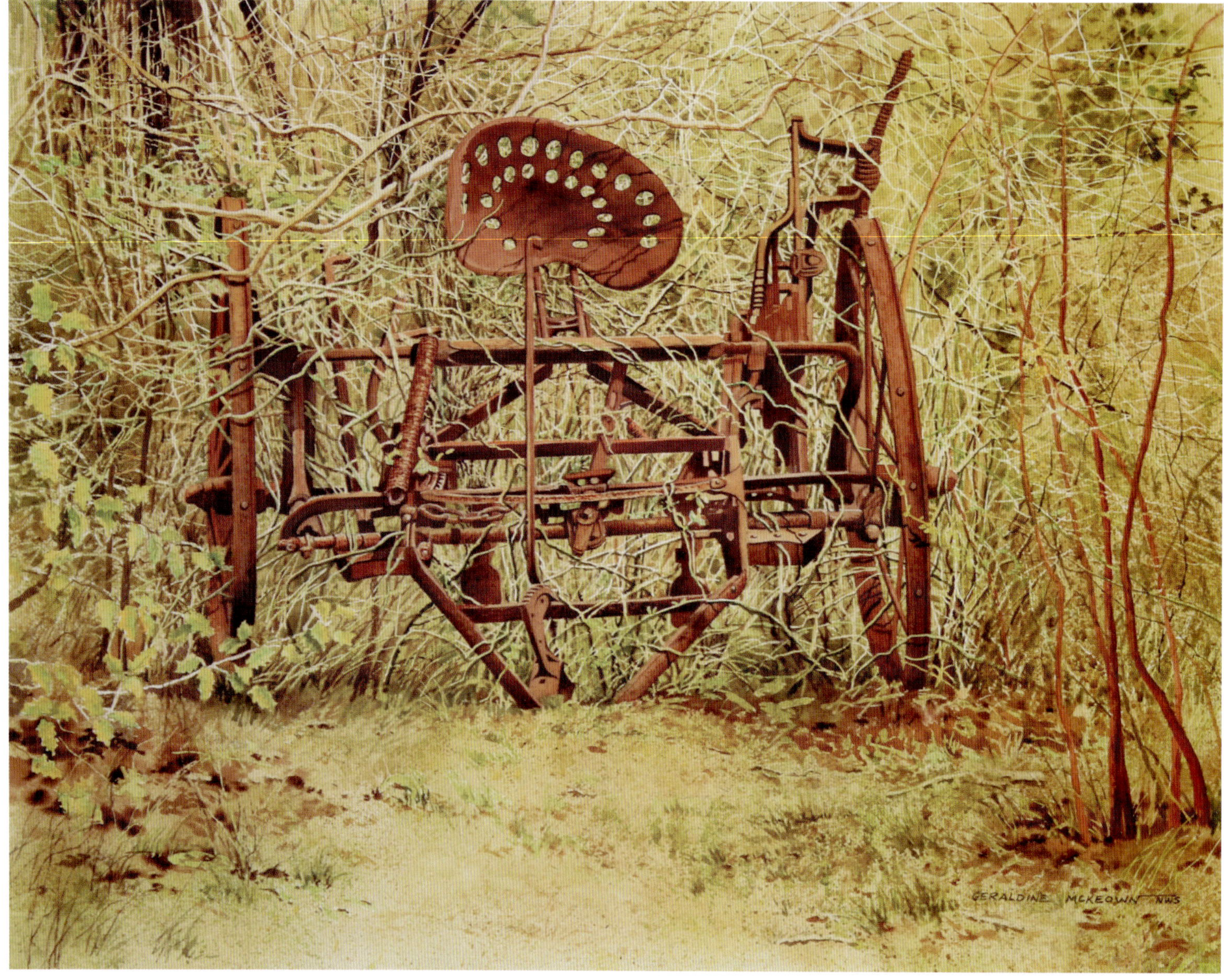

ENTWINED | GERALDINE MCKEOWN
Transparent watercolor, 20" × 26" (51cm × 66cm)

The inspiration for *Entwined* came unexpectedly while photographing an old carriage house. My eye was drawn to the rich colors of an old, horse-drawn hay rake left to rust in a jungle of twisting vines beside the building. In the studio, after a value study, a detailed drawing was made on stretched watercolor paper. To convey the depth of the layers of vines and the details on the rake, multiple washes of color were applied over areas protected by masking fluid. For fresh color, spray bottles filled with a variety of color mixtures were used instead of a brush. My vision was to express the essence of spring and new life bursting forth.

For me the joy of painting is to see beauty in the ordinary and create enriched fragments of life which might never be seen except through the eye of the artist.

Geraldine McKeown

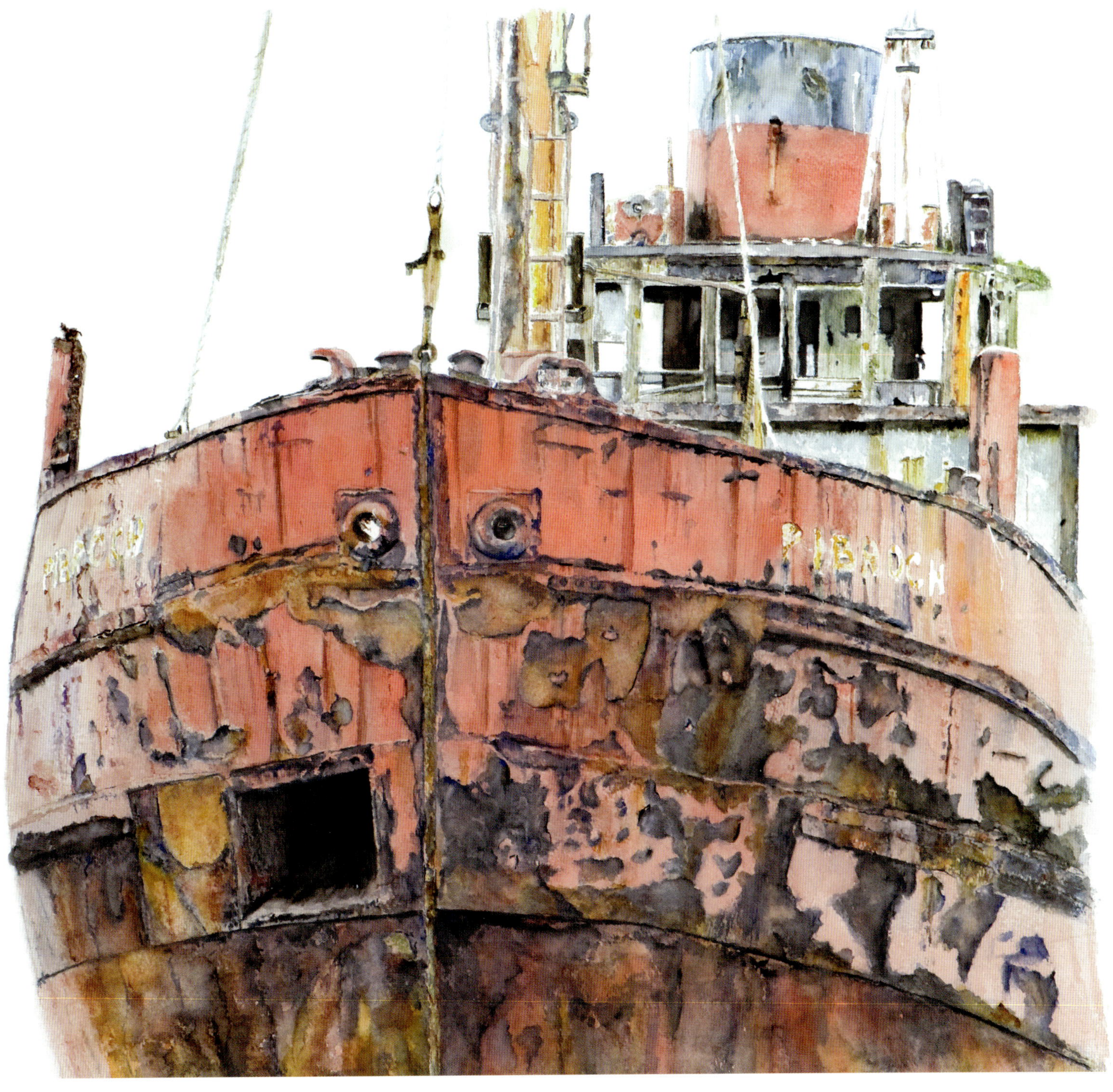

RUSTIC BEAUTY | VERNA HENDRICKS
Transparent watercolor on 300-lb. (640gsm) Arches, 19¾" × 21" (50cm × 53cm)

This old boat docked in Ireland in the middle of nowhere had a "wow" factor that inspired the painting. The beauty of its bygone glory excited me. Working from photos I tried to capture the patina of vibrant colors and to portray the texture of metal and rust by applying several layers using mainly wet-into-wet. I wanted people to feel they could peel back the layers and explore the beautiful colors peeking through.

To see paper transform through paint is a magical journey that makes the heart sing.

Verna Hendricks

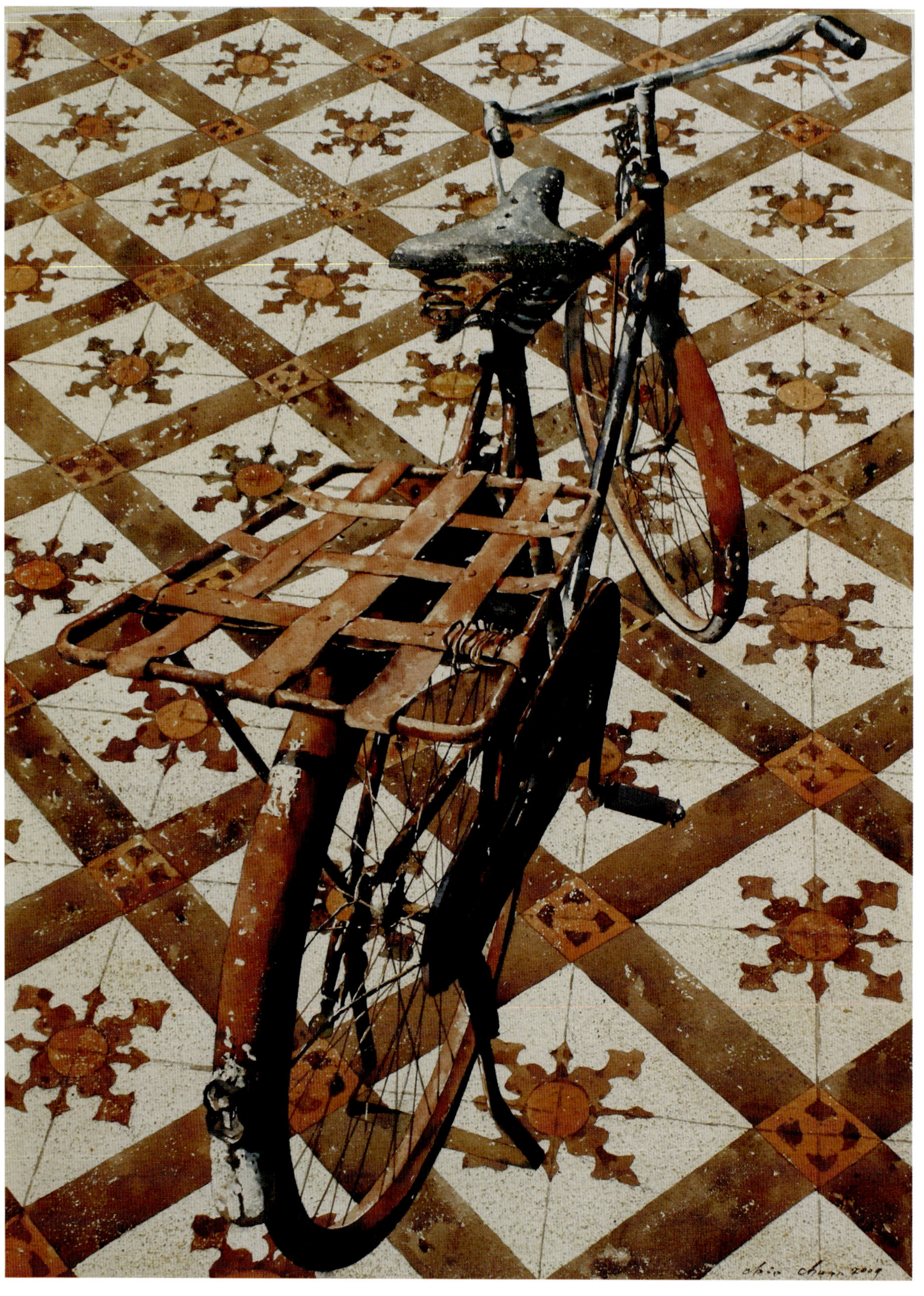

FLOWER CORRIDOR 3 | CHOW CHIN CHUAN
Transparent watercolor on paper, 30" × 20" (76cm × 51cm)

AT HOME | CHOW CHIN CHUAN
Transparent watercolor on rough cold-pressed Arches, 30" × 20" (76cm × 51cm)

Flower Corridor 3 was done in the studio from a photo. The main subject was placed in a position where no shadow was visible. This was a new idea. After a detailed sketch, I applied masking fluid in the small areas to allow for smooth washes. Burnt Sienna was used greatly in this painting.

At Home was painted first on location, then I created a more detailed version in the studio. After initial sketches, I applied masking fluid in the small areas to create texture on the ground. The background door in yellow helps bring out the lighting effect.

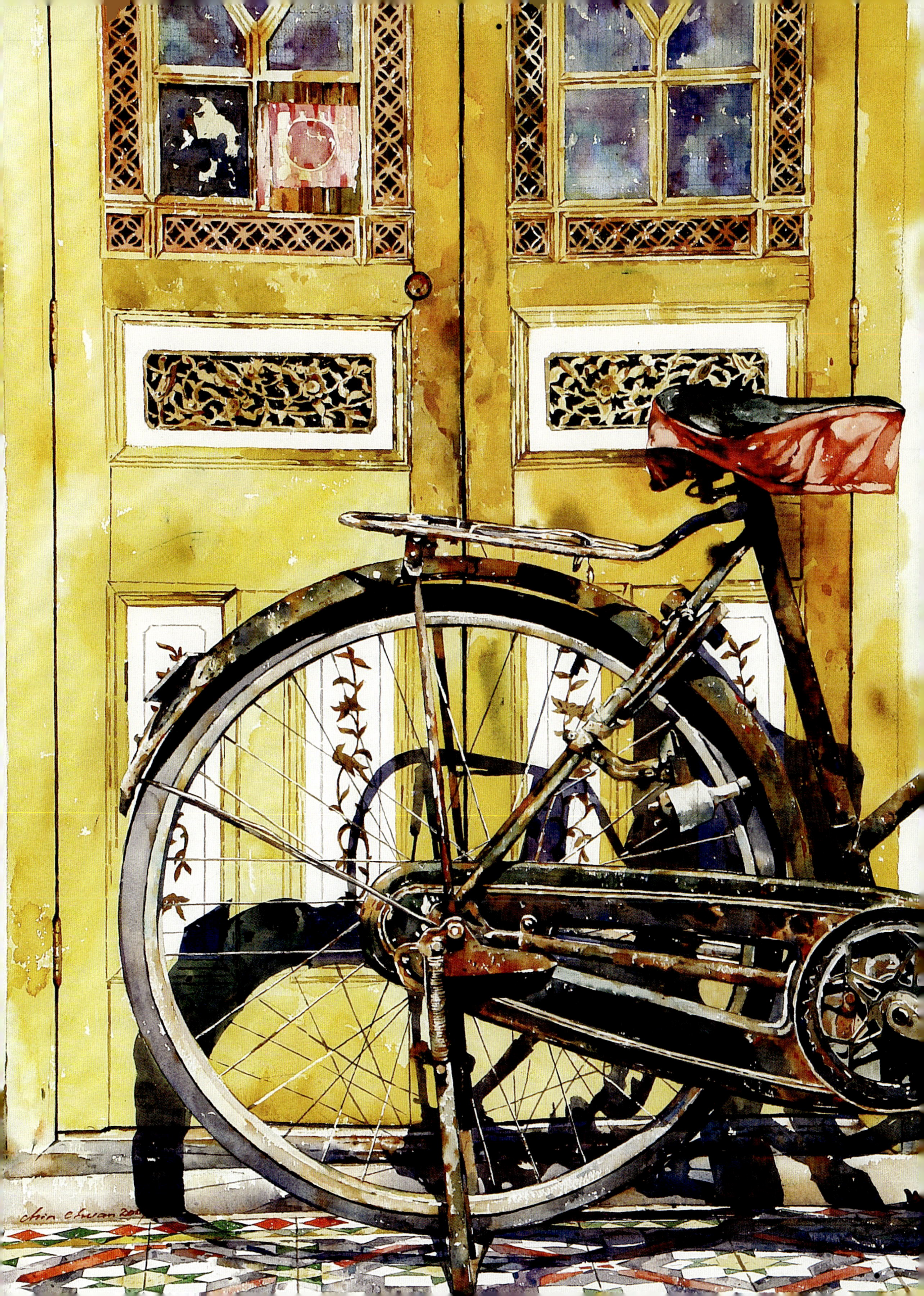

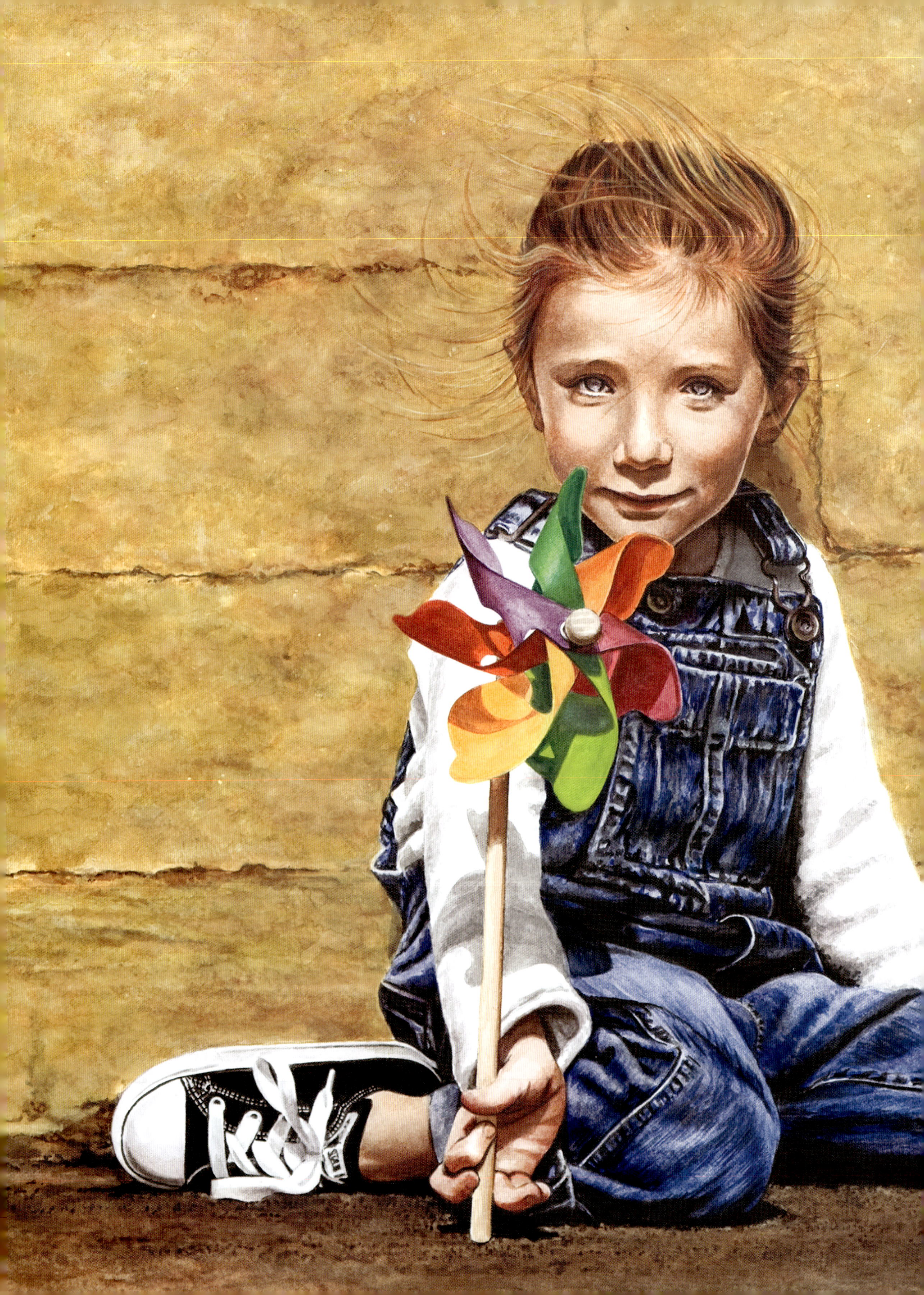

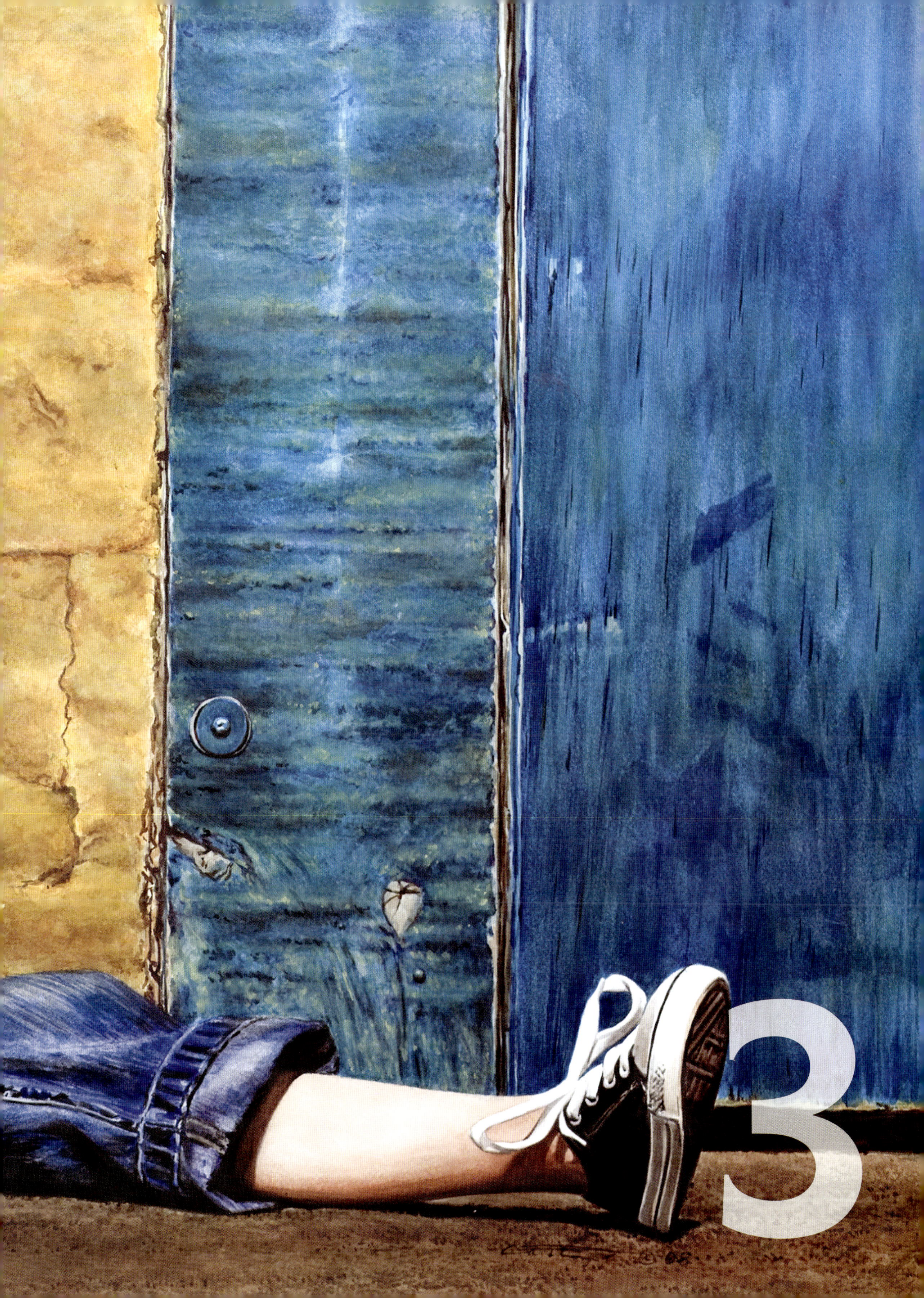
3

3 | PEOPLE

{ art on previous spread }

GIDEON'S PINWHEEL | KARA CASTRO

Transparent watercolor on paper, 20" × 30" (51cm × 76cm)

Gideon's Pinwheel is a painting that made itself. I had another painting in mind, but Gideon was bored with posing and slumped to the ground against the wall in a little triangular blue heap. She had a patient smile in the center of the triangle and three blocks of color in a "pinwheel" around her. It's the part of a painting that happens effortlessly that I find most satisfying. In this instance, adding color and watching Gideon push out from the flat surface of the paper were the parts I loved. It happened as though someone else was painting and I was an observer.

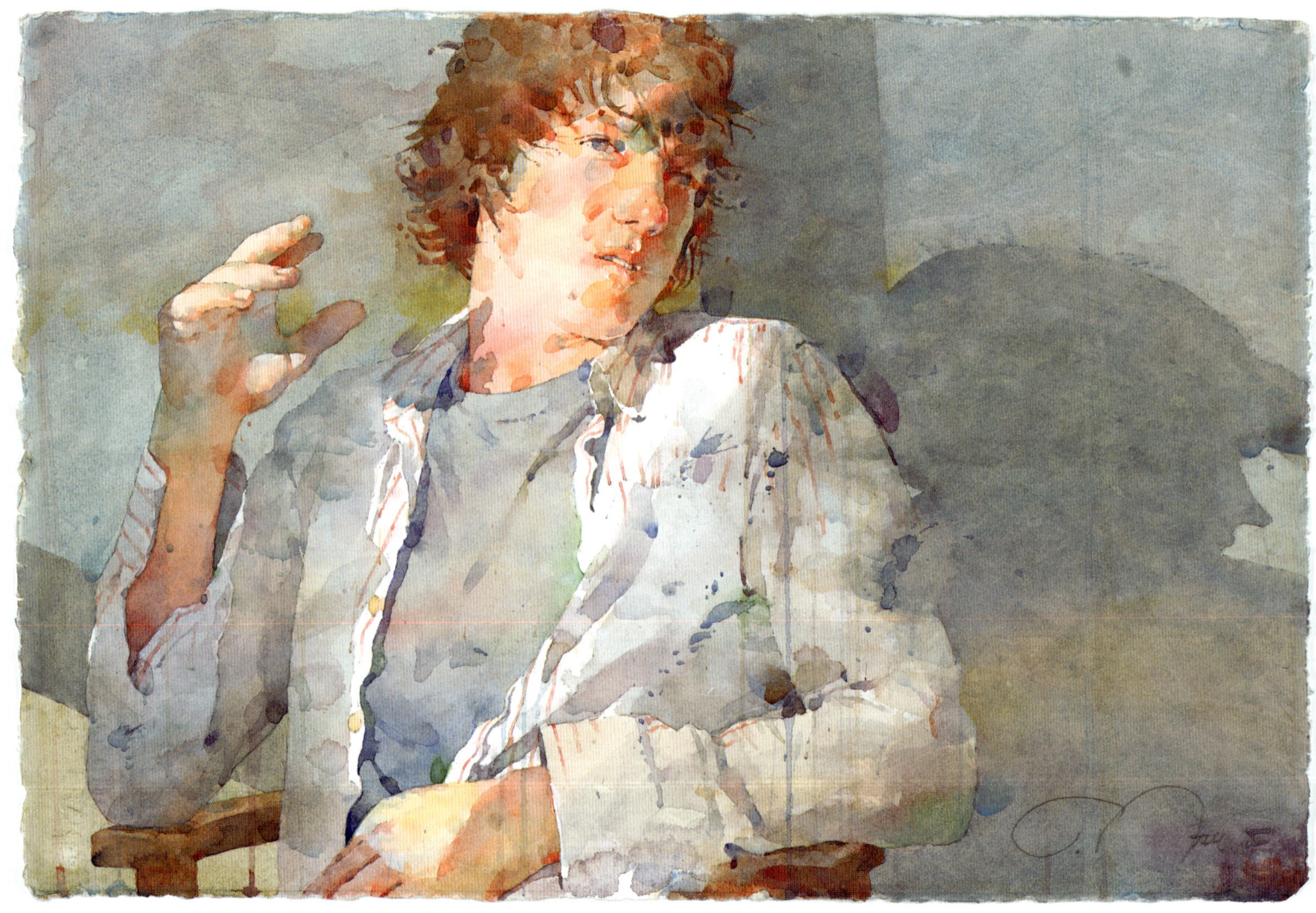

LIGHT AND SHADOW | TED NUTTALL

Transparent watercolor on paper, 15" × 22" (38cm × 56cm)

My artistic vision sees people paintings as landscapes of expression and emotion. In order to express a fleeting moment, I spend a great deal of time in preparation. I first put a lot of thought into the arrangement of the page—the composition. Then I do my drawing with an HB pencil directly on the watercolor paper with the use of a very simple grid. The process is very time intensive (four to six hours), but this careful investment in time allows me great freedom when I begin to apply the watercolor. The look of spontaneity and looseness—the drips, blossoms and accents of color—works because of the thought and time given to the drawing.

WHISPERING SMITH
TED NUTTALL

Transparent watercolor on paper
15" × 11" (38cm × 28cm)

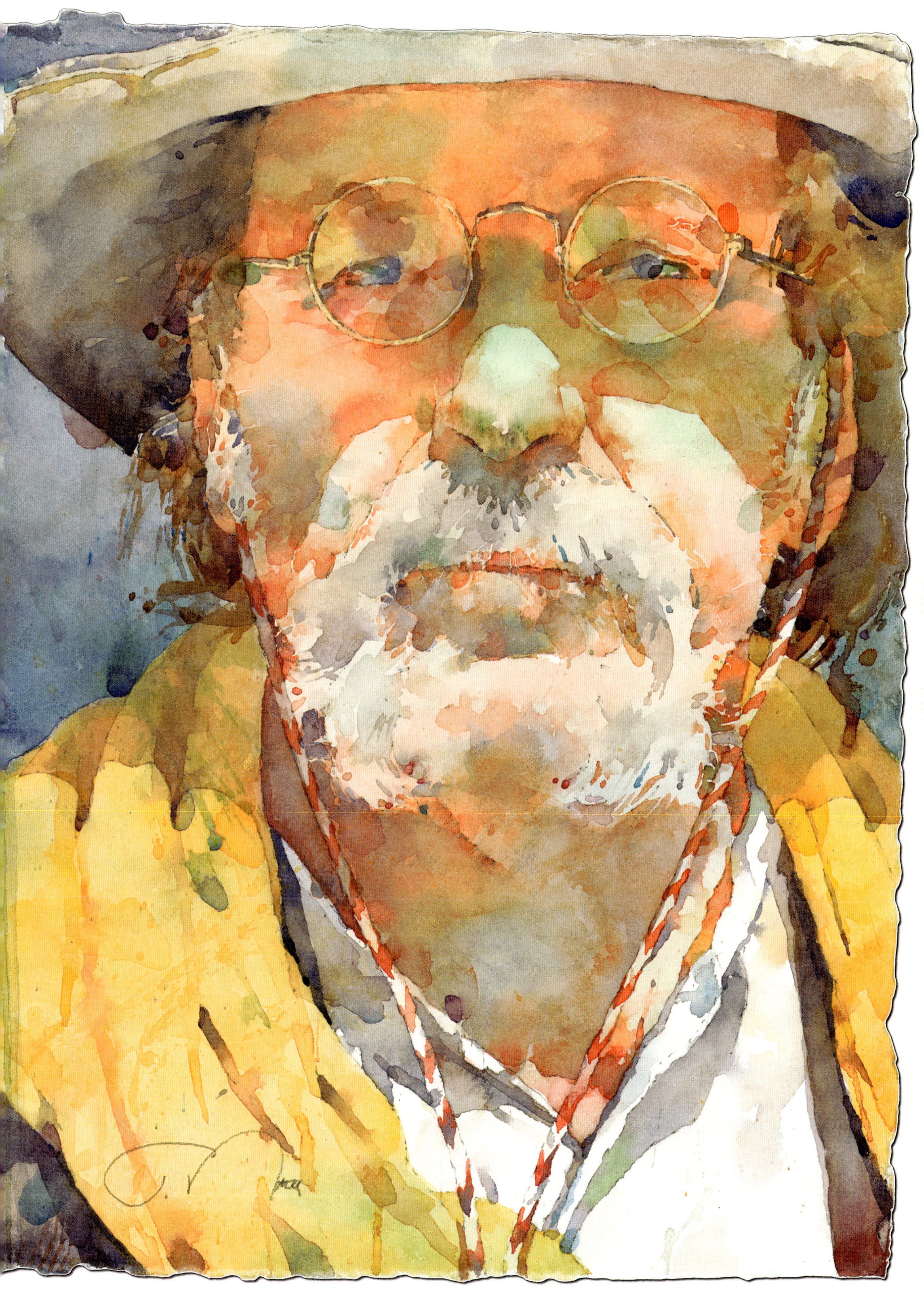

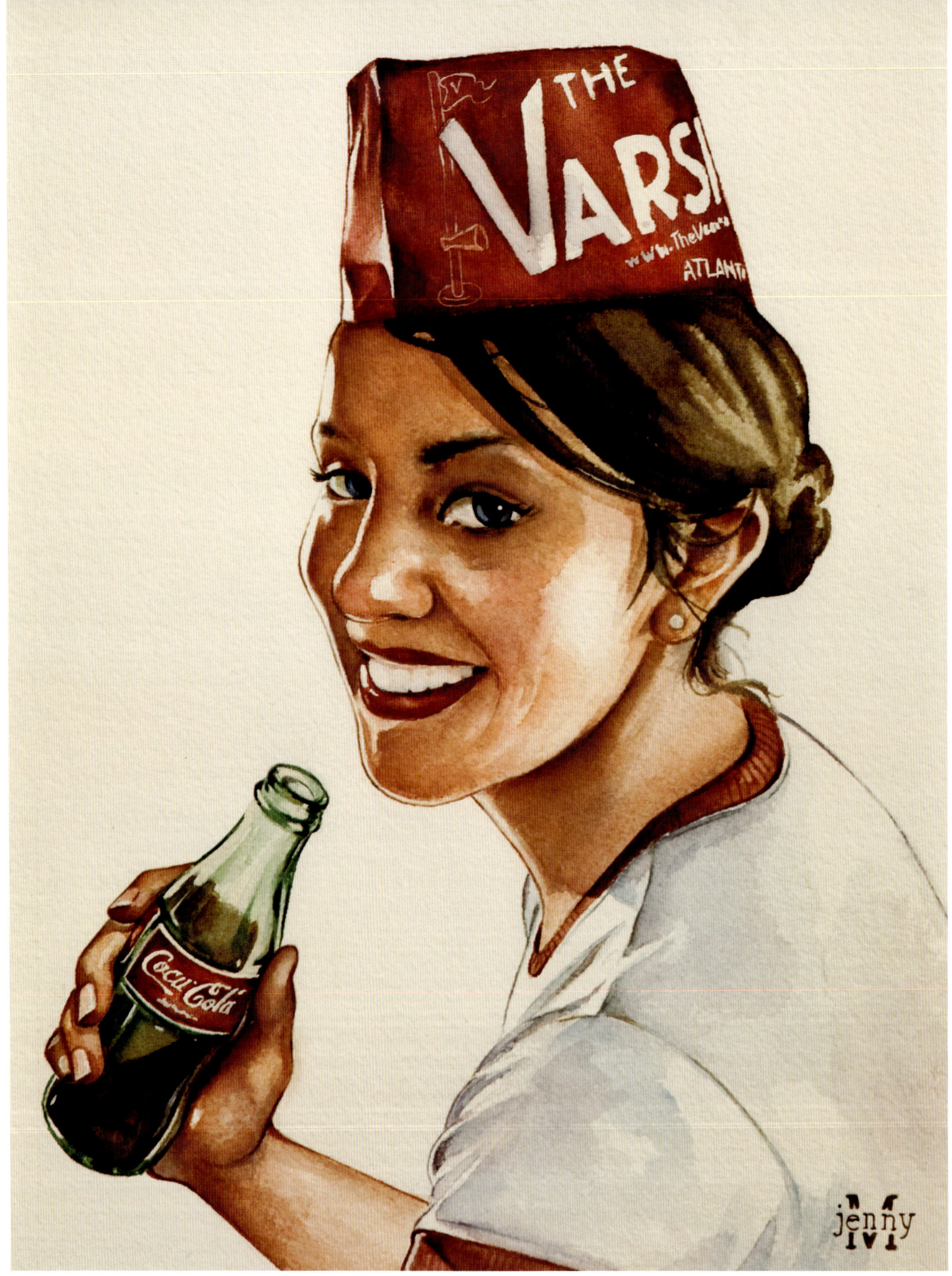

WHAT'LL YA HAVE | JENNY MEDVED

Transparent watercolor on 300-lb. (640gsm) rough watercolor paper, 16" × 11½" (41cm × 29cm)

The model in this portrait is a friend whose timeless and classic look always reminded me of the illustrations in ads of decades ago. This vintage-style portrait is a tribute to one of my favorite historical landmarks in my hometown of Atlanta, Georgia. I painted this at a time I was feeling a little nostalgic and homesick, longing for the smell of hamburgers lingering in the cold city air and listening to my grandmother sip on a Coke.

All of our dreams can come true if we have the courage to pursue them.

Walt Disney

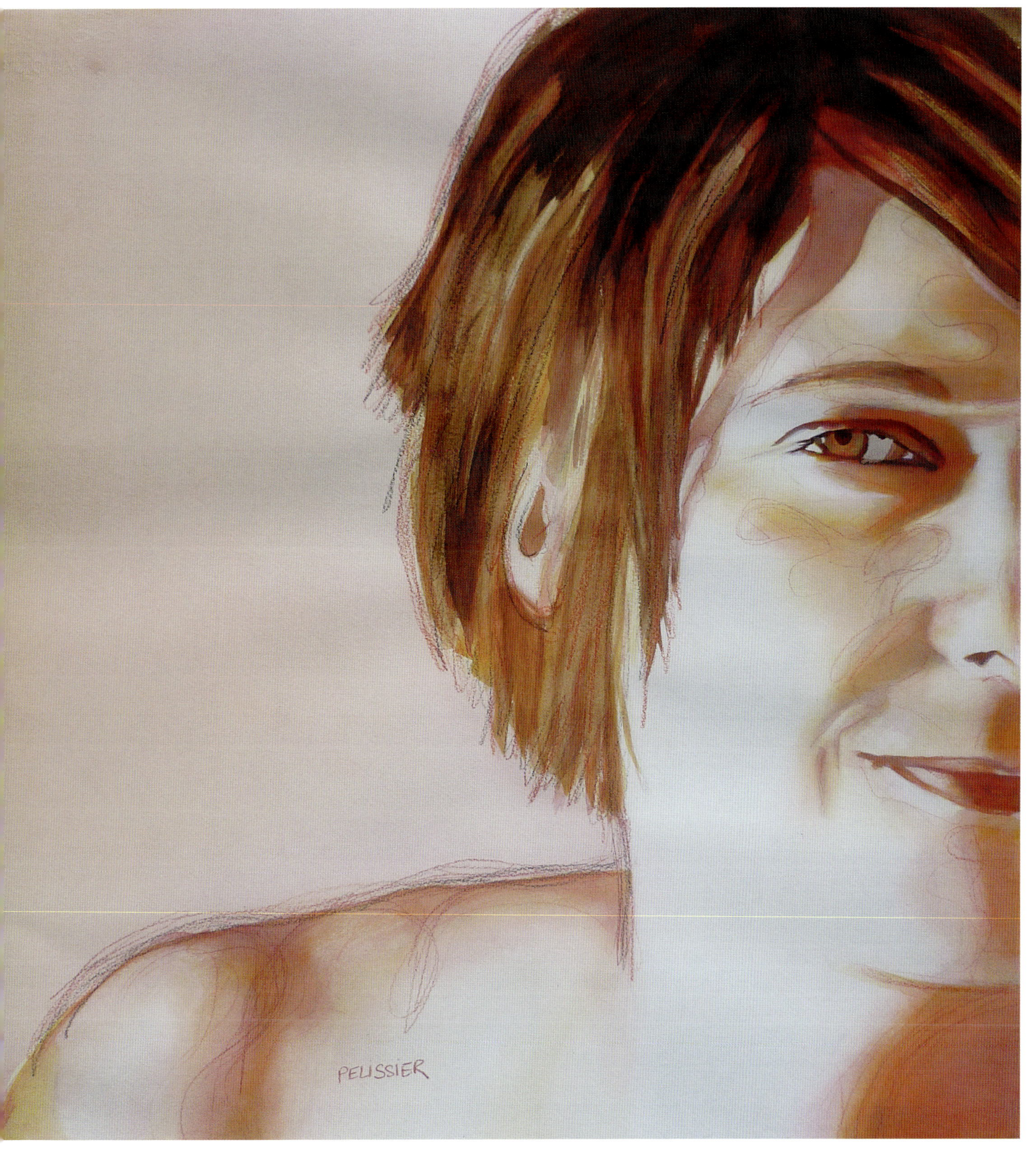

AUTO PORTRAIT #4 | SANDRINE PELISSIER
Watercolor and watercolor crayons on paper, 20" × 20" (51cm × 51cm)

Artistic vision comes naturally when you get into the habit of painting regularly, expressing your own style in the act of creation.

— Sandrine Pelissier

I used layering to create this auto portrait because applying colors separately allows me to focus on tone and edge quality. After the layering process, I make corrections—softening some edges, scrubbing out and adjusting color. Using a watercolor pencil, I added an extra layer of drawing on top of the painting to add energy and movement. I was in a happy mood when my friend Paula took the photograph from which this portrait was painted.

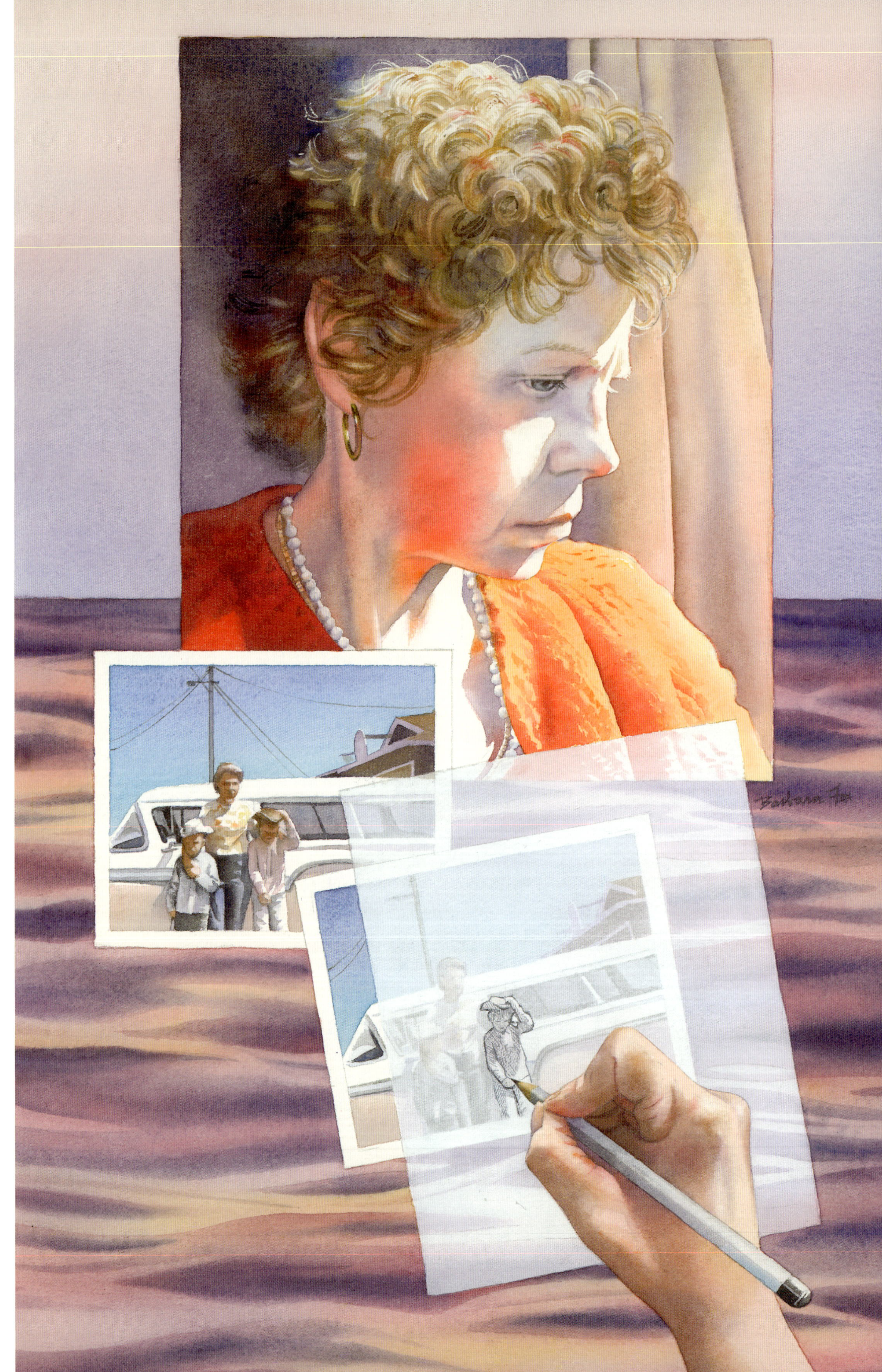
Barbara Fox

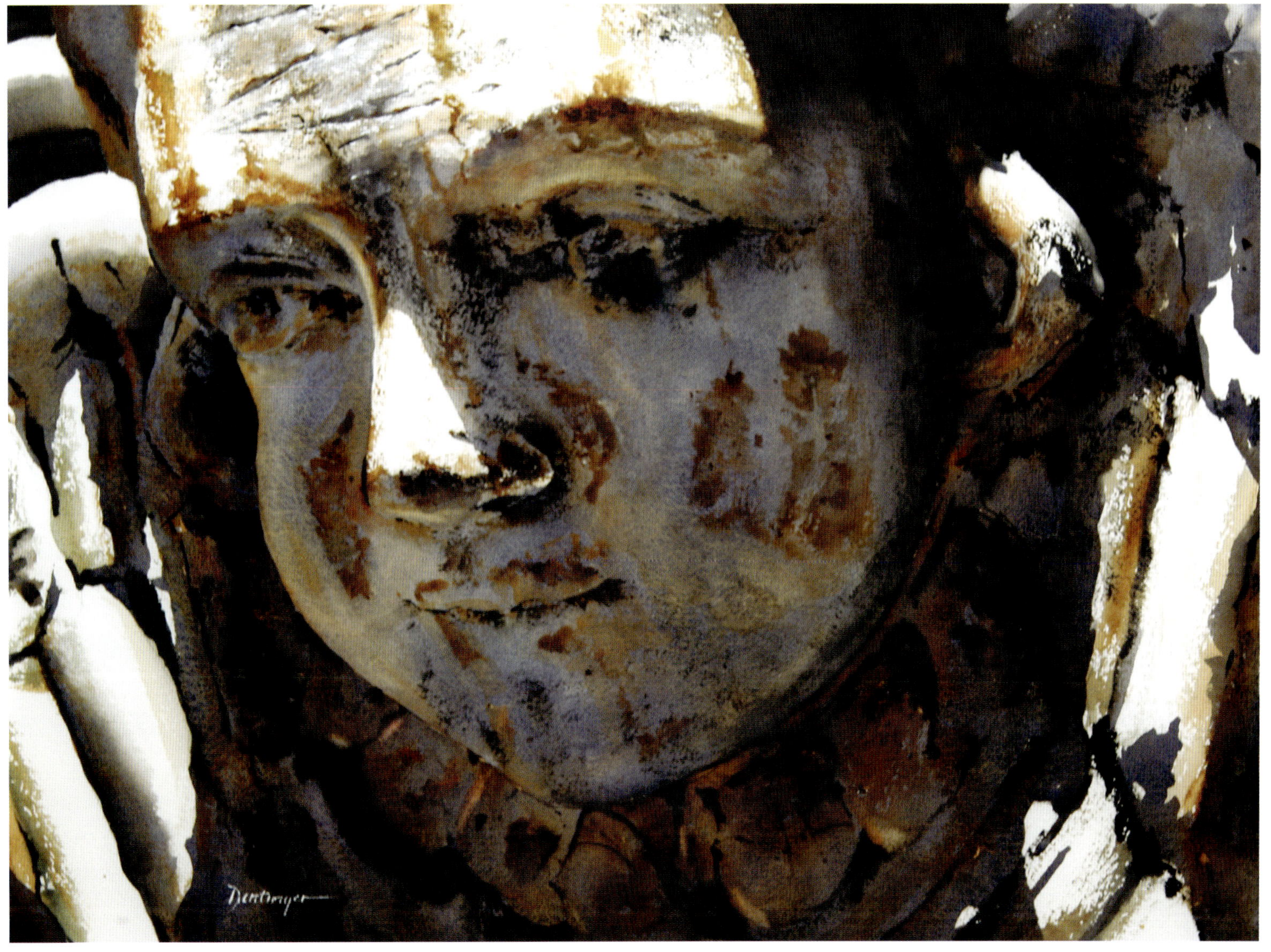

LITTLE WING | RIC DENTINGER

Watercolor with gouache on 300-lb. (640gsm) cold-pressed Arches, 21" × 28¼" (53cm × 72cm)

I painted the *Little Wing* portrait in my studio from a photograph, part of a series of angels perched on the doorway façade of Mission San José in San Antonio, Texas. Built in 1720, the mission lands were given to the Native Americans in 1794. The Mission is now part of the San Antonio Missions National Historical Park and I have spent many hours painting on the grounds over the years. After thumbnail sketches and a detailed drawing, I painted the darkest darks using Ultramarine and Burnt Sienna mixed very thick. Most of the painting was done quite thick, almost dry-brush. I added the final details using gouache Titanium White. My artistic vision celebrates an emotional connection with my subject. The all-knowing, almost sad, face of the little wing angel never ceases to move me.

ANCHORED | BARBARA FOX

Watercolor with gouache on 300-lb. (640gsm) cold-pressed watercolor paper, 22" × 15" (56cm × 38cm)

In this self-portrait, I painted myself at different ages, giving a trompe l'oeil illusion of layers, arranging the images into a quirky composition. I use a fairly traditional watercolor method: light to dark, applying many transparent glazes to achieve rich, luminous color. Creating strong and dark colors is challenging and takes a lot of time, but watercolor is worth it.

The future belongs to those who believe in the beauty of their dreams.

• *Eleanor Roosevelt*

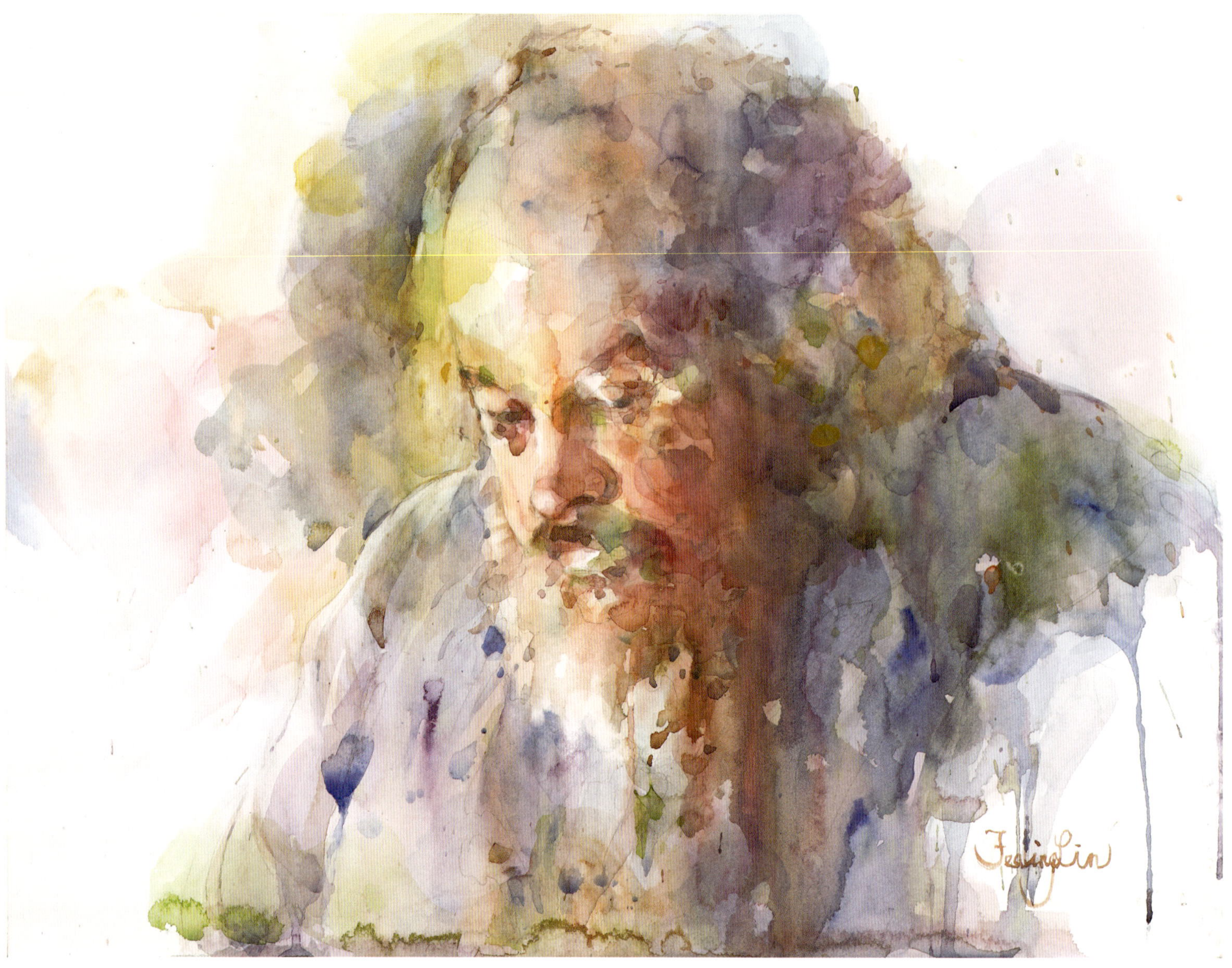

LOBSTER FISHERMAN | FEALING LIN
Transparent watercolor on hot-pressed paper, 12" × 16" (30cm × 41cm)

My passion is to paint characters who have unique expression and attitude. By using a zoom lens, I am able to capture these fleeting moments. Most of my portrait paintings start as demonstrations for classes and workshops and are finished in my studio. An accurate and careful drawing provides a solid foundation for my painting. Then a loose and light underwash sets the mood. After the paper is dry, I paint the large shapes to start with and then glaze the smaller shapes on the top of them. Making interesting shapes is always my emphasis since I am not a realistic painter. My goal is to focus on the essence of a particular character.

A watercolorist's vision:
To plan like a chess player.
Be calm like a Zen master.
Execute like a fine surgeon.
Be graceful like an ice skater.

Fealing Lin

FARMER GEORGE | FEALING LIN
Transparent watercolor on cold-pressed paper, 16" × 12" (41cm × 30cm)

Every breath is a gift. Every brushstroke is a joy.

Fealing Lin

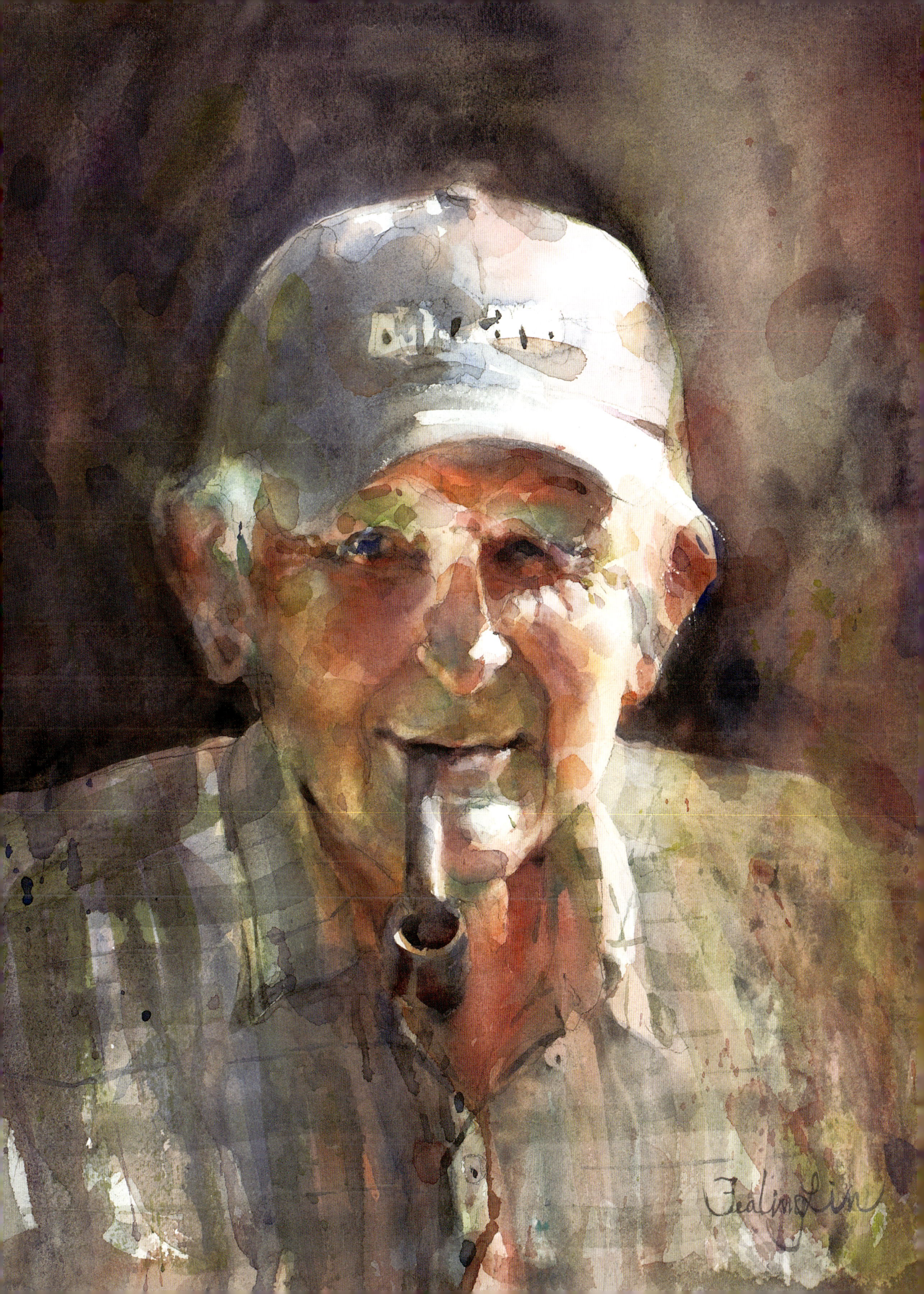
Fealing Lin

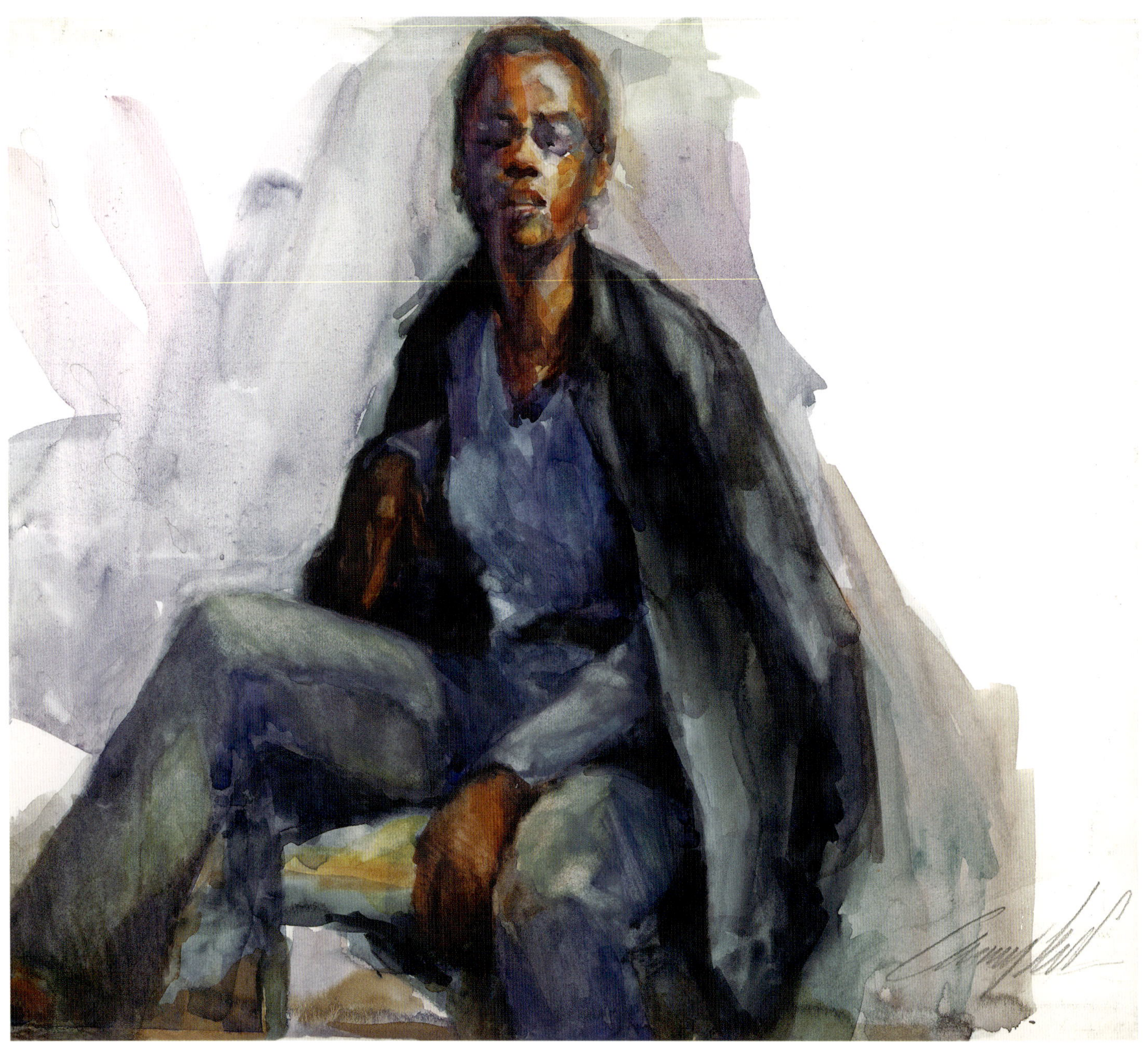

BLUENOTE | NAOMI CAMPBELL
Transparent watercolor on paper, 10" × 12" (25cm × 30cm)

"Let your soul do the singin' ..." (Ma Rainey to Bessie Smith). This piece does not reference music directly, but implies it. Painted from life, *Bluenote* emerged through a preoccupation with jazz in the city I call home—that is New York City. Taking the expressive nature of this transparent aqueous medium, I have bound it together with my idea of musicality. The process of smoky layering creates an ethereal tension for the subliminal senses in this existentialist view of living in the metropolis, where paradoxes are everywhere.

The body inherently takes its place in my work in response to the environment eliciting a vernacular of the senses.

Naomi Campbell

RAIL YARD FLAPPER FANTASY | LAEL H. NELSON
Opaque watercolor on 300-lb. (640gsm) paper, 29" × 19" (74cm × 48cm)

Sifting through old photographs of family and friends from the 1880s to the 1940s, I found a photograph of my mother taken in 1929. All the small towns at that time had freight trains, and my mother climbed up to show off her new outfit made by my grandmother. Using a dry-brush technique I mix white gouache with watercolors until I get an opaque mixture. I first do a detailed drawing on the watercolor paper and then a Burnt Umber underpainting. I then add the details on top, similar to oil technique.

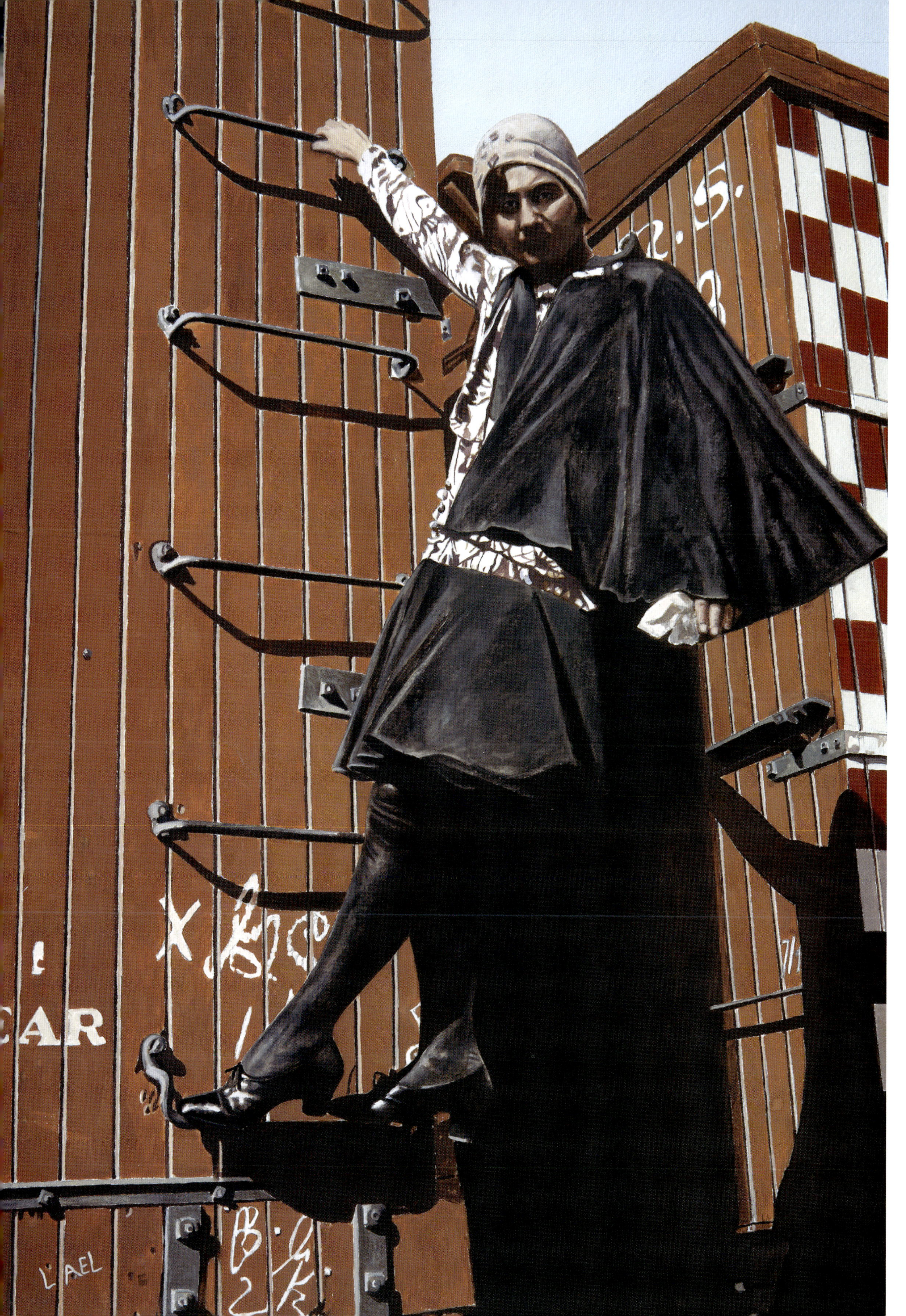
CAR

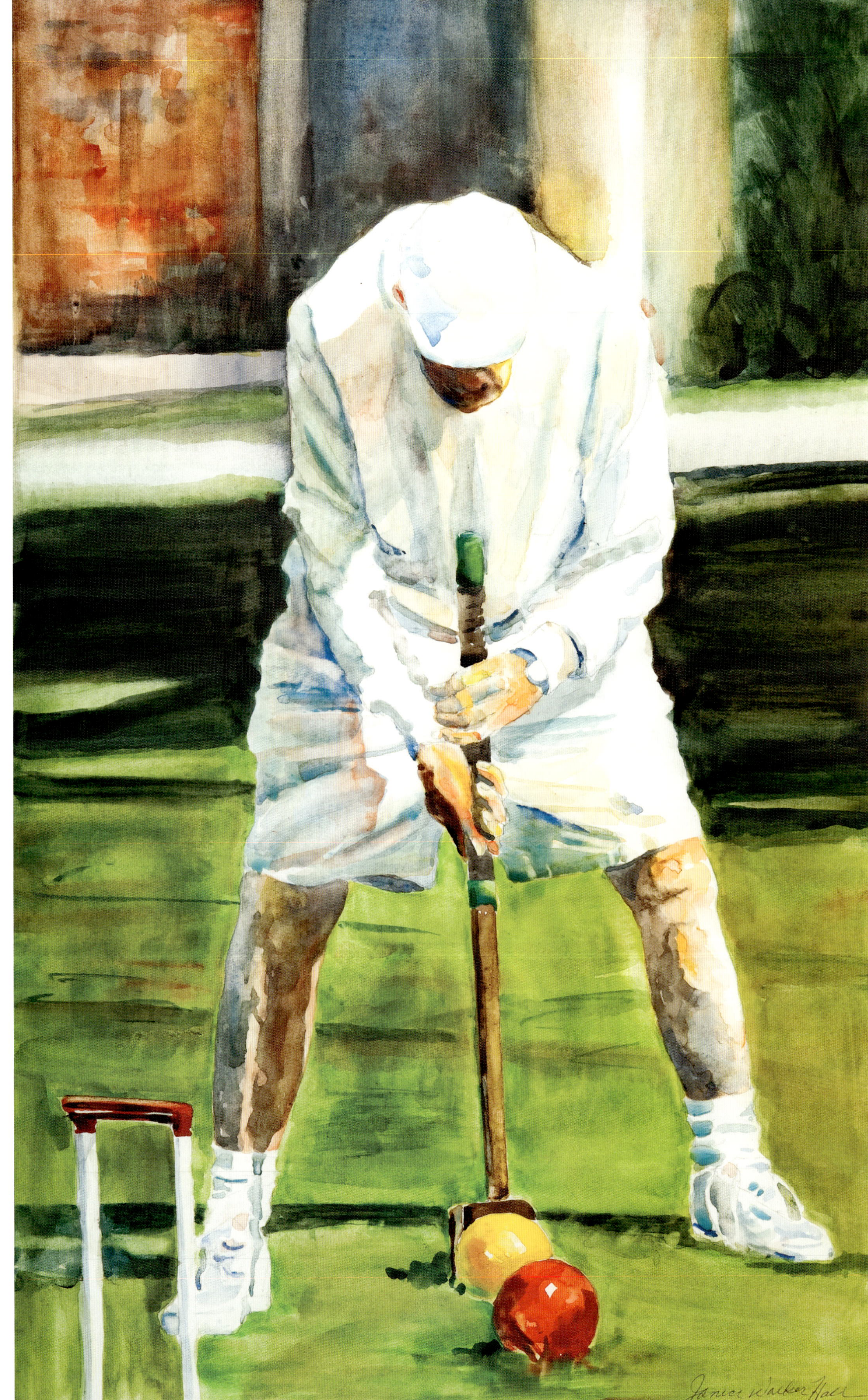
Janice Walker Hall

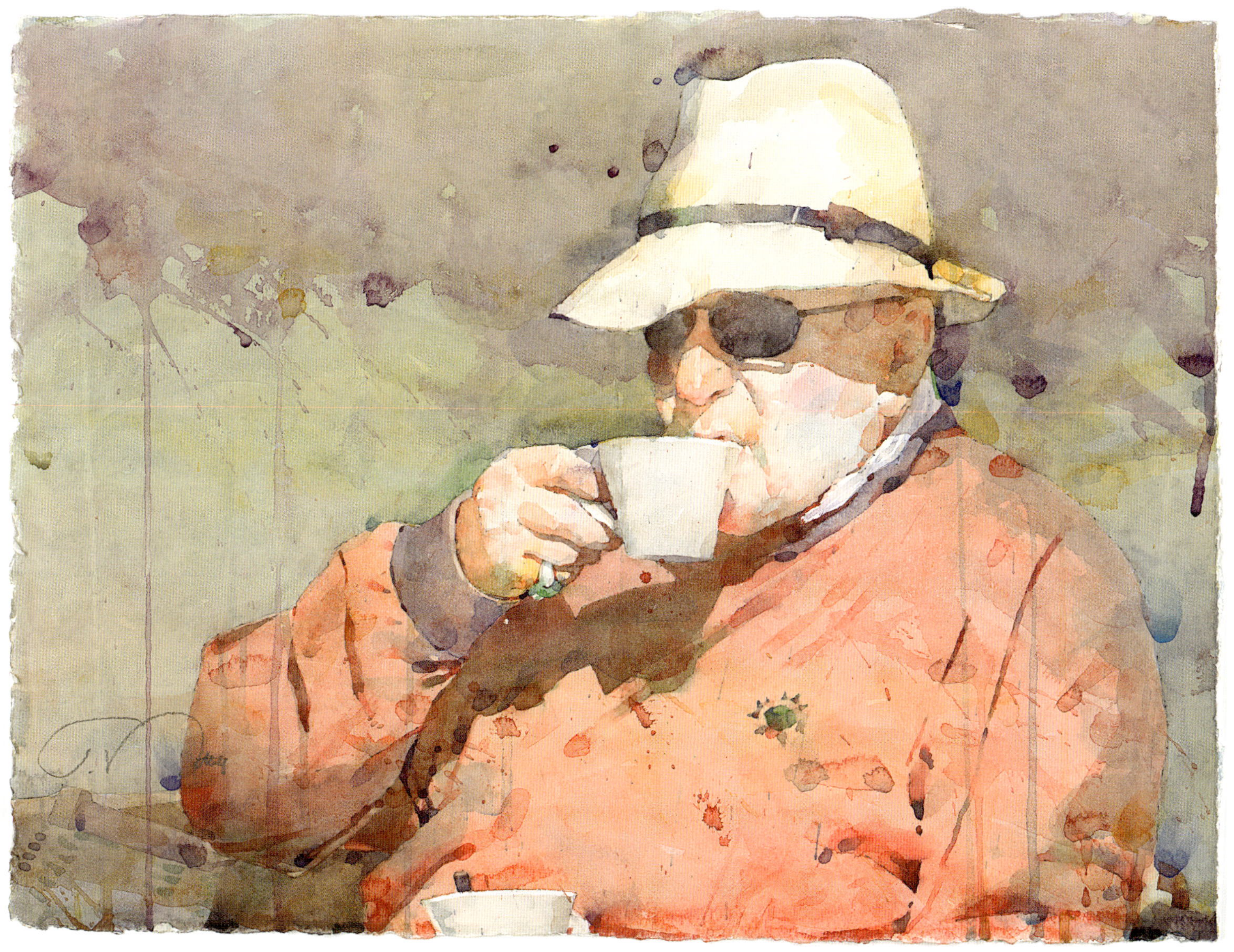

COSI' COMINCIA IL GIORNO | TED NUTTALL
Transparent watercolor on paper, 15" × 20" (38cm × 51cm)

This gentleman was seated outside a wonderful café on the piazza in San Gimignano, Italy. I was immediately attracted to the play of morning light on his face and jacket. I was also intrigued by the empty cup on the table in front of him. I left it in the foreground of the painting as I felt it suggested more to the story.

CROQUET: STRAIGHT SHOT | JANICE WALKER HALL
Watercolor on hot-pressed paper, 21" × 13" (53cm × 33cm)

I came across a serious game of croquet while traveling in England. Trying not to disturb the players, I shot a few photos of an older gentleman in his white apparel concentrating on his shot. I couldn't wait to get back to my studio to create this painting. The initial drawing was very important to me, making certain his stance was perfect, illustrating his sense of determination. As I laid down light washes of color, I was careful to keep my whites. Adding more layers, I enjoyed the learning process of moving paint around on the challenging hot-press surface. My vision in creating this painting was to bring a smile to those who view *Croquet: Straight Shot.*

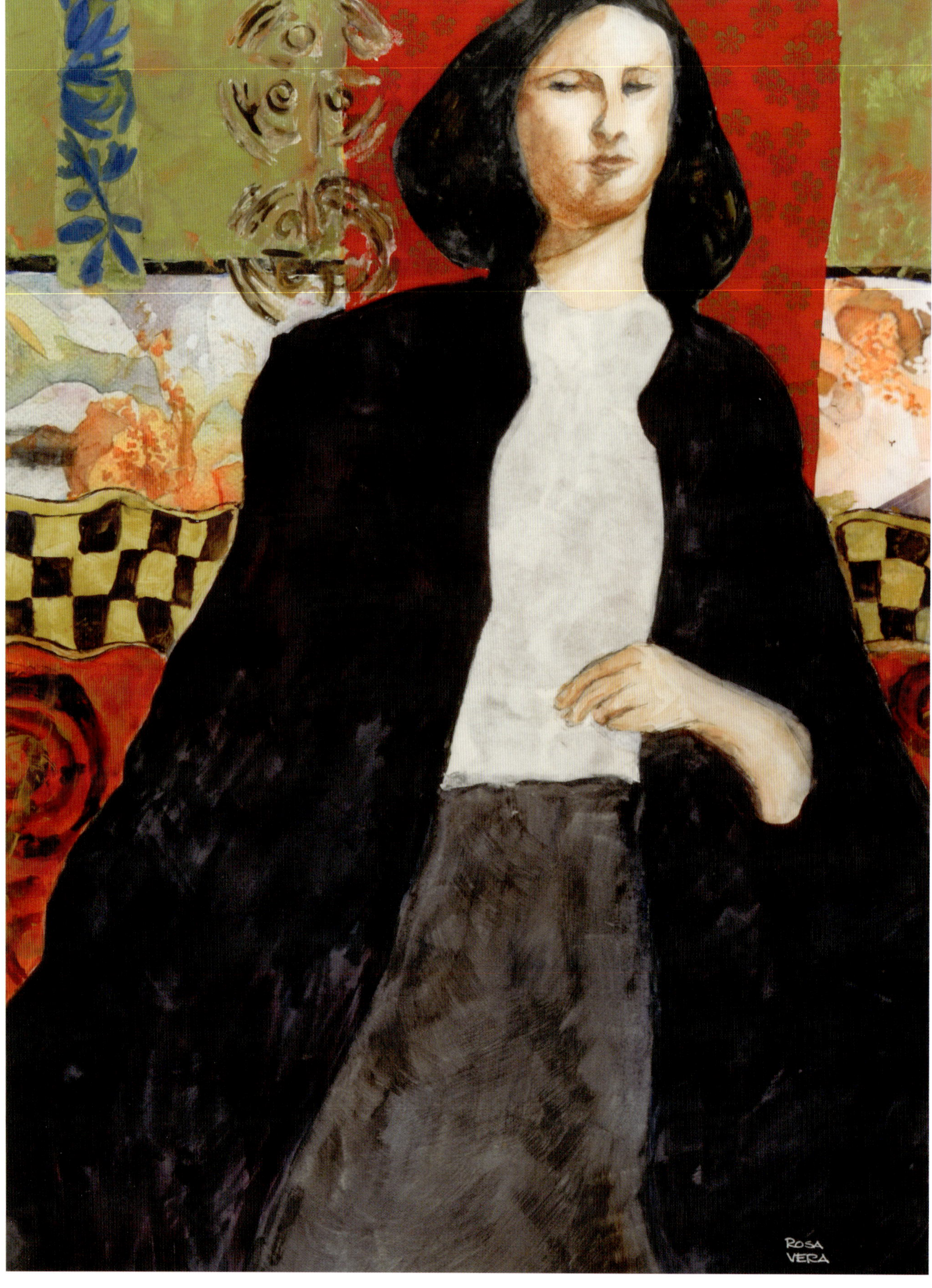

WHAT SHE MISSED | ROSA INÉS VERA

Watercolor, acrylic, gouache and collage on paper, 22½" × 16½" (57cm × 42cm)

This is a very personal painting for me. It was inspired by an old photo of my mother that I found in my grandmother's photo album. Several layers of acrylic were applied and then covered up as I tried to work out the theme. As the figure is the main focus, the collage was cut around it. Under the figure's blouse are old family photos that I covered up because they didn't work in the composition. The symbols all have individual meaning. For example, the flower in the background is from an earlier painting.

Everything is collage, even genetics.

— *Michael Ondaatje*, Divisadero

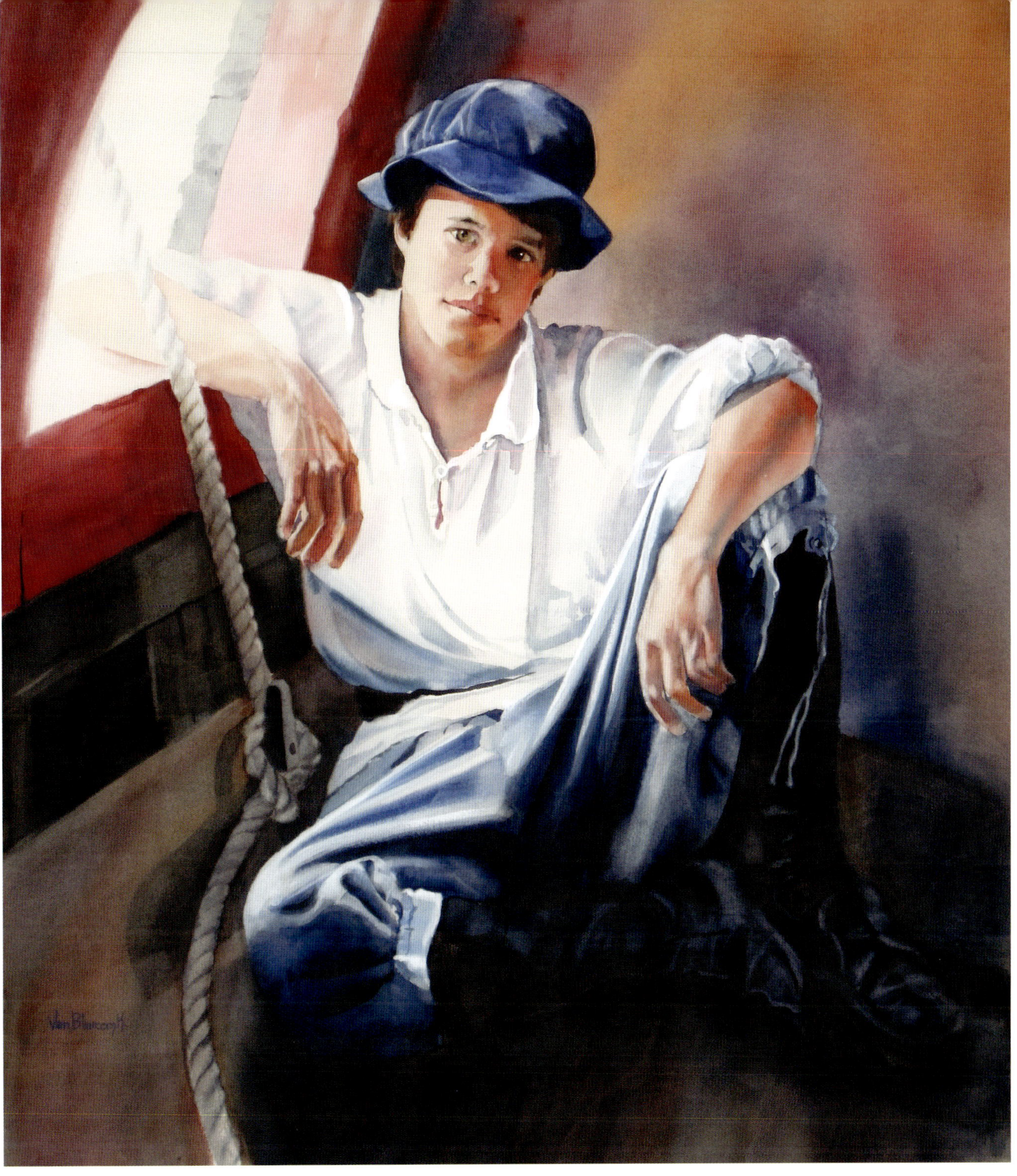

BOSUN'S MATE | ANNE VAN BLARCOM KUROWSKI
Watercolor on Arches rag paper, 24" × 22" (61cm × 56cm)

Life's treasure hunt produces souvenirs of incongruities and contradictions, feelings and perceptions that I can translate into celebrations of my love of individuality and the human spirit.

— *Anne Van Blarcom Kurowski*

Bosun's Mate was inspired by the nonchalant attitude portrayed by this young man who was a guide aboard the *Elizabeth II*, docked in Manteo, North Carolina. The dramatic light from the porthole created the perfect atmosphere. I feel the action and attitude of my subjects vicariously, visualize the painting first, and then take photos I can use as reference in my studio. I painted an initial layer of random colors to enrich and add complexity to all areas.

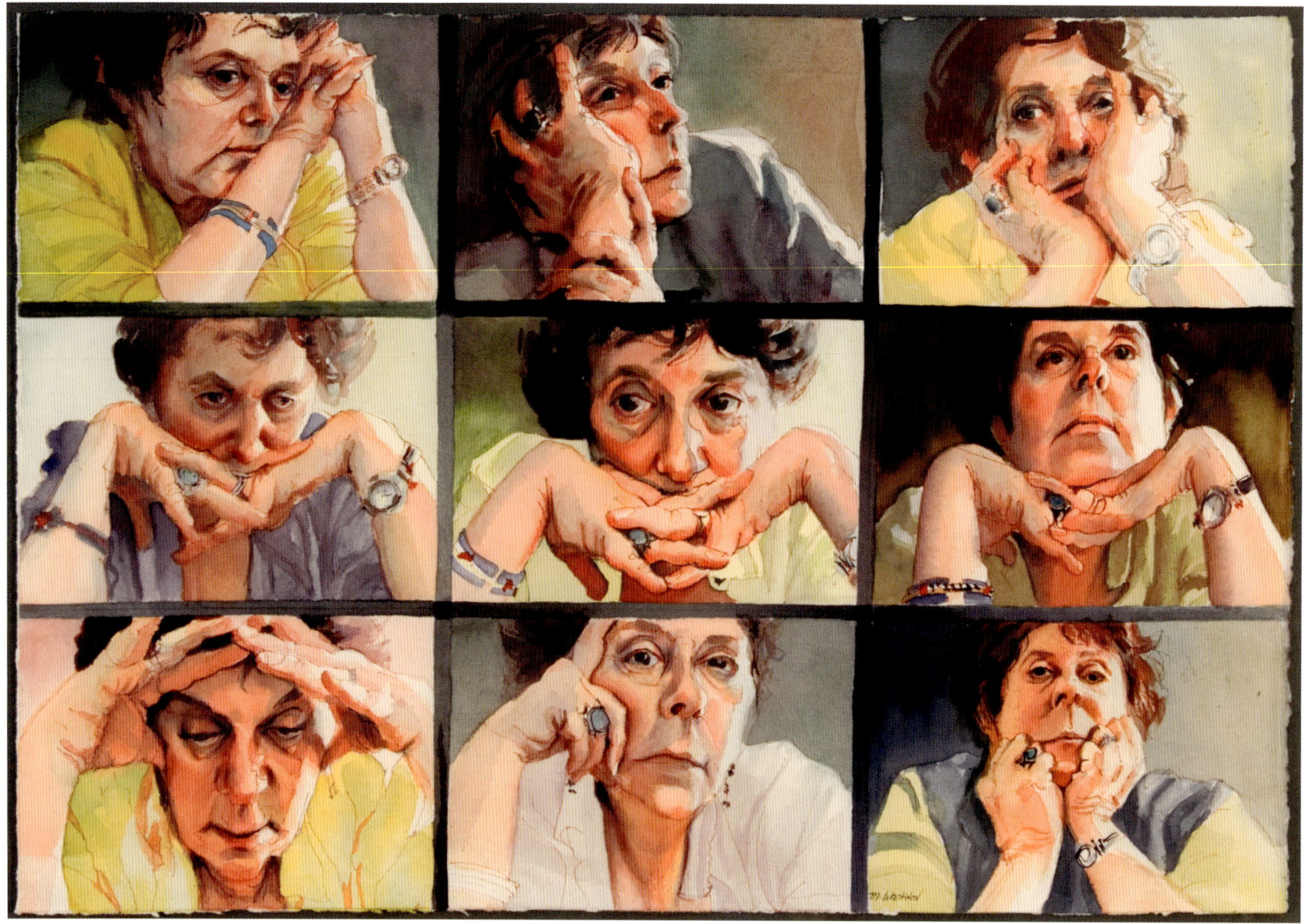

REFLECTIONS ON TURNING 65 | MYRNA S. WACKNOV

Transparent watercolor over sepia ink drawings on watercolor paper, 15" × 21" (38cm × 53cm)

Faces are compelling. My portraits are about expression more than accuracy. They tell a story. During my sixty-fourth year there were daily reminders, with angst, that I was fast approaching official "senior" status. Self-portraits have become a way to make peace with the disparity between how I feel internally and what I see externally. I use my own photographs as reference. Without projection, tracing or pencil guidelines, on a single half sheet of watercolor paper, I drew nine sepia ink images in the modified contour manner, then painted in transparent watercolor.

Learning to draw is important. When you draw instead of project or trace, you impart your DNA into your work, making it uniquely yours, just as your handwriting is unique to you, alone.

Myrna S. Wacknov

THE JARVIS GIRLS | DANA FOX JENKINS

Watercolor and graphite on 180-lb. (400gsm) cold-pressed Cartiera Magnani, 8" × 6" (20cm × 15cm)

And above all, watch with glittering eyes the whole world around you because the greatest secrets are always hidden in the most unlikely places. Those who don't believe in magic will never find it.

Roald Dahl

I am most energized by juicy color, strong value contrast and line, and I want the graphite to be obvious in the completed painting. But without a narrative the painting would be meaningless. *The Jarvis Girls* is from a series of more than one hundred paintings done to illustrate my self-published book, *Red Cherries and Blue Mountains: A Family Food Memoir from the Shenandoah Valley.* The book visually describes a proud tradition of creative, hard-working people who taught life lessons to the next generation as they raised, prepared and enjoyed food around family tables, celebrating a heritage of self-respect and generosity. Painting in a theme over a period of many months lets me engage in research and take advantage of serendipitous opportunities such as finding old photographs, listening to stories and assembling artifacts.

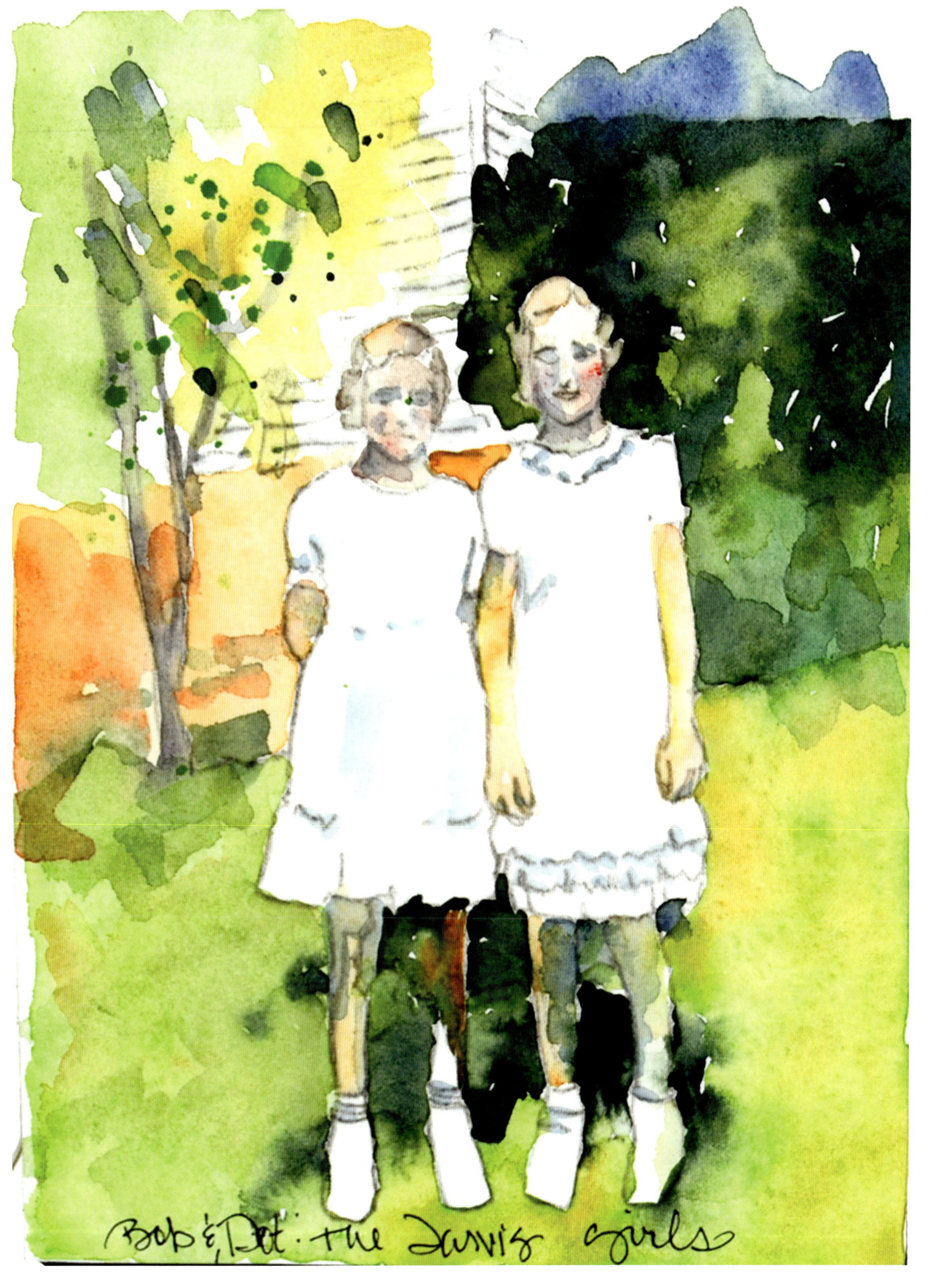
Bob & Dot: the Jarvis girls

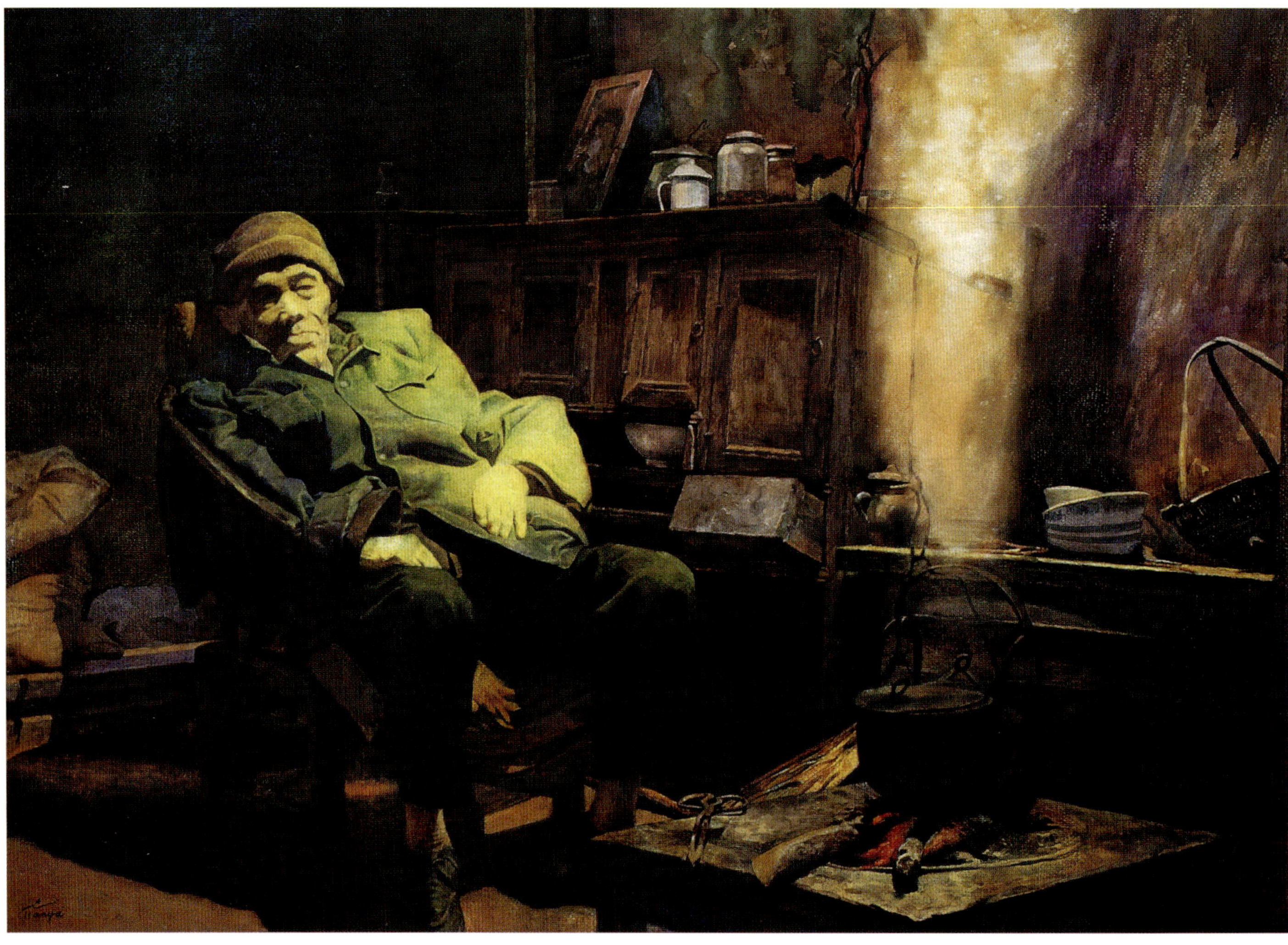

THE LIGHT FROM THE HEAVEN | ZHOU TIANYA
Transparent watercolor with oil pastel on Baoding watercolor (China) paper, 29½" × 41" (75cm × 104cm)

For this painting I used a unique technique that I call "washing off," which allows me to achieve the effects of rich, strong darks that still breathe. I wet the paper on which a detailed sketch has been made, and apply a thin layer of paint to the whole picture wet-into-wet. When it dries, I apply a thick layer of paint to all the details (dry-into-dry), but preserve light areas. The layer of paint is so thick that it covers all the pores of the paper and the colors lose their transparency. After it dries, I spray a mist of water and gently wash off the paint with a soft brush to reveal the tooth of the paper without removing all the paint. This thick paint application and washing-off process is repeated several times until the colors become rich and strong but remain translucent, and the paper texture is also preserved. Finally, here, I applied a light layer of white oil pastel to accent the paper texture where it was less visible. The result is a painting that shows the sky light from an unrevealed opening, seeming to reveal a hidden message about our existence in which we praise the fortitude of life, and we sigh for its fragility.

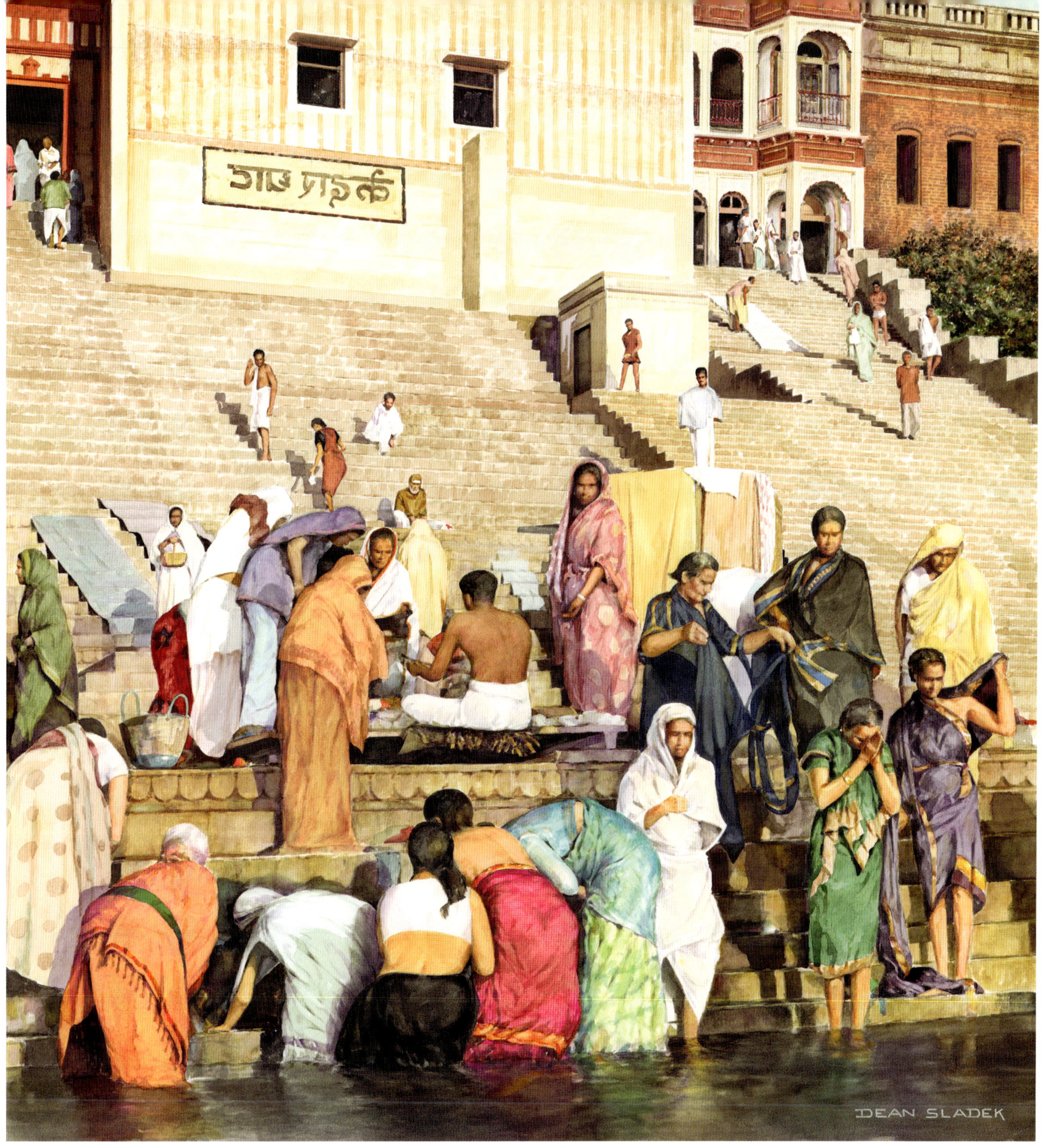

WASHING IN THE GANGES | DEAN W. SLADEK
Transparent watercolor on 140-lb. (300gsm) Arches, 28" × 25½" (71cm × 65cm)

> If the drawing is not right, the painting is not right!
>
> — *Dean W. Sladek*

Washing in the Ganges is from a photograph taken by a friend while in India. The painting was a challenge from the beginning because of the detail required in the drawing. I like working on stretched Arches watercolor paper because its sizing and surface texture permits subtle corrections. Working in transparent watercolor allows for layering and altering colors without getting a muddy or dull image. Prior to starting, I drew the center three lower figures onto another piece of Arches and rendered them. Once I was satisfied with that exercise, it set the tone and I was ready to paint.

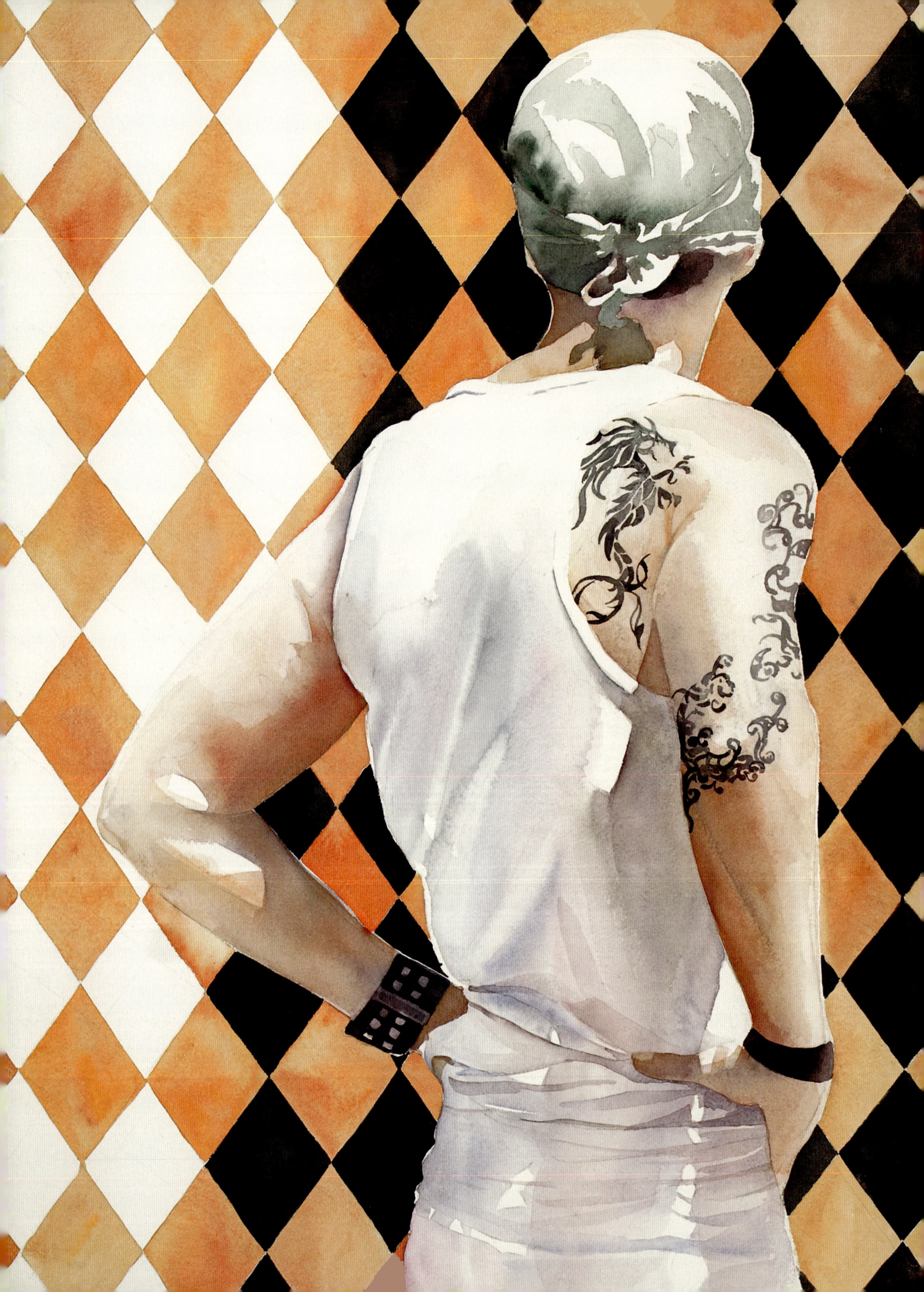

HARLEQUIN | LYNN FERRIS

Transparent watercolor on cold-pressed paper, 30" × 22" (76cm × 56cm)

Harlequin began with a glimpse of body language that felt familiar. I photographed the pose, and created the character in my studio from my imagination. As with all of my work, I used a limited palette of transparent pigments to build up multiple layers and subtle color changes. The outcome is a study in contrasts. One arm is tattooed and set against black diamonds; the other arm, softer and faded by the strong sunlight, is unadorned, creating a lost edge into a white diamond. While the figure is a man, it has a gentleness that feels almost feminine. The faceless stranger should seem at once familiar and foreign.

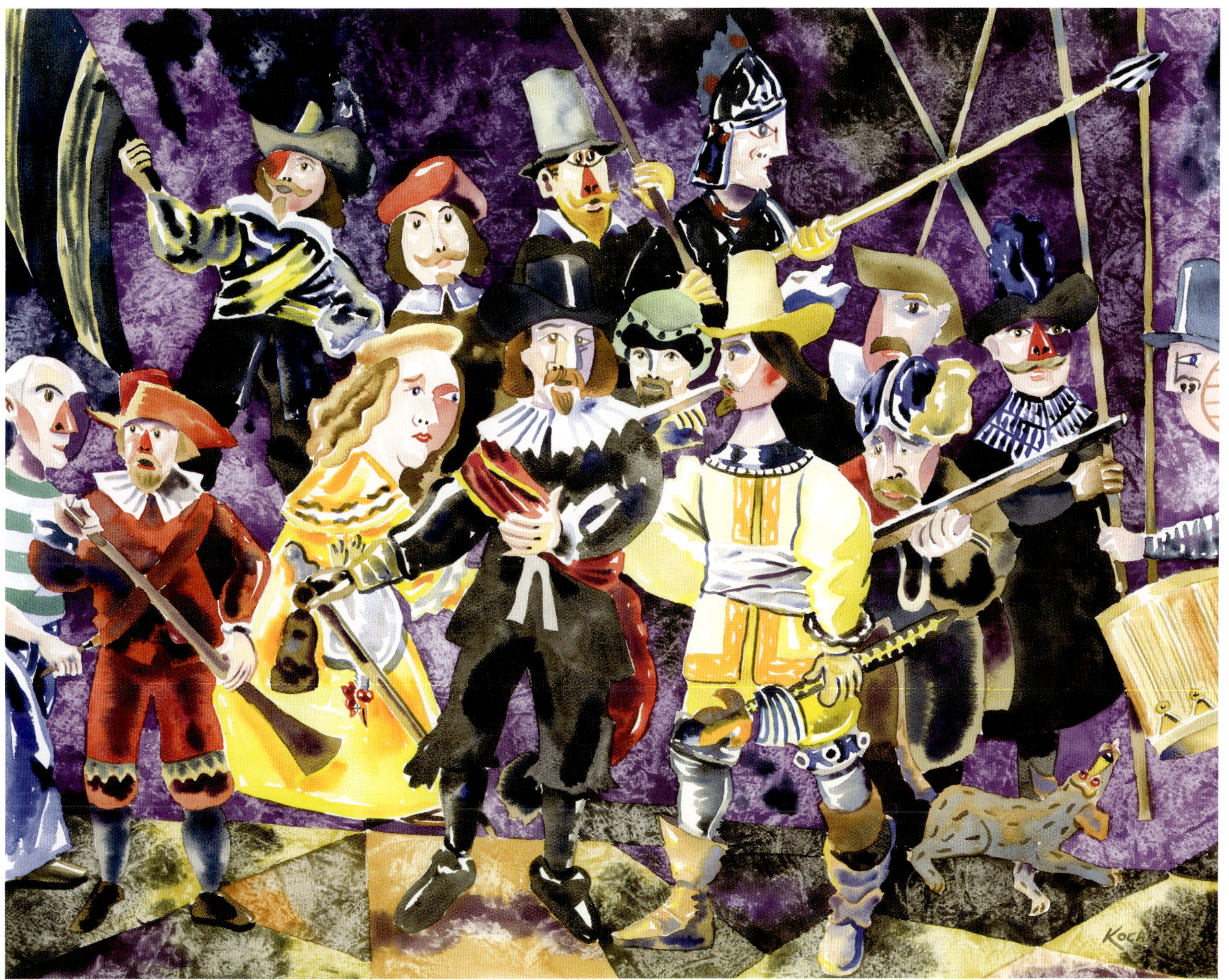

PABLO'S NIGHTWATCH
GEORGE F. KOCAR
Transparent watercolor on paper
18" × 24" (46cm × 61cm)

For many years I have been painting artistic parodies based on the work of Pablo Picasso. Picasso himself reinterpreted numerous masterpieces during his lifetime. *Pablo's Nightwatch* is my version of how I thought Picasso would interpret Rembrandt's *Night Watch*. I used the Rembrandt as a source for numerous studies, distorting the people and the composition and adding Cubist elements. Once I worked out the composition, I transferred the drawing to watercolor paper. I painted straightforward transparent watercolor; the only trick was using balled-up paper towels to remove wet color from the background and give it some texture.

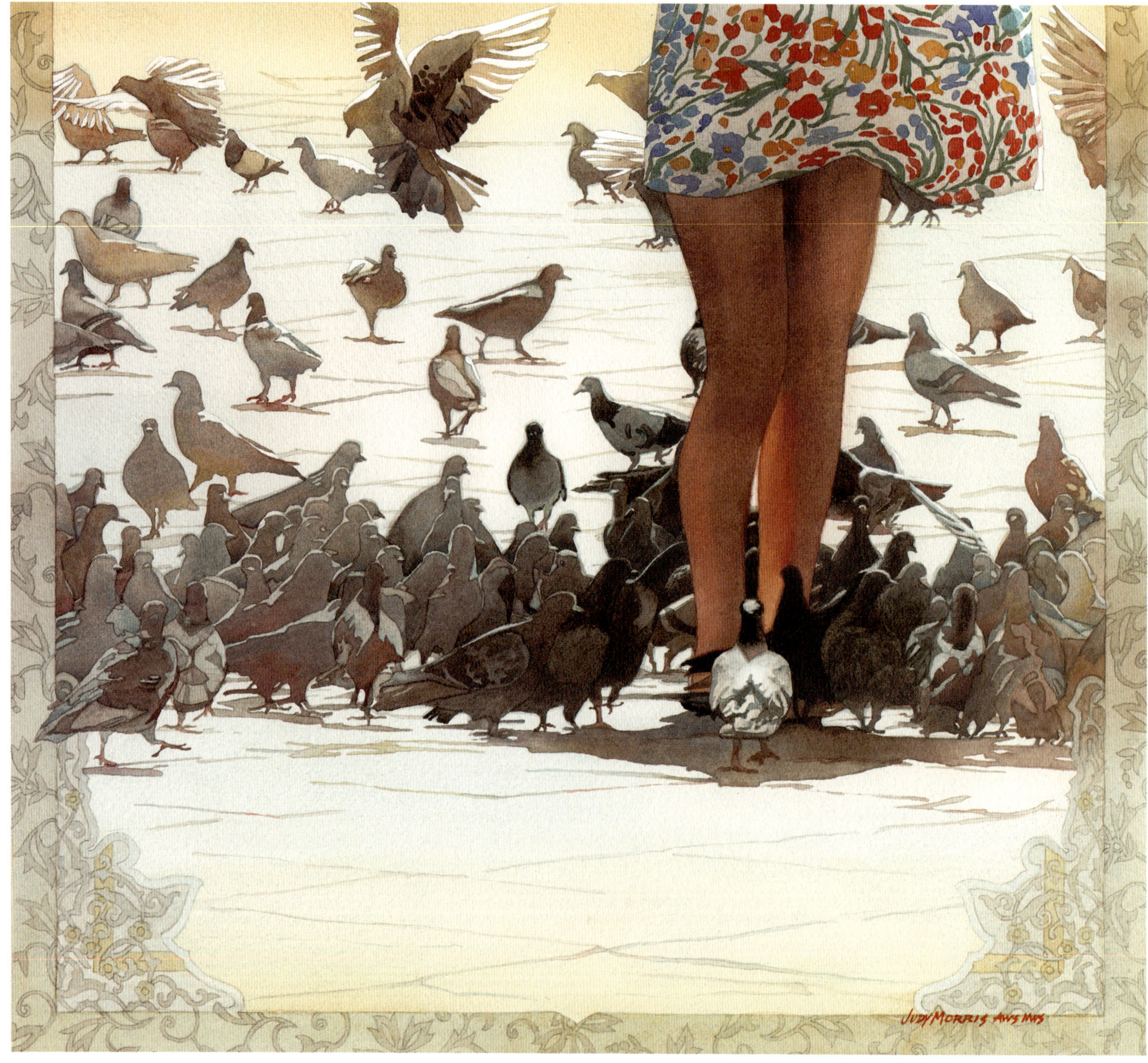

PIGEONS IN THE PIAZZA | JUDY MORRIS

Transparent watercolor on 300-lb. (640gsm) cold-pressed Arches, 21" × 23" (53cm × 58cm)

Finding painting inspiration is like shopping at a flea market. You never know what you want until you see it. Either way, learn to expect the unexpected. On a recent trip to Venice, I expected to see pigeons in Piazza San Marco. I didn't expect to capture their feeding flurry surrounding the legs of a young lady! I intentionally created a 4-inch (10cm) low-contrast zone on the left, bottom and right edges of the painting. Notice how the darkest darks and lightest lights are concentrated around the legs and on the back of the pigeon in front of the girl's feet. This helps direct the viewer's eye to the focal point in a painting.

Don't be satisfied with ordinary subject matter. Look for the unexpected!

Judy Morris

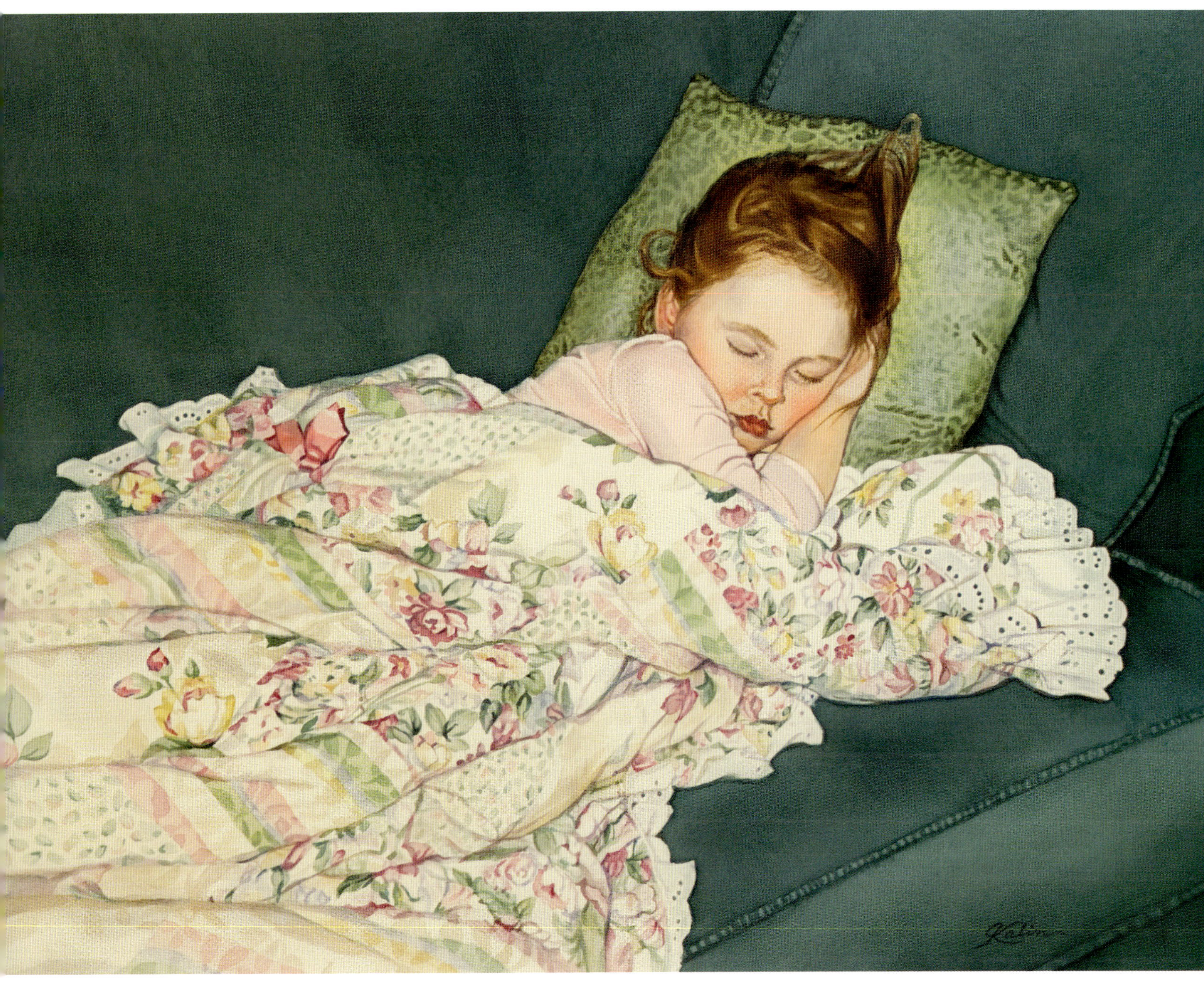

SIESTA AT THREE | JEAN KALIN
Transparent watercolor on 140-lb. (300gsm) cold-pressed paper, 17½" × 23½" (44cm × 60cm)

I'm a people watcher and storyteller. My fascination with people began during years of life drawing. I like to work from my unposed photographs of subjects. Establishing composition and design with value studies, I may combine several photographs. My vision for this painting was to express the innocence and trust of a child. Working in layers of transparent watercolor, I build up color and value. To emphasize the center of interest, the soft folds of the comforter lead to the greatest contrast and harder edges surrounding her face and hair. Dry-brush details are added to finish.

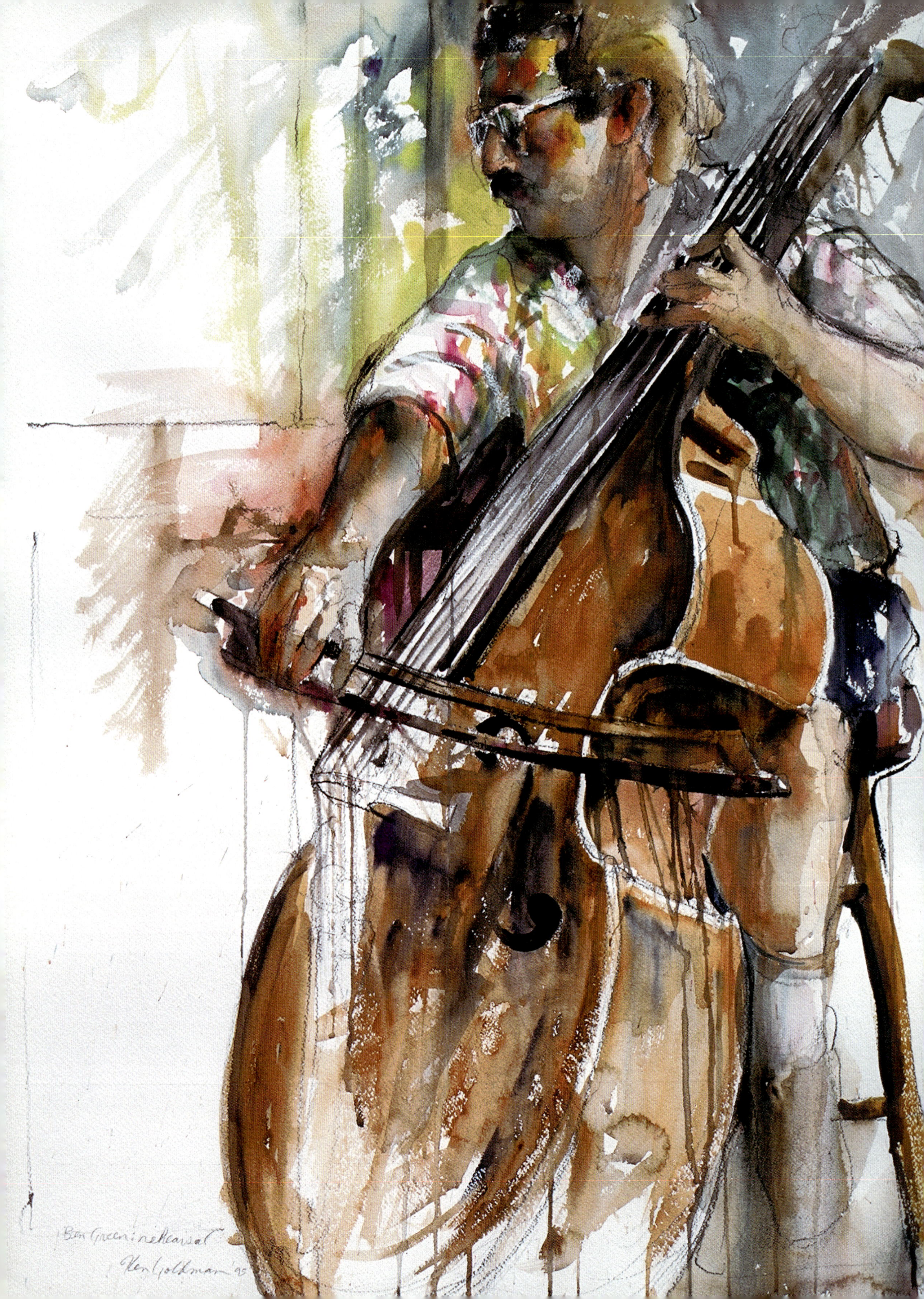
"Ben Green in Rehearsal"
Ken Goldman '95

LIVE REHEARSAL | KEN GOLDMAN

Transparent watercolor on Arches, 30" × 22" (76cm × 56cm)

Standing behind an upright French easel, I painted from the live model who was rehearsing for a symphony audition in my studio. With a no. 2 graphite pencil, I sketched quickly but carefully, then painted freely with a #36 Robert Simmons Goliath brush. This painting represents a double artistic vision: that of my model the musician, and my own artistic aspiration—an attempt to capture in watercolor the essence of his vital passion for music.

Don't try to make it perfect, just make it better and better.

Ken Goldman

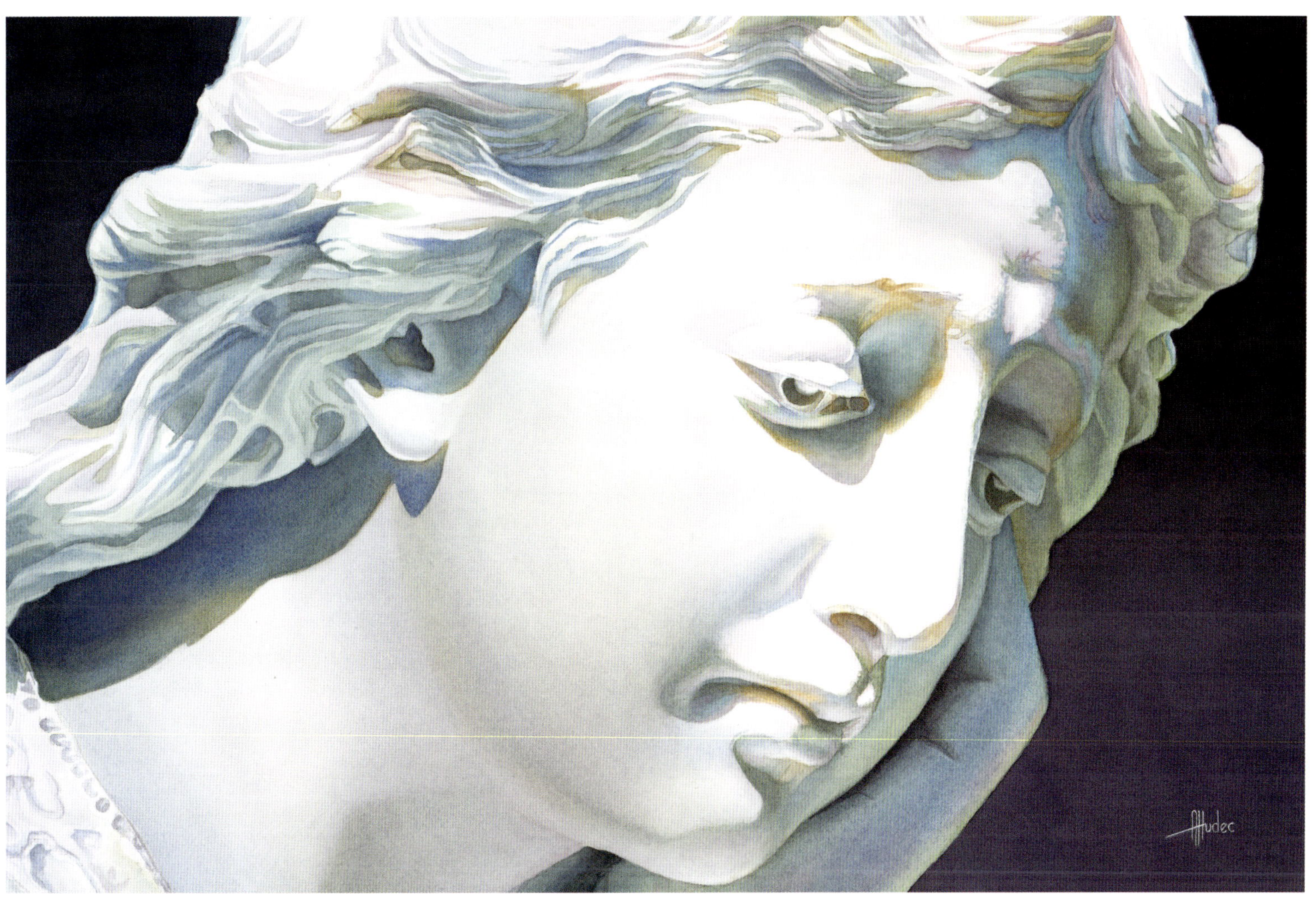

EMPATHY | ANNE HUDEC

Transparent watercolor on 140-lb. (300gsm) cold-pressed paper, 12" × 18¼" (30cm × 46cm)

Accentuating colors brings interest and individuality to your subject as long as you maintain correct values to create form.

Anne Hudec

On a recent trip to Europe I encountered the original sculpture that *Empathy* is based upon. I was immediately overcome by a tremendous sense of peace and tranquility. The thought-provoking downward gaze evokes empathy as well as reflection. The strong light with contrasting light and shadow challenged me to use my artistic vision to infuse warmth into something that is otherwise viewed as cold: stone. I photographed her from various vantage points and later painted from my reference materials. *Empathy* was painted with many thin glazes in the sunlit areas while shadows were enhanced with a variety of colors.

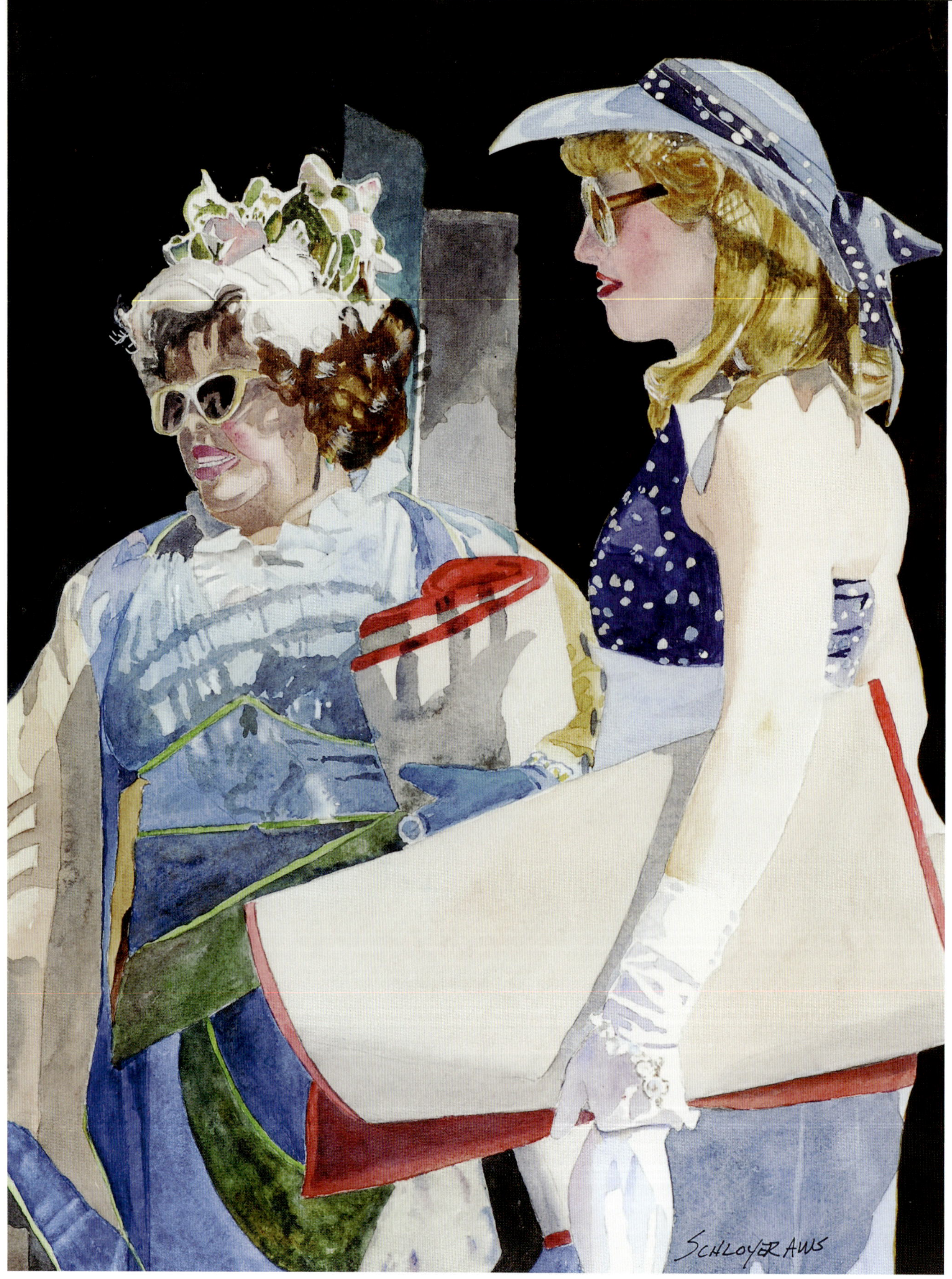

MAT-TERIAL GIRLS
RONALD A. SCHLOYER
Transparent watercolor on
300-lb. (640gsm) hot-pressed Arches
19" × 14" (48cm × 36cm)

For a very long time in my painting life, I purposefully avoided painting figures or even including them in my landscapes. But, more recently, it has energized my work to draw and paint persons who are a bit beyond the commonplace. The subjects of this painting were spotted in a popular theme park. It was the colorful costumes and rolled mats that caught my attention. I used my camera as a sketchbook, downloaded the image into Photoshop, and adjusted it to suit my compositional tastes. When the image closely matched my vision, I printed it. Then, using the grid method, I transferred the image to watercolor paper and painted it with a wet-into-dry watercolor method.

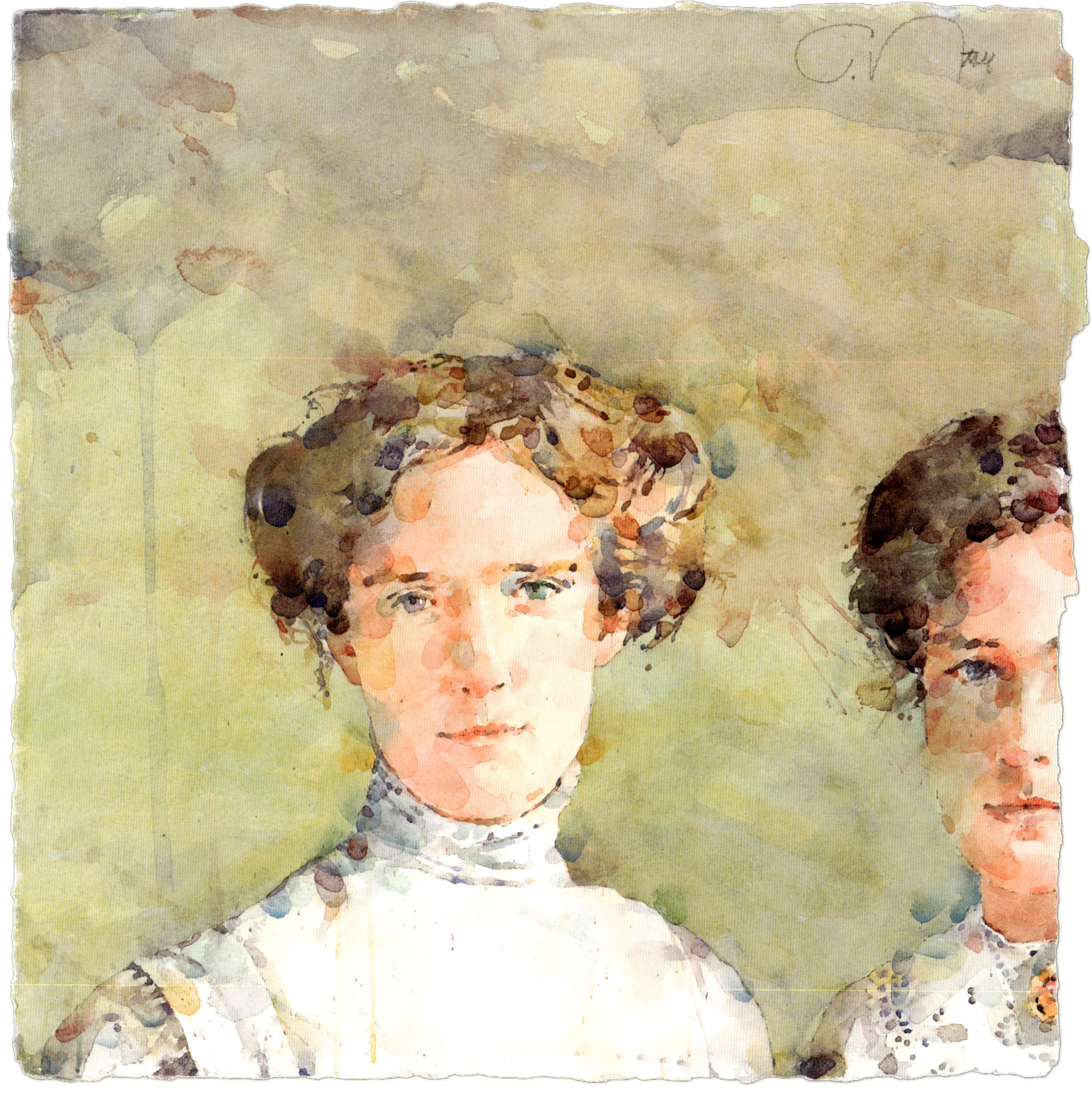

SISTERS | TED NUTTALL

Transparent watercolor on paper, 15" × 15" (38cm × 38cm)

"Loosening up," or whatever you want to call it, is a state of mind, not a state of brush. Splashing paint on paper or canvas with the hand without splashing it on with the head first will just make a mess.

Charles Reid

The image in the vintage family photograph was pretty straightforward—a full figure shot of the two women (actual sisters). I decided to crop and compose the picture as I did to give the painting more of an edge and suggest an overtone to their relationship.

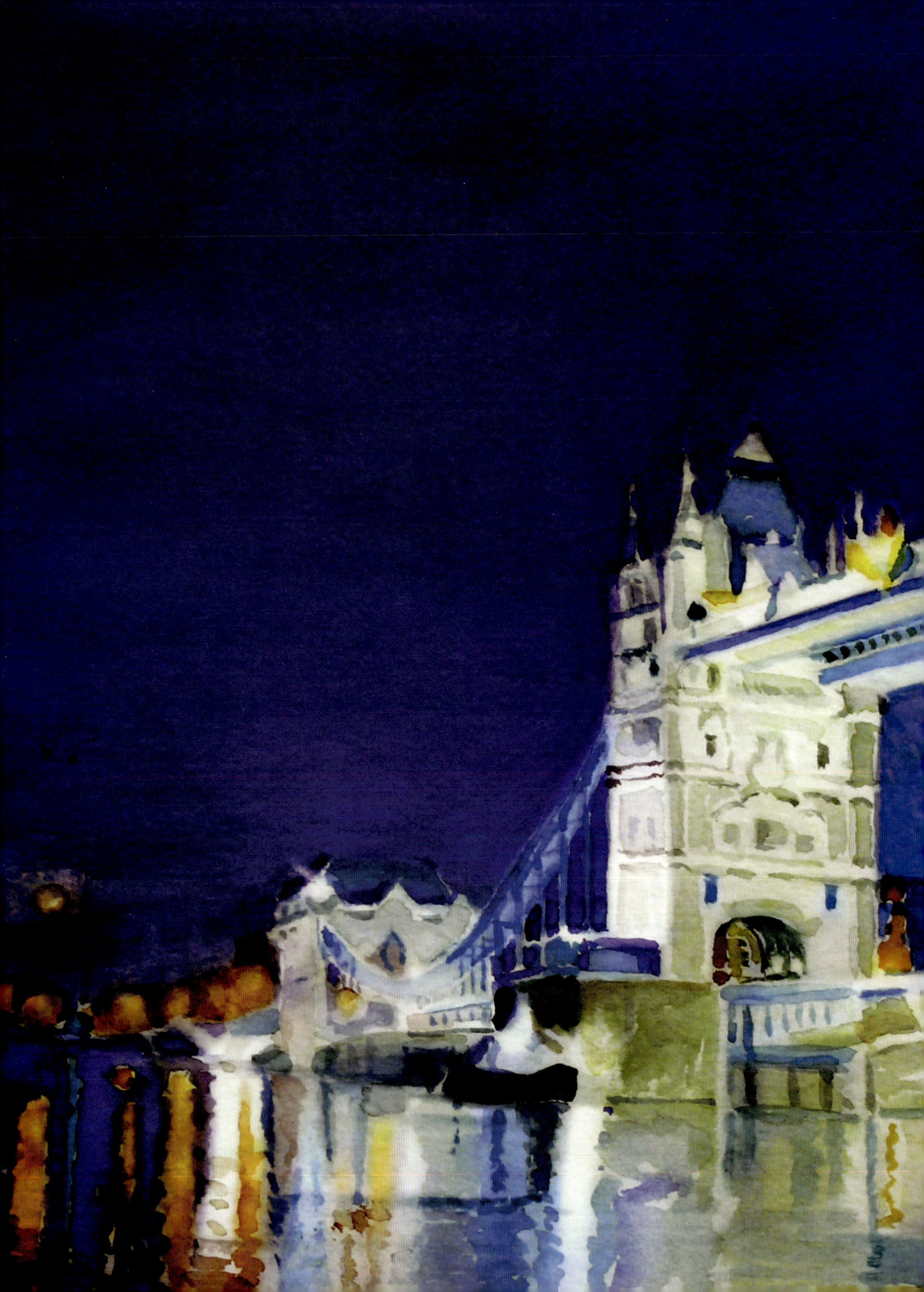

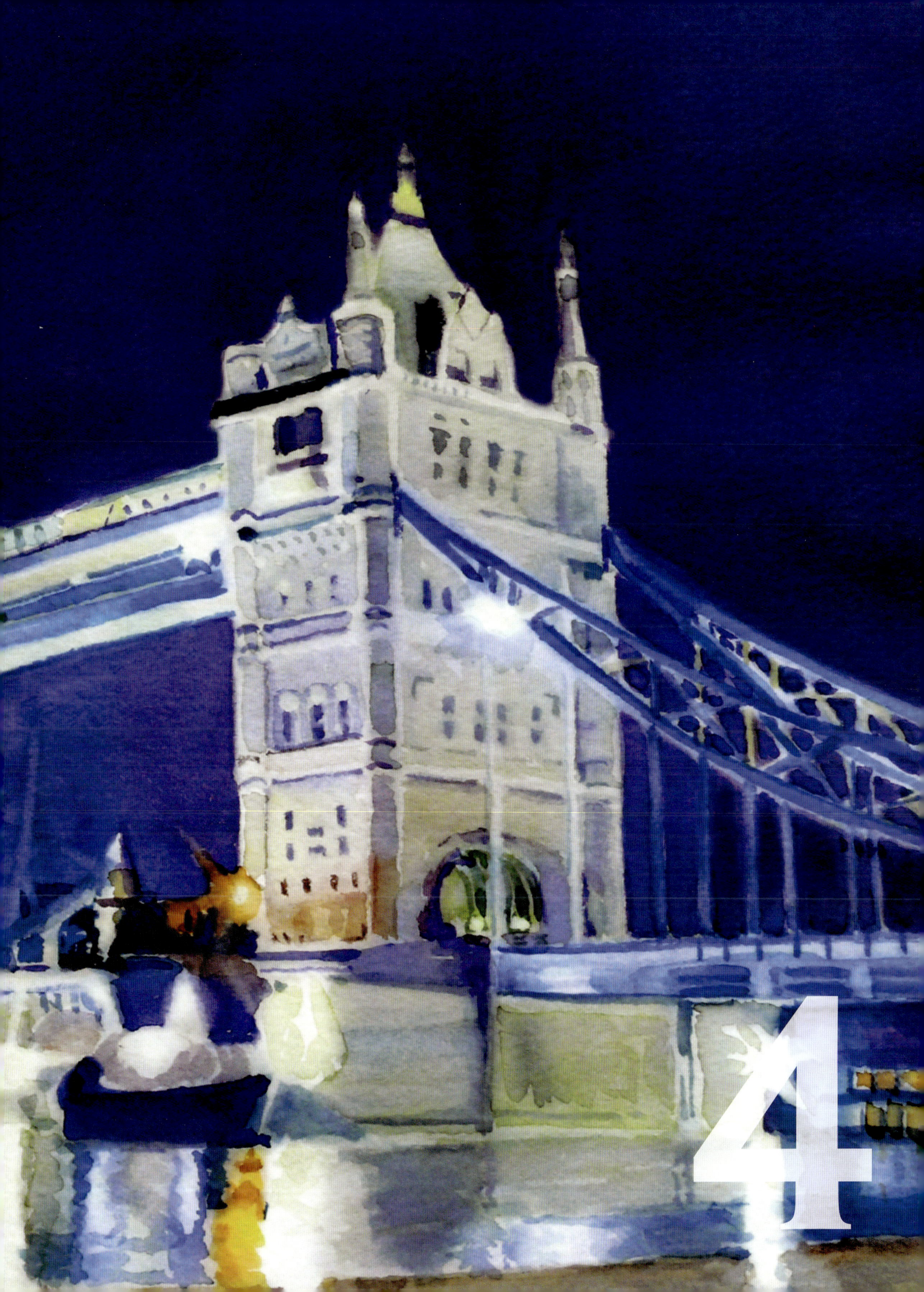
4

4 | TOWN AND COUNTRY

It is how an artist sees rather than what an artist sees that makes a painting interesting.

— Nancy Fortunato

{ art on previous spread }

LONDON'S GEM | NANCY FORTUNATO

Transparent watercolor on 140-lb. (300gsm) cold-pressed Fabriano, 9" × 13" (23cm × 33cm)

Several years ago, my students challenged me to teach them to paint a night scene, something I had never attempted in watercolor, so I started studying night paintings. *London's Gem* was inspired by looking at many van Gogh paintings of night scenes; the glow he achieved was my driving force. It had been many years since I had been in London, but I'd always wanted to paint the bridge at night. There are many glazes of pink and shades of blue that make up the sky. I used large no. 12 and no. 14 round brushes for this effect.

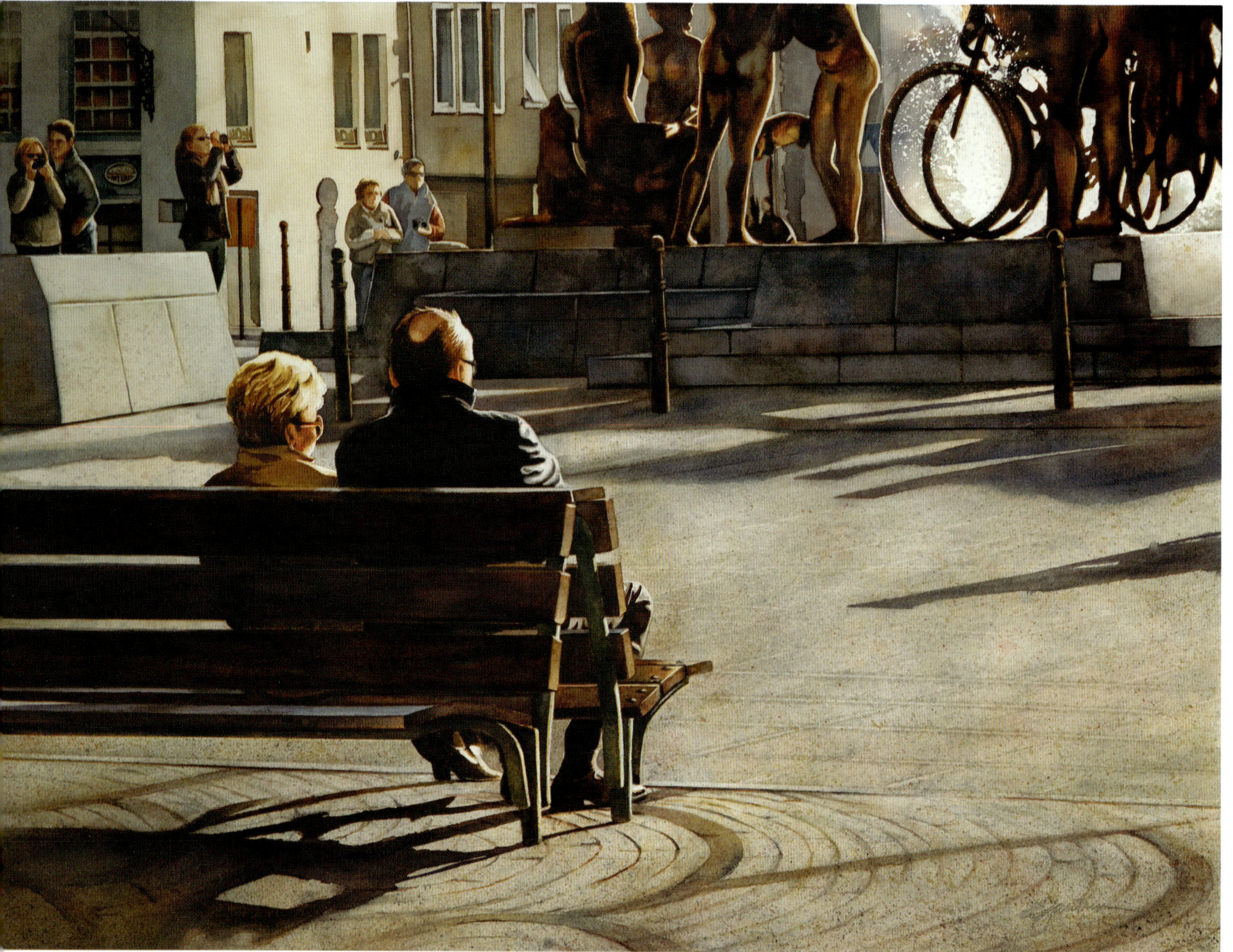

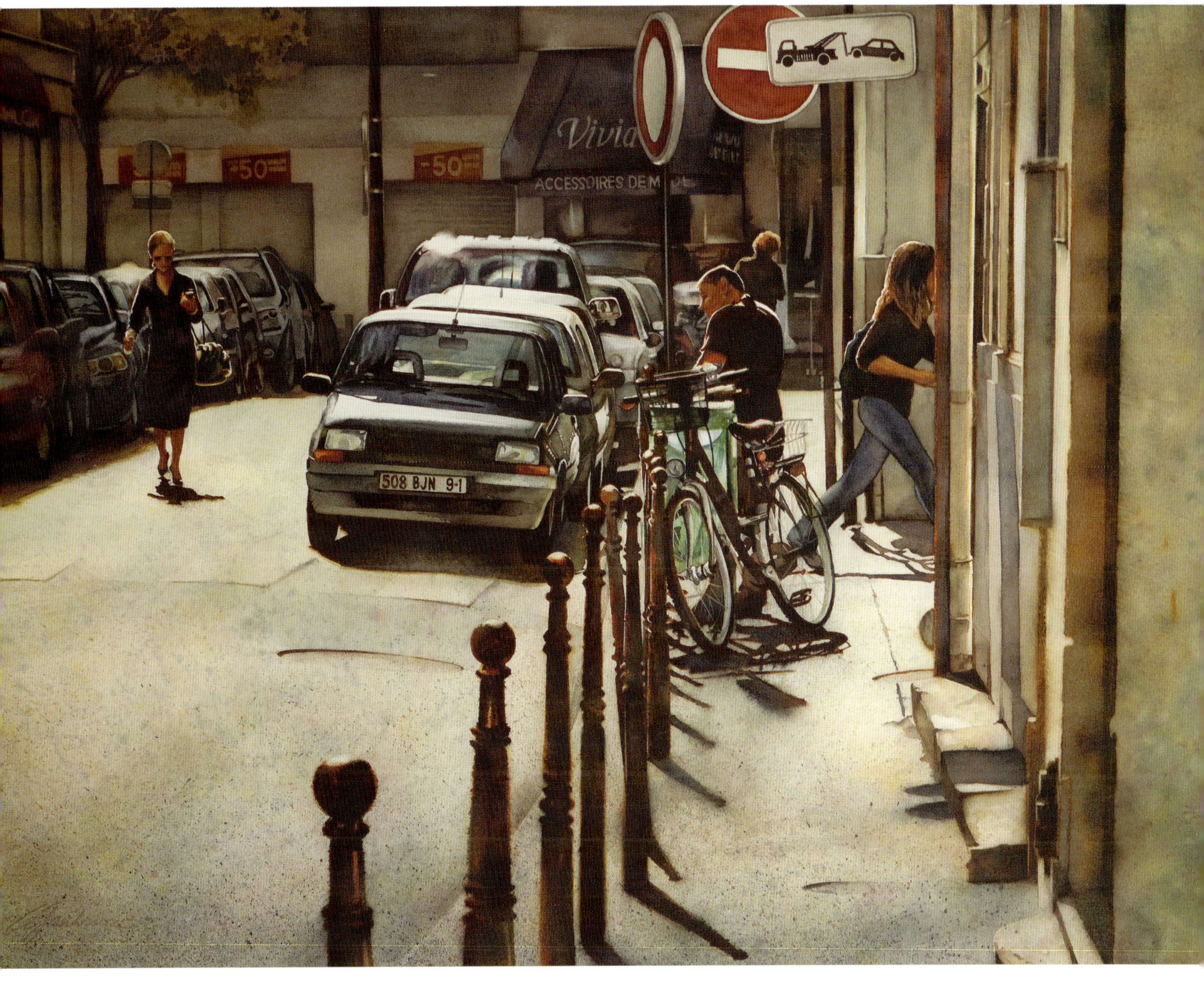

LATE AFTERNOON, BRUGGE | CARLA GAUTHIER
Watercolor on paper, 22" × 30" (56cm × 76cm)

NORTH, SOUTH, EAST AND WEST | CARLA GAUTHIER
Watercolor on paper, 22" × 30" (56cm × 76cm)

For me, the painting process starts with camera in hand. Backlighting captures my imagination; I love to create rich colors in areas almost completely in shadow and to find that thread of highlight that will define the focal areas. Using a four-color palette for almost every painting (Quinacridone Gold, Permanent Rose, Idanthrene Blue and occasionally Manganese Blue Hue) gives me freedom to concentrate on shapes and values knowing I have color unity. The subject matter? Always people! I watch scenes unfold and enjoy capturing candid shots, refining the composition later. Strong lighting and shadows are the backdrop to the figures, their surroundings and their stories.

Just keep painting ... even the paintings that flop are stepping-stones to one that will take your breath away!

• *Carla Gauthier*

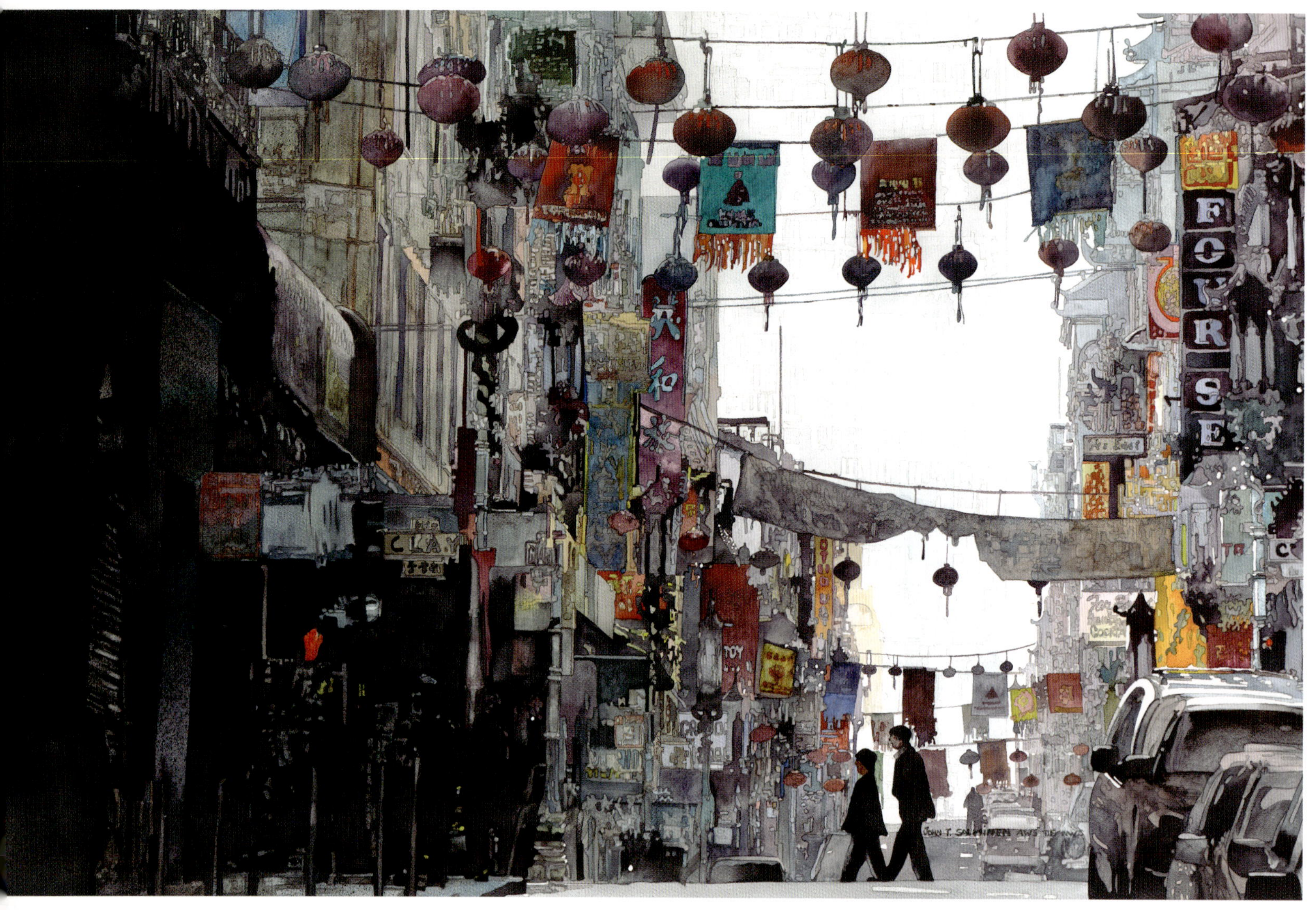

GRANT LANTERNS | JOHN SALMINEN
Transparent watercolor on paper, 26" × 38" (66cm × 97cm)

I love painting urban scenes because of the organizational challenge it presents. The more complex the subject, the better. I use photos because the amount of detail I include would take too long to sketch. The camera, however, doesn't discriminate or prioritize. It simply records information, but fails to tell a story. That's where I come in. Taking the raw data of the photo, I add emotional content in my personal interpretation of the subject. My hope is to transfer to the viewer the same emotional impact and intrigue that continues to draw me to the urban scene.

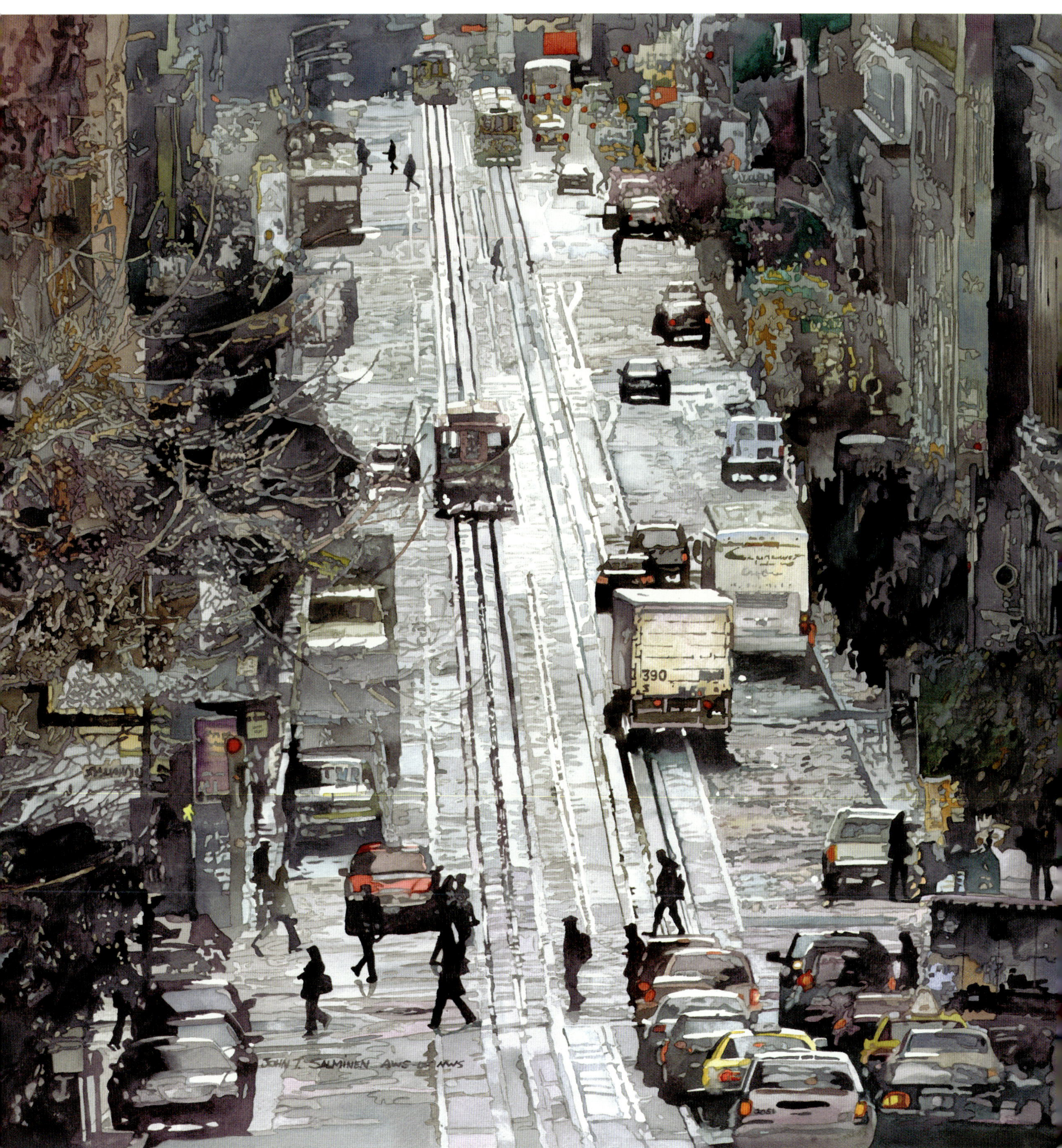

CABLE CAR | JOHN SALMINEN
Transparent watercolor on paper, 24" × 23" (61cm × 58cm)

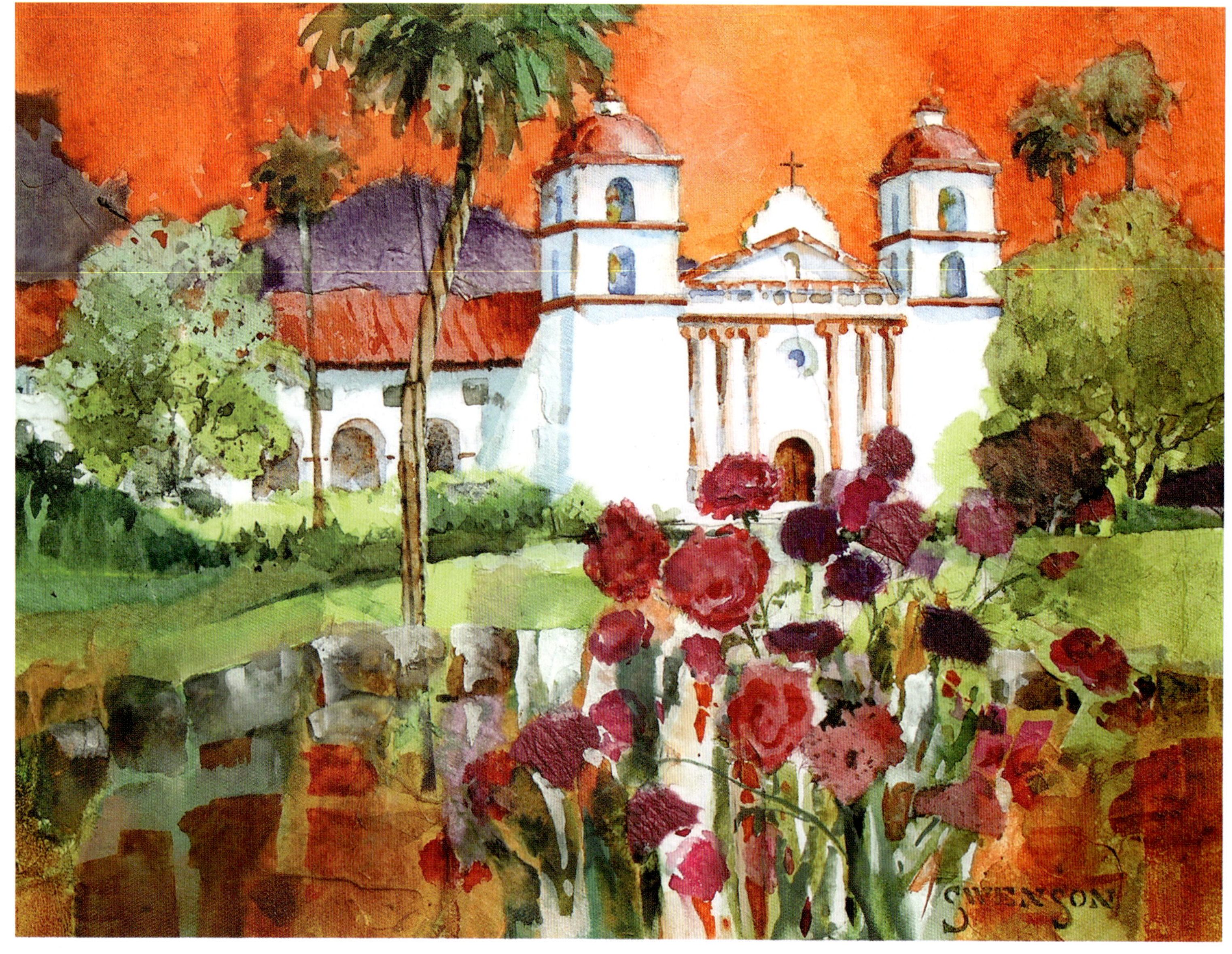

MISSION COLORS | BRENDA SWENSON
Watercolor-stained paper collage on 300-lb. (640gsm) watercolor paper, 11" × 15" (28cm × 38cm)

Recently I had the opportunity to visit the Santa Barbara Mission where I did numerous small watercolor sketches that I used as a springboard for this painting. I used Japanese papers stained with watercolor to block in the image. Only when the surface of the watercolor paper is completely covered do I begin to paint. This technique helps me to simplify the subject matter with larger shapes and focus more on design.

RUST COVERED MEMORIES | BRENDA SWENSON
Watercolor-stained paper collage on 300-lb. (640gsm) watercolor paper, 19" × 14" (48cm × 36cm)

The artist should be intoxicated with the idea of the thing he wants to express.
— Robert Henri

When I stumbled across this old bicycle, it brought back a flood of memories. I remembered the freedom I felt with my first bike, carefree summer days, the sting of skinned knees, riding double and getting my toes in the spokes. All the joys and woes of being a child! The challenge I faced with this painting was the design. I devised the idea of using a plant vine as a way to move the eye from the top of the painting around the wheel and back again. The design is the S-curve. I used a double complementary palette for this painting, blue/orange and red/green, and the same basic technique as for my painting *Mission Colors*.

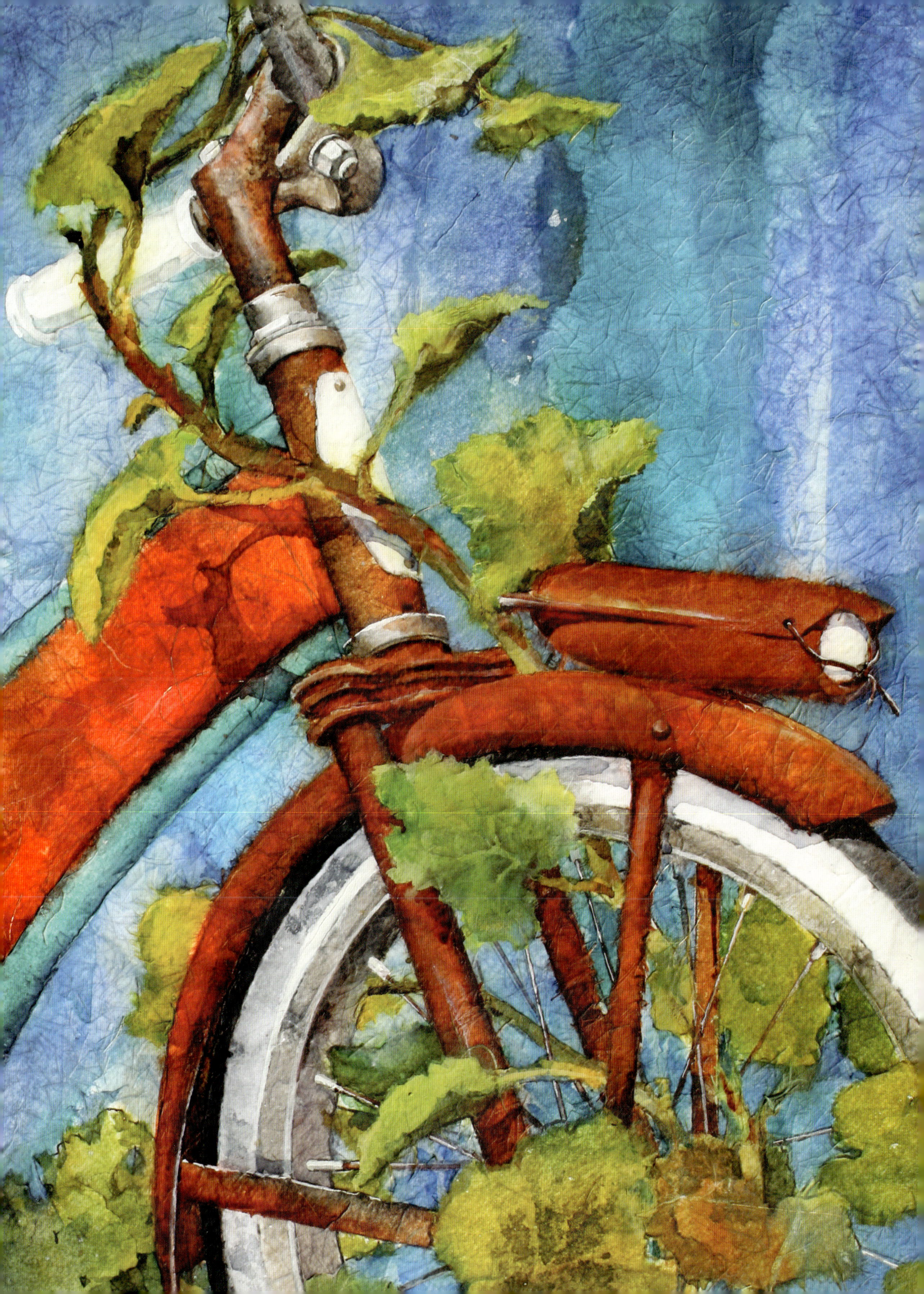

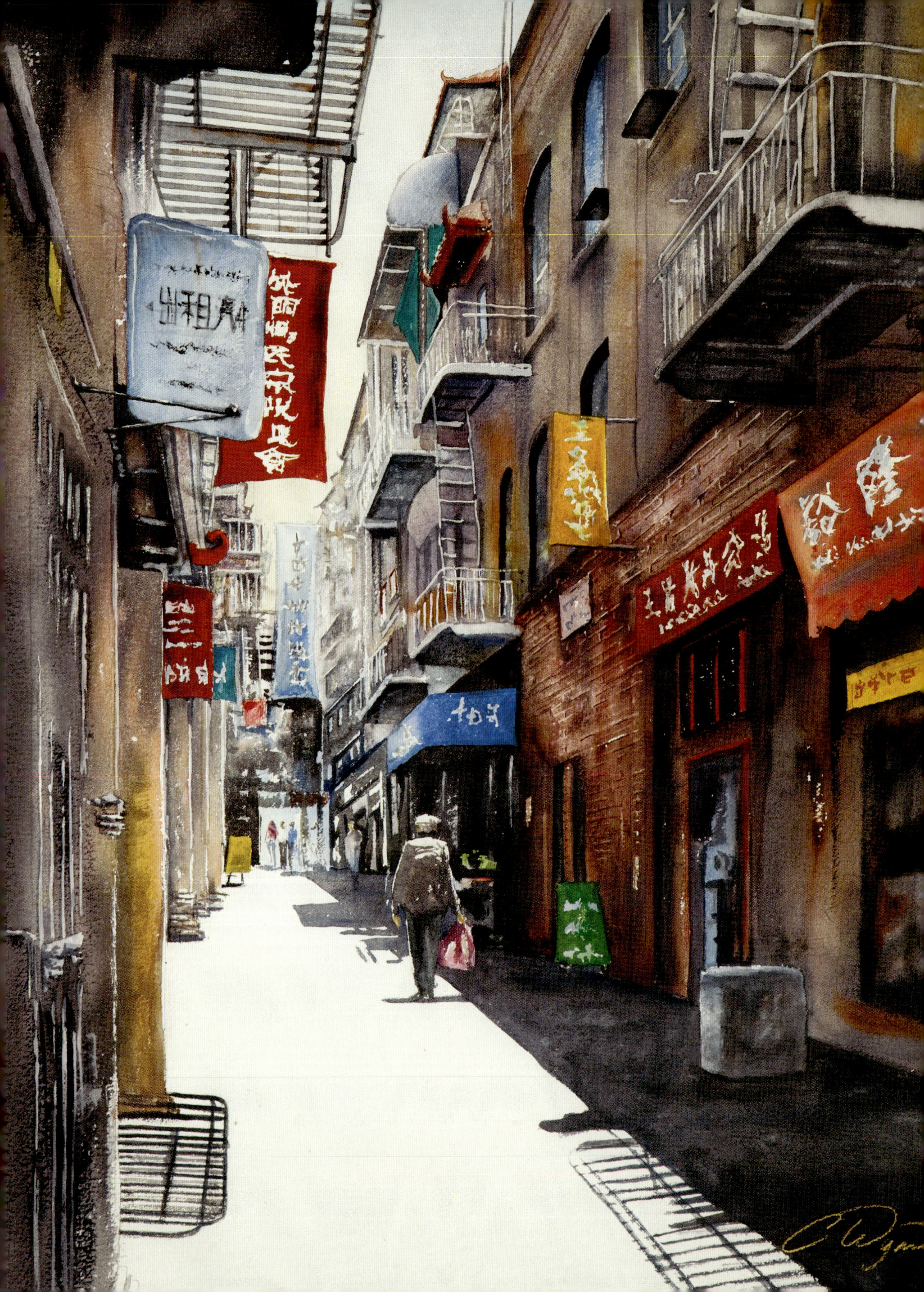

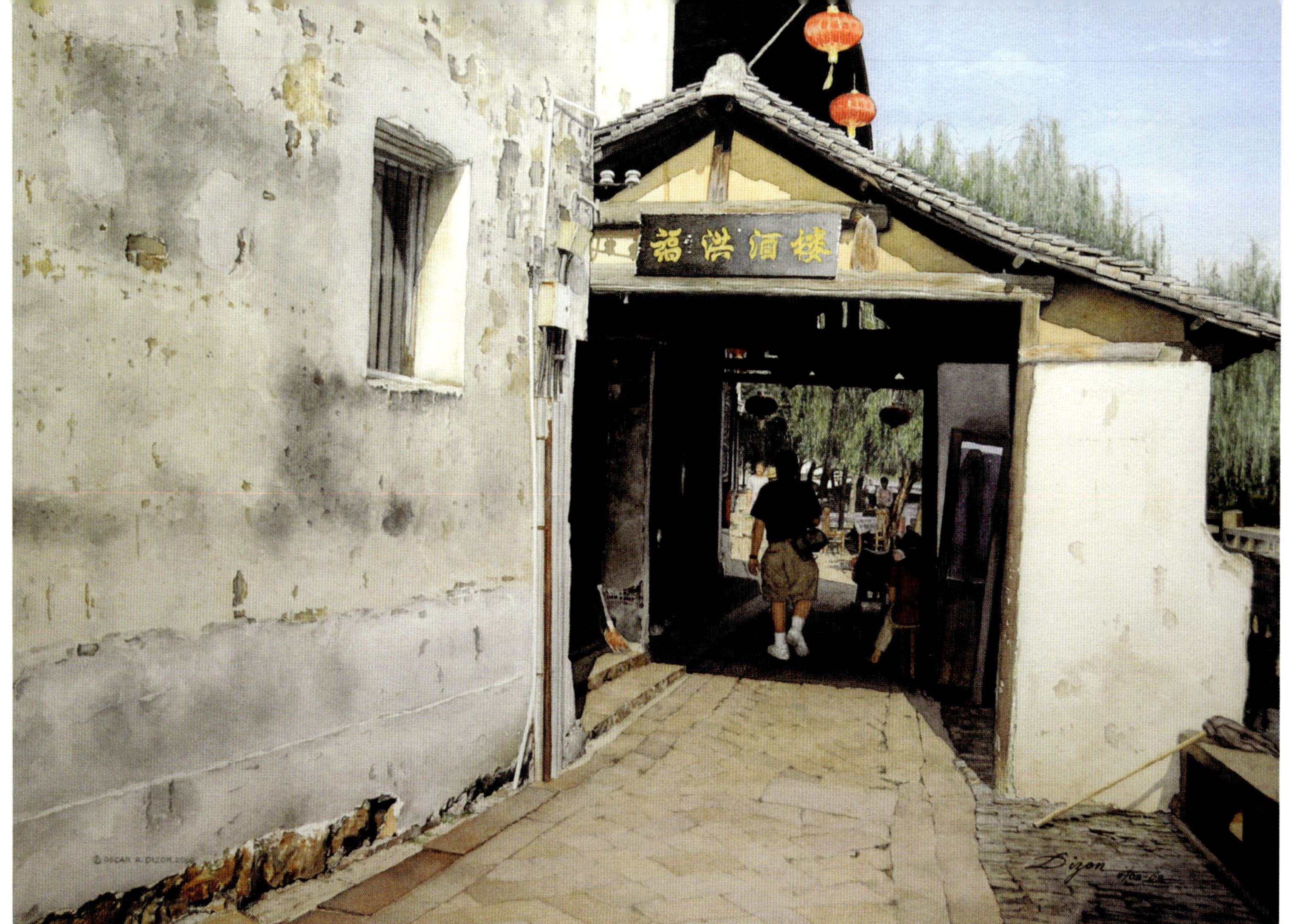

PASSAGE TO THE PARK | OSCAR R. DIZON
Transparent watercolor on Arches, 22" × 29" (56cm × 74cm)

Paint what you see, not what you think.

Oscar R. Dizon

The figure under the shade between the bright sunlight of both the foreground and the background seemed as interesting as it was challenging. The red lanterns against intense dark, the weathered sign and the character of the stonework on the left convinced me to take the challenge. The foreground value was established after working meticulously on the detailed stonework on the left. The diagonal shape leads the eye to the figure under the shade. I then completed the façade of the building, the background and the sky, leaving the middle ground shade for last so I could determine how much dark was needed to balance the composition. I build up color slowly to ensure the right value.

THE SECRET OF ALLEYS | CHRISTOPHER WYNN
Transparent watercolor on paper, 28" × 21" (71cm × 53cm)

Growing up in California, I was always fascinated with San Francisco's Chinatown—the back alleys in particular. In 2009, I returned to California for a brief visit, and the concepts for a series on Chinatown developed. I wanted my artistic vision to convey my original boyhood sense of the mystery and intrigue of it all. What's behind the curtain, so to speak. The elements of the painting are simple and the brushstrokes are loose. The contrast of sunlight (simply the white paper) to deep shadows adds a sense of drama and draws the eye to the end of the alley. The sense of mystery is further enhanced by the lone man walking away from the viewer.

Sometimes watercolor paintings lack depth because of the exclusion of a full complement of 1 to 10 values. Keep a rich, mixed black on your palette to prevent that.

Christopher Wynn

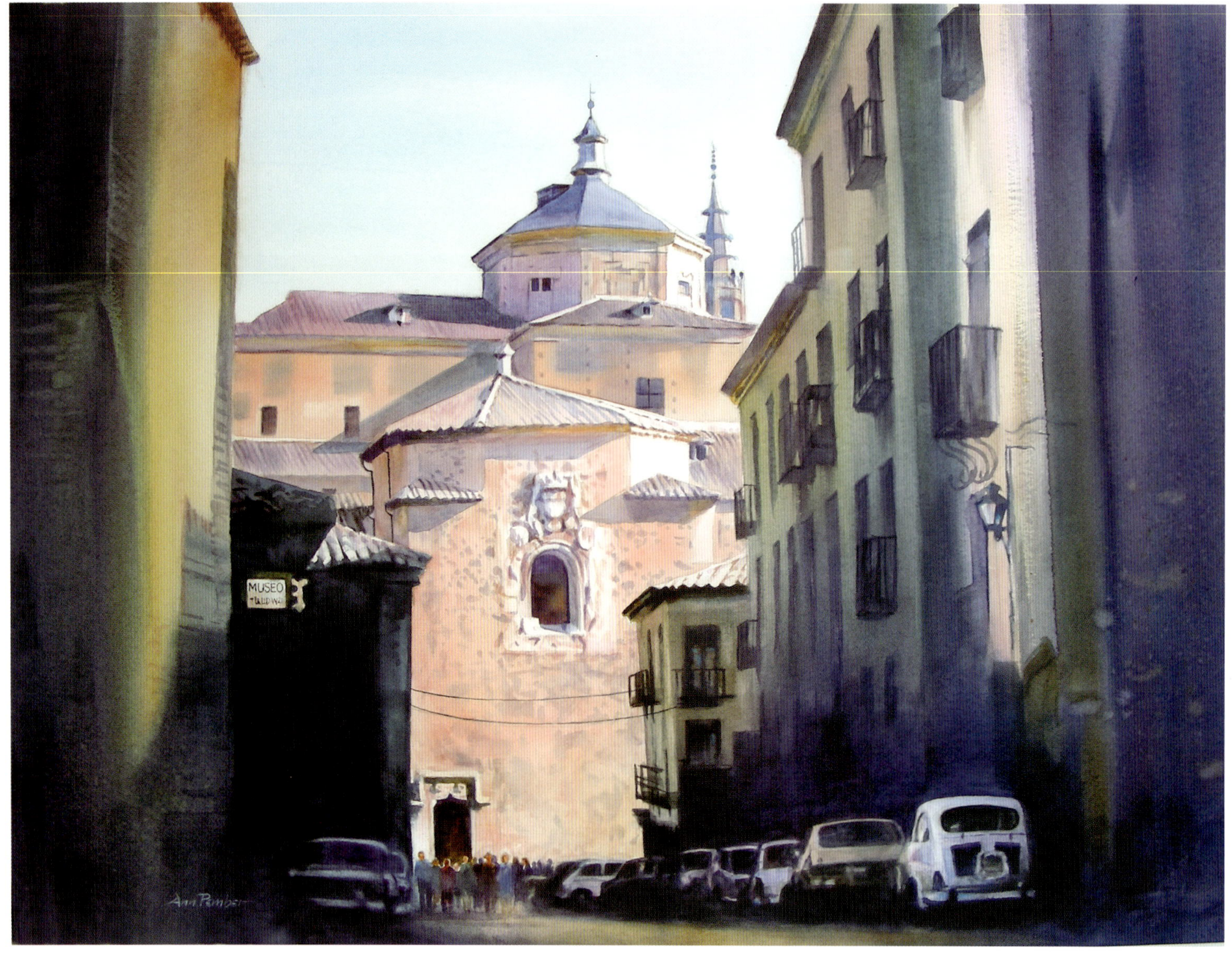

MUSEO MAJESTUOSO | ANN PEMBER

Transparent watercolor on 300-lb. (640gsm) cold-pressed Lanaquarelle, 21" × 29" (53cm × 74cm)

A few years ago, I photographed this image in Spain as I approached through a narrow street, hoping to capture the dramatic lighting and buildings in a painting one day. I was excited by it once again as I recently made the drawing. I designed the painting to bring the viewer in to the museum building with its staccato shapes, textures and angles struck by sunlight. The tall, dark buildings along the narrow street form a framework for the museum. People and cars add a human element and provide directional movement without being too important. I painted with large round brushes and transparent pigments, mingling them on the paper for luminous color. Darks were charged into washes before they dried.

BRIDGE OF SIGHS | LYNN HOSEGOOD

Watercolor on paper, 28" × 19" (71cm × 48cm)

Artistic vision is a journey, not an event.

— *Lynn Hosegood*

Bridge of Sighs has been painted by artists for centuries. Crossing the bridge, prisoners caught their last glimpse of natural light before spending the remainder of their lives in the dungeons. My challenge was to create something different using a somewhat clichéd location. Using Photoshop, I select areas from my photo to create a high-contrast design. I then simplify shapes and create asymmetrically balanced value and color contrasts. To keep all the dark areas transparent, I use transparent greens, reds, blues and violets and apply them separately to mix on the paper, not on the palette.

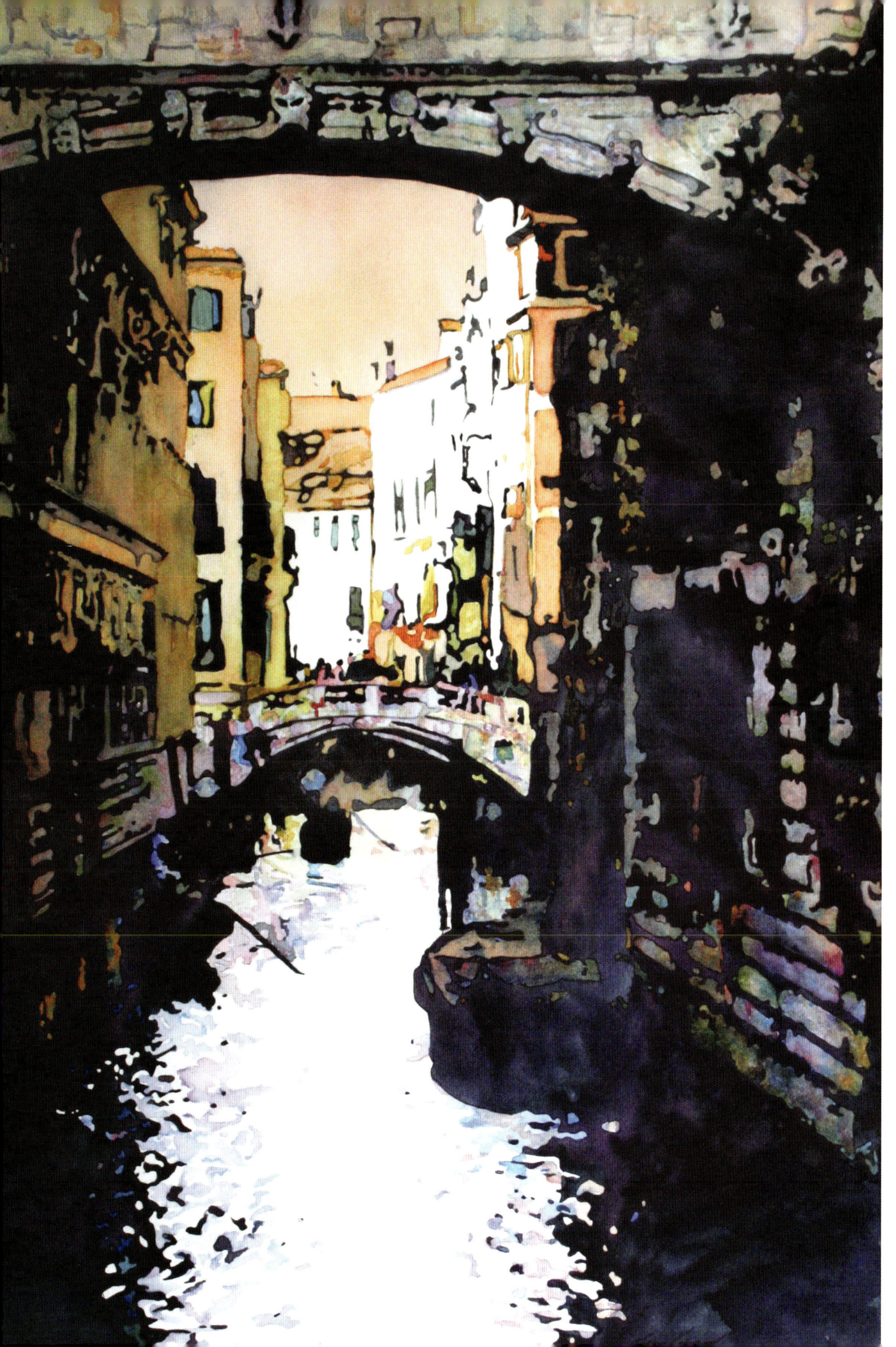

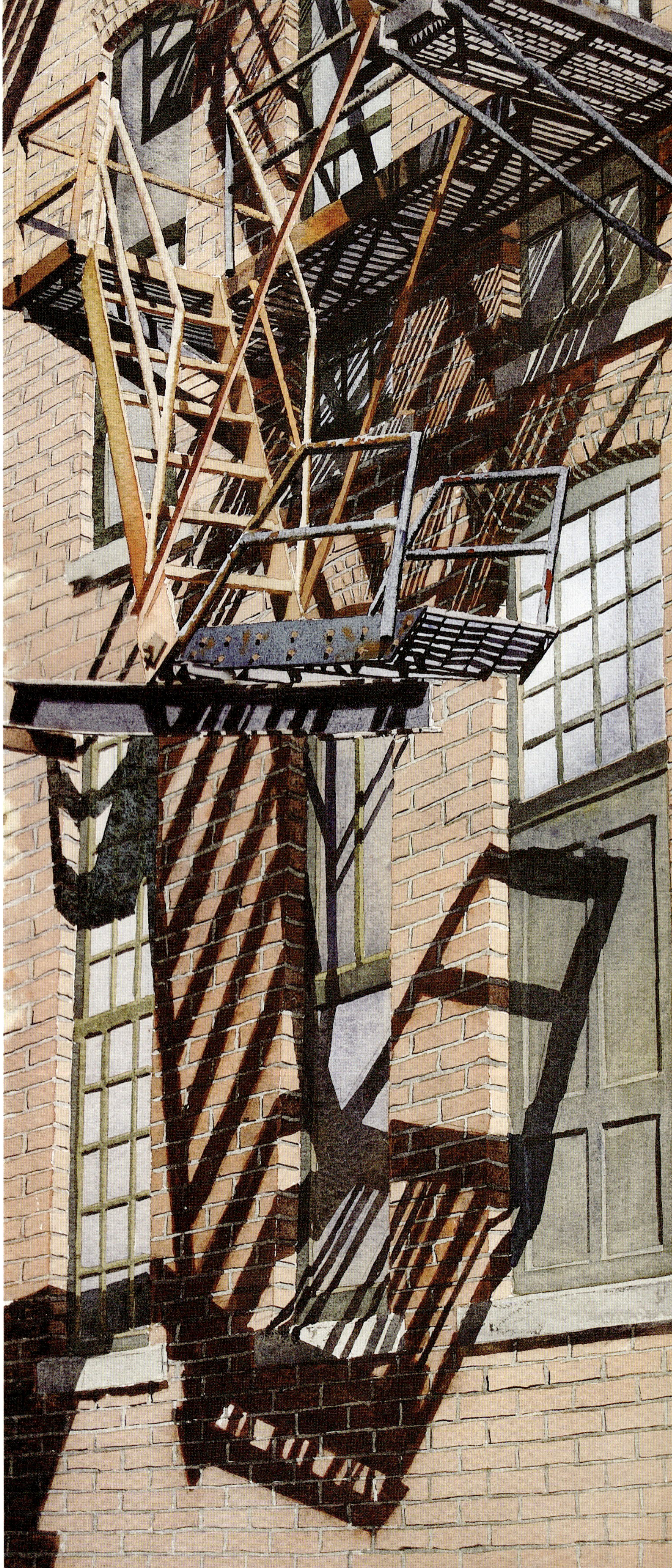

LADDER AND SHADOWS
SCOTT HARTLEY
Transparent watercolor on paper
23" × 10" (58cm × 25cm)

After carefully arranging the composition to feel most evocative, I applied transparent pigments with as few layers as possible, working from light to dark, but with the placement of some darkest darks first to help establish values. I deliberately courted granulation to help suggest texture. I look for subjects that are not picturesque and find many layers of meaning in them. The solidity of the rectangular forms is juxtaposed against the angular, precarious forms of the fire escape and shadows. This evokes the feeling one might have using a fire escape, as the composition causes the viewer to be without firm grounding, looking up at the structure.

My vision consists of choosing an unusual and meaningful subject and shaping the composition to enhance the mood and focus, to create a unique and powerful image.

Scott Hartley

FOUNTAIN, SONOMA PLAZA
MICHAEL REARDON
Transparent watercolor on 140-lb. (300gsm) cold-pressed Arches
22" × 11" (56cm × 28cm)

During the 2009 Sonoma Plein Air event I wandered around Sonoma Plaza in frustration. I couldn't find anything worth painting. About to give up, I glanced at the fountain and there it was! I sat in the grass and began to paint. First I did an underpainting. Then working wet-into-wet, I started at the tower top, continuing down to the grass at the bottom in one unbroken wash. I took some factual liberties, such as diffusing the background building to create an illusion of distance. Since the plein air version sold, I re-created it in my studio, painting it the same way as I did while sitting in the grass.

Once you have a strong vision and a striking composition of values and shapes, you can hardly go wrong.

Michael Reardon

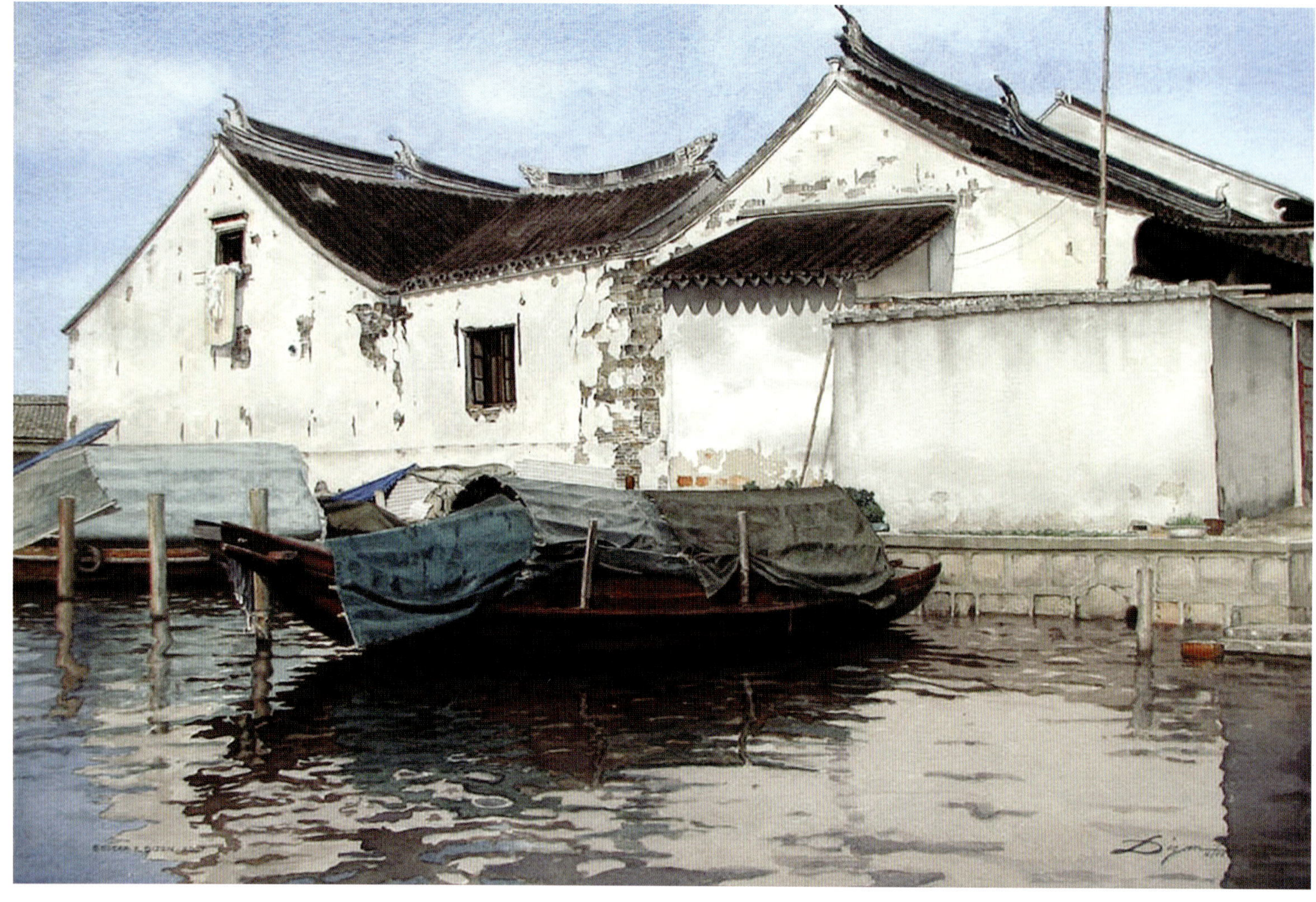

LATE SUMMER AT ZHOUZHUANG, 2006 | OSCAR R. DIZON
Transparent watercolor on Arches, 21" × 29" (53cm × 74cm)

On our visit to Shanghai, I was attracted to the rich culture and remarkable ancient architecture of the Watertown. This building with decorative roof, and the antiquated boat with three generations of weathered canvases, captivated my attention. Structures characterized by their history, coupled with richness of texture, interest me most. I compose my painting through the camera, freezing the moment, thereby synchronizing the shadows in one direction. In my studio, I started with the main focal point (I refer to it as my inspiration point), working on all of the boat details. Satisfied with the results, I then continued to work with mounting inspiration to the finish. I work exclusively with transparent watercolor and utilize masking fluid for the white.

A SIDE CANAL, VENICE | JAMES TOOGOOD
Watercolor on paper, 14" × 11" (36cm × 28cm)

In this painting I wanted a strong feeling of midday sunlight. To do this I made a middle-value sky to contrast with both the light and shadow of the surrounding buildings. Dappled light reflects onto the yellow building from the gentle movement of the water. I also wanted a contrast of color, shape and texture. The rectilinear shapes of the buildings contrast nicely with the graceful curvilinear patterns in the water. The red bricks complement the color and spiky texture of the green asparagus ferns in the foreground. This pattern of contrast continues with the use of vegetation as you look farther down the canal.

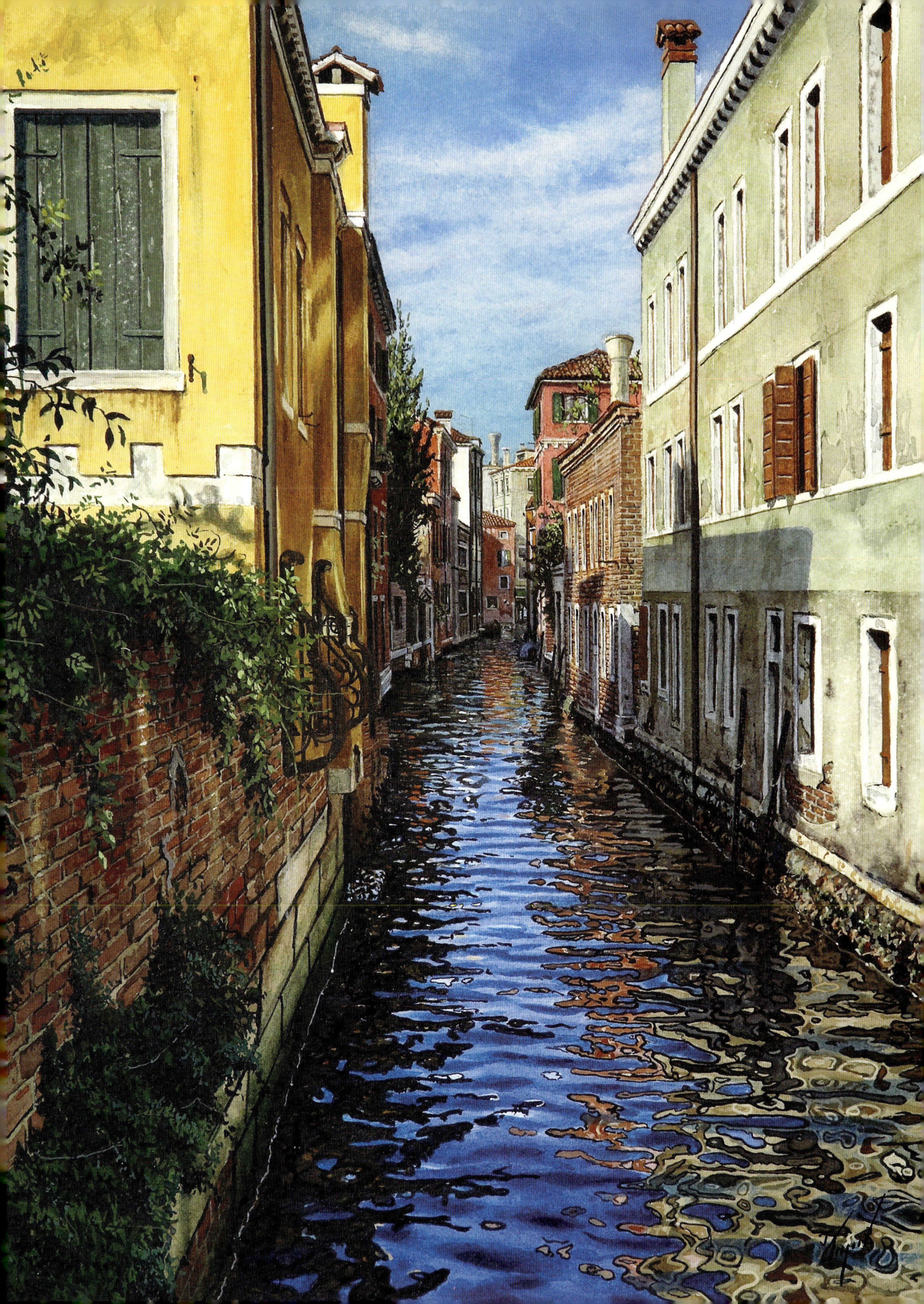

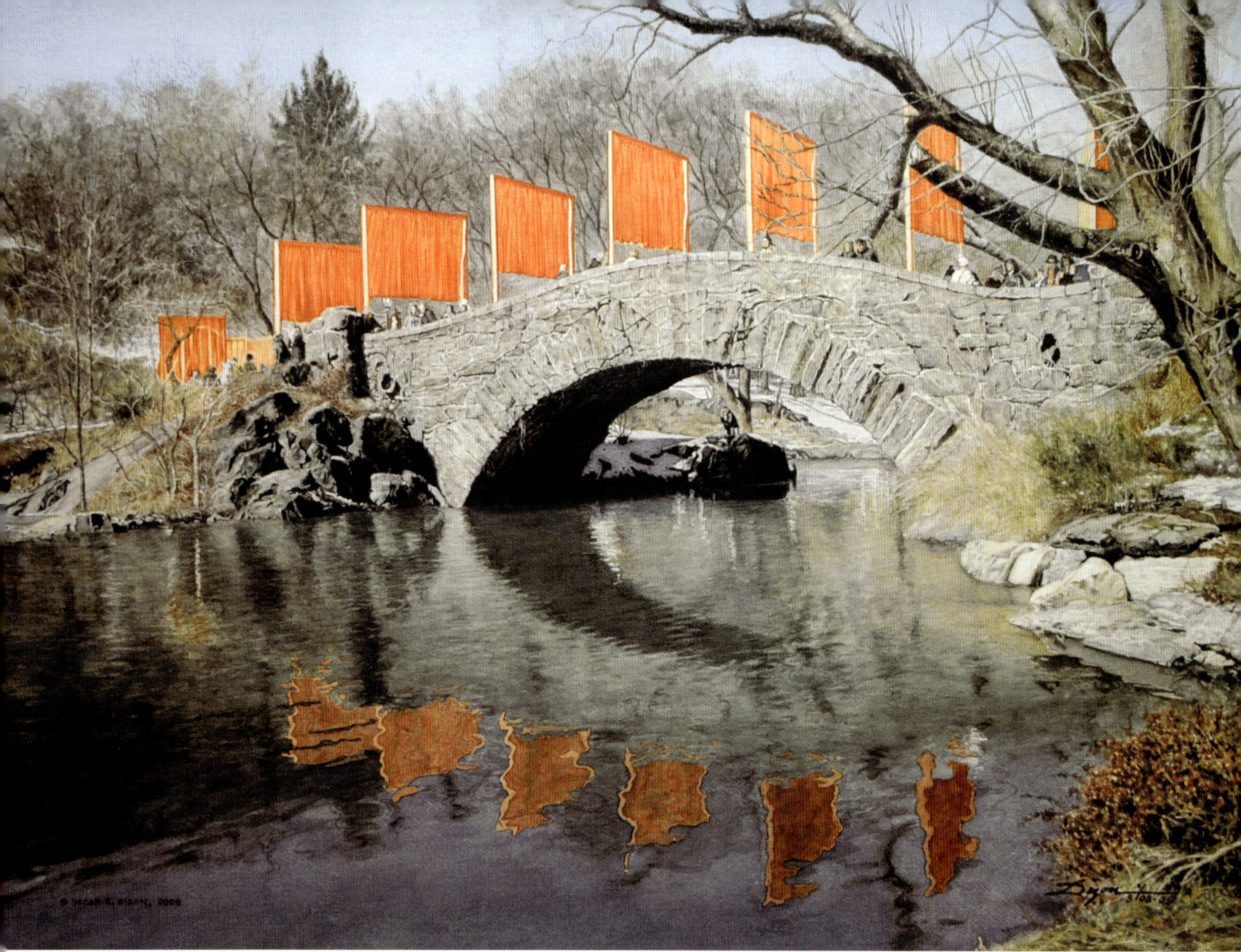

BRIDGE WITH "GATES" | OSCAR R. DIZON

Transparent watercolor on Arches, 22" × 29" (56cm × 74cm)

My artistic vision is to record the scene or events of today for tomorrow.

Oscar R. Dizon

The half-frozen Central Park lake becomes a winter mirror for the stone bridge and *The Gates* exhibit of Christo and Jeanne-Claude. After working on my composition, I started with the bridge's stonework to establish the first of three values, while showing the intricate details in the process. I then masked the overlapping tree branches. The trees on the left and tall grasses on the right were masked repeatedly after each wash of color. The bridge's reflection was done last to see how much dark was needed.

LUMBER SCOW | STUART GIVOT

Transparent watercolor on paper, 22" × 15" (56cm × 38cm)

I follow the advice I give my students: "Be patient, let it dry."

Stuart Givot

The scow schooner was a type of boat locally developed on San Francisco Bay in the nineteenth century. There were hundreds built and used like trucks are used today: carrying lumber, hay, sand, grain and all kinds of bulk cargo. My painting depicts a scow schooner with a cargo of lumber. It is based on dozens of drawings I made from old photographs, books and copies of plans. My painting process consisted of increasingly darker glazes over a multicolored flat wash for the atmospheric effect. The painting is on Twinrocker paper, which is quite nice for scrubbing out lighter areas, allowing me to avoid masking fluid. I like to take unusual subjects and put them in interesting atmospheric conditions such as fog or rain to create a specific mood.

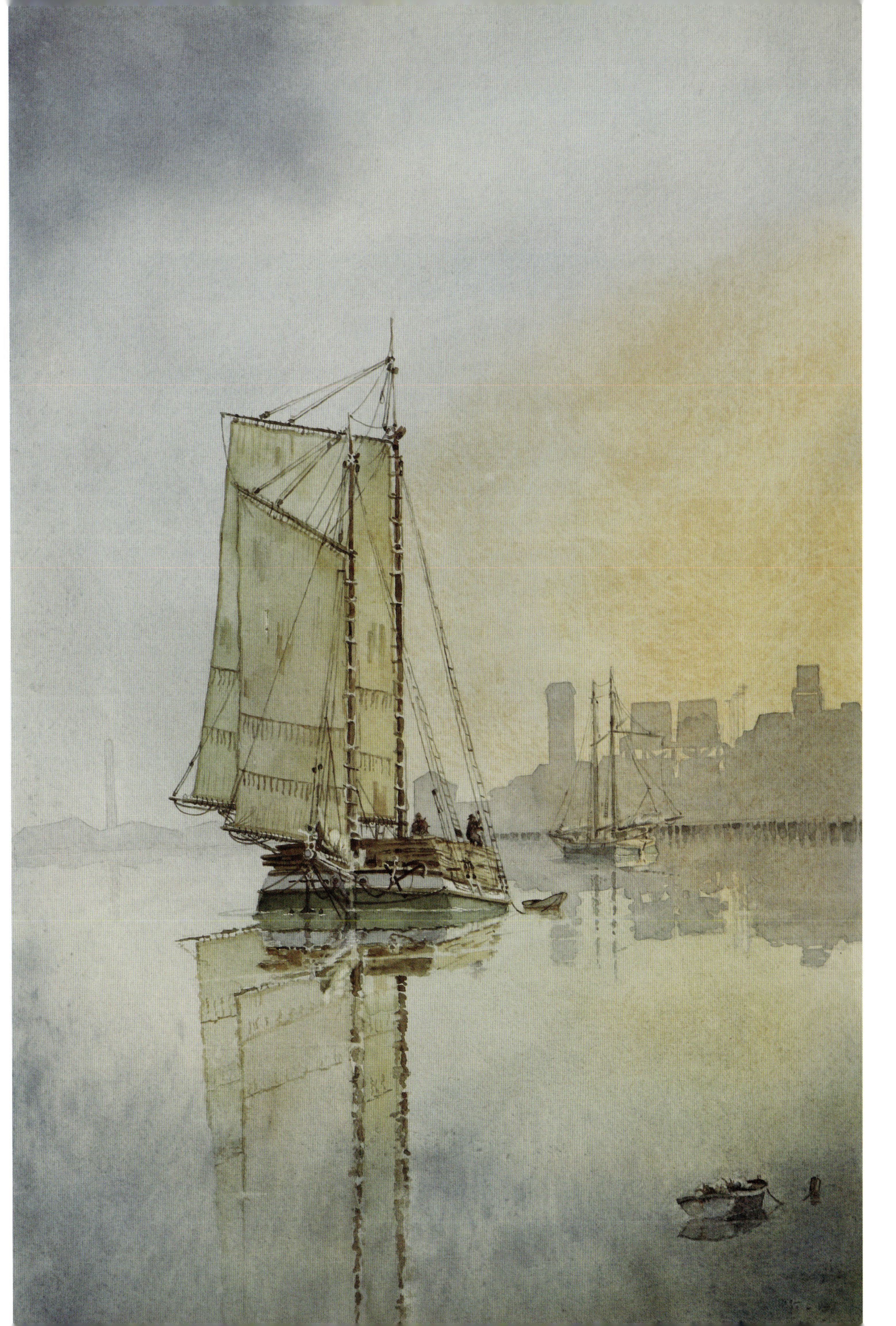

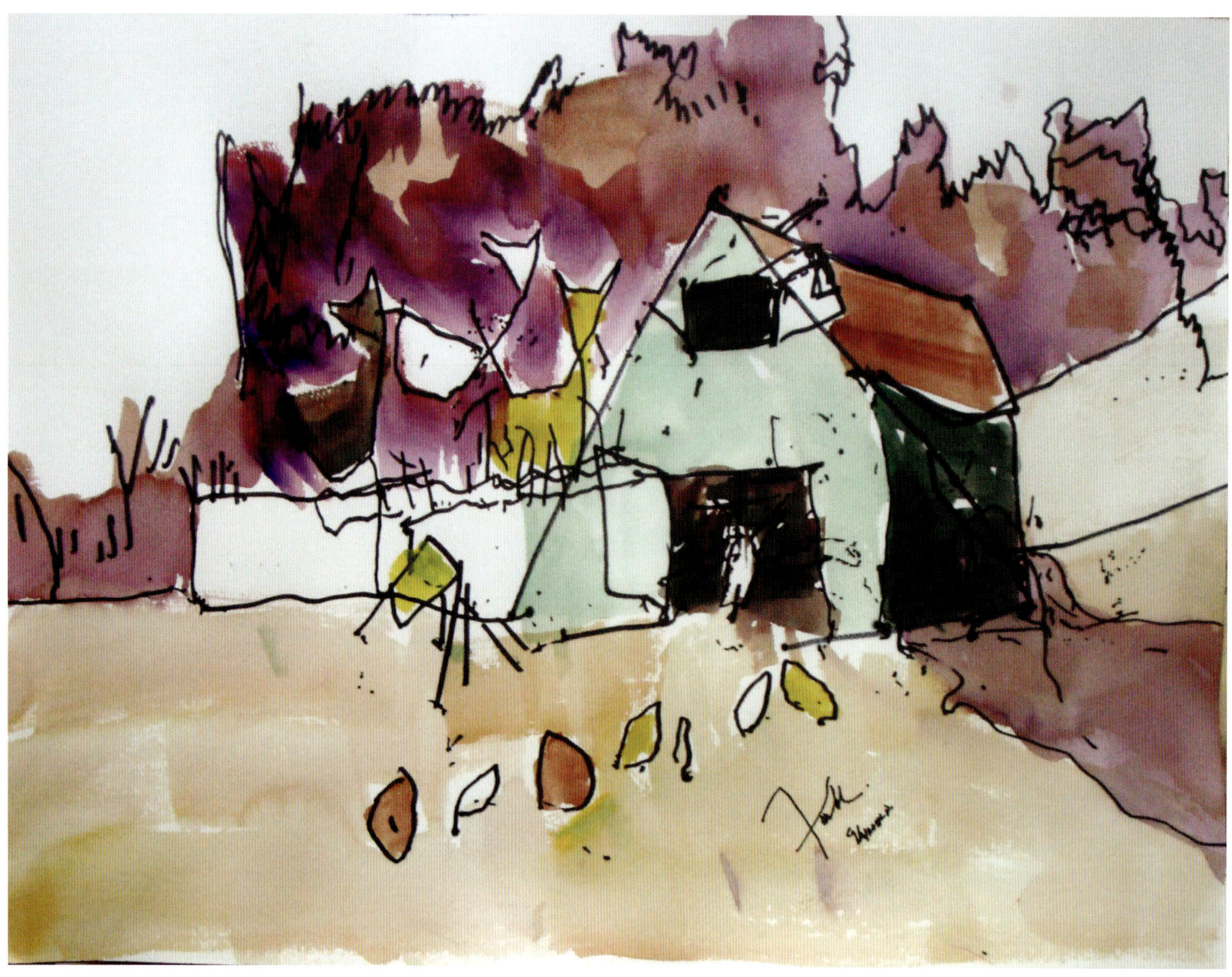

ROWLAND HEIGHTS BARN
HENRY FUKUHARA
Transparent watercolor with felt pen assisted by Ettore Andreani
18" × 24" (46cm × 61cm)

Don't be a reporter; be an entertainer.

— Henry Fukuhara

At age 96 Henry Fukuhara was completely blind and bedridden in a nursing home when he painted this image in October 2009. The image is derived from his visual memory; he had painted this scene on-site many times. Neither age nor loss of eyesight diminished Henry's artistic vision. He merely made a transition to painting "by feel" and needed an assistant to hand him tools and to provide verbal feedback. For this painting he was assisted by friend and fellow artist Ettore Andreani. Henry used his familiar butcher tray palette, a 2-inch (51mm) flat brush and a calligraphy brush. To situate himself spatially he switched to a watercolor block whose sides he could feel. Despite his blindness, Henry's work retained its characteristic simplicity and lightheartedness and his signature linework. Fukuhara was a very popular and highly respected teacher as well as painter. He passed away in January 2010 during the production of *Splash 12*.

Written by Albert C. Setton, Fukuhara's friend and fellow artist

ROOFTOPS NEW YORK
LAURIN MCCRACKEN
Transparent watercolor on 300-lb. (640gsm) soft-pressed Fabriano
25" × 18" (64cm × 46cm)

I painted this from a photograph that I had taken from a hotel window in midtown Manhattan in New York City, from about 39th Street looking south. I was intrigued with the repetitive shapes of the water storage tanks and the skylights, especially the triangular shapes. The light was at the right angle. I projected the image onto my paper and did a very detailed drawing. Starting from the top, I worked back and forth across the sheet to the bottom, adding detail as I advanced down the sheet. This painting illustrates that sometimes the rooftops are more interesting than the bustling streets.

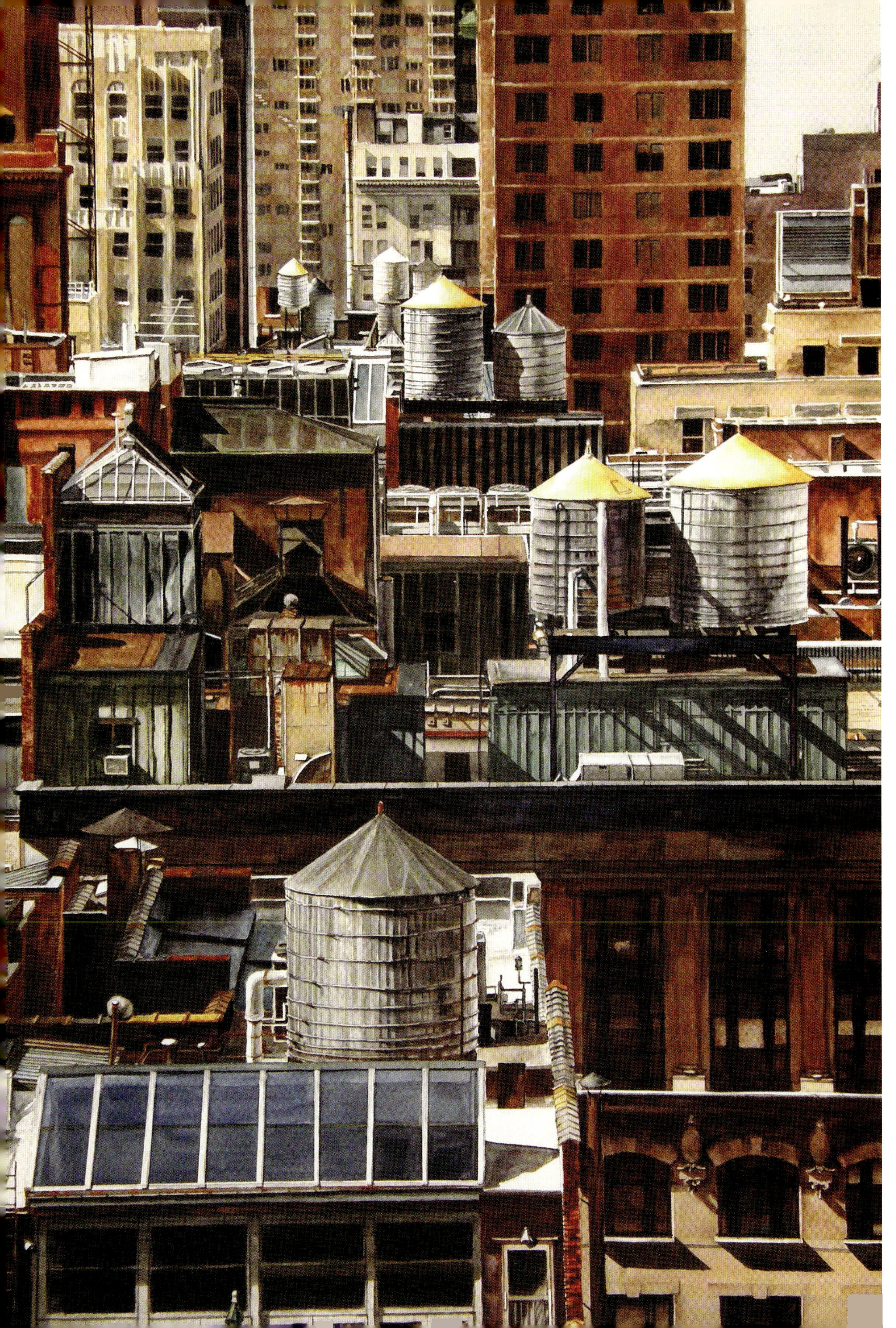

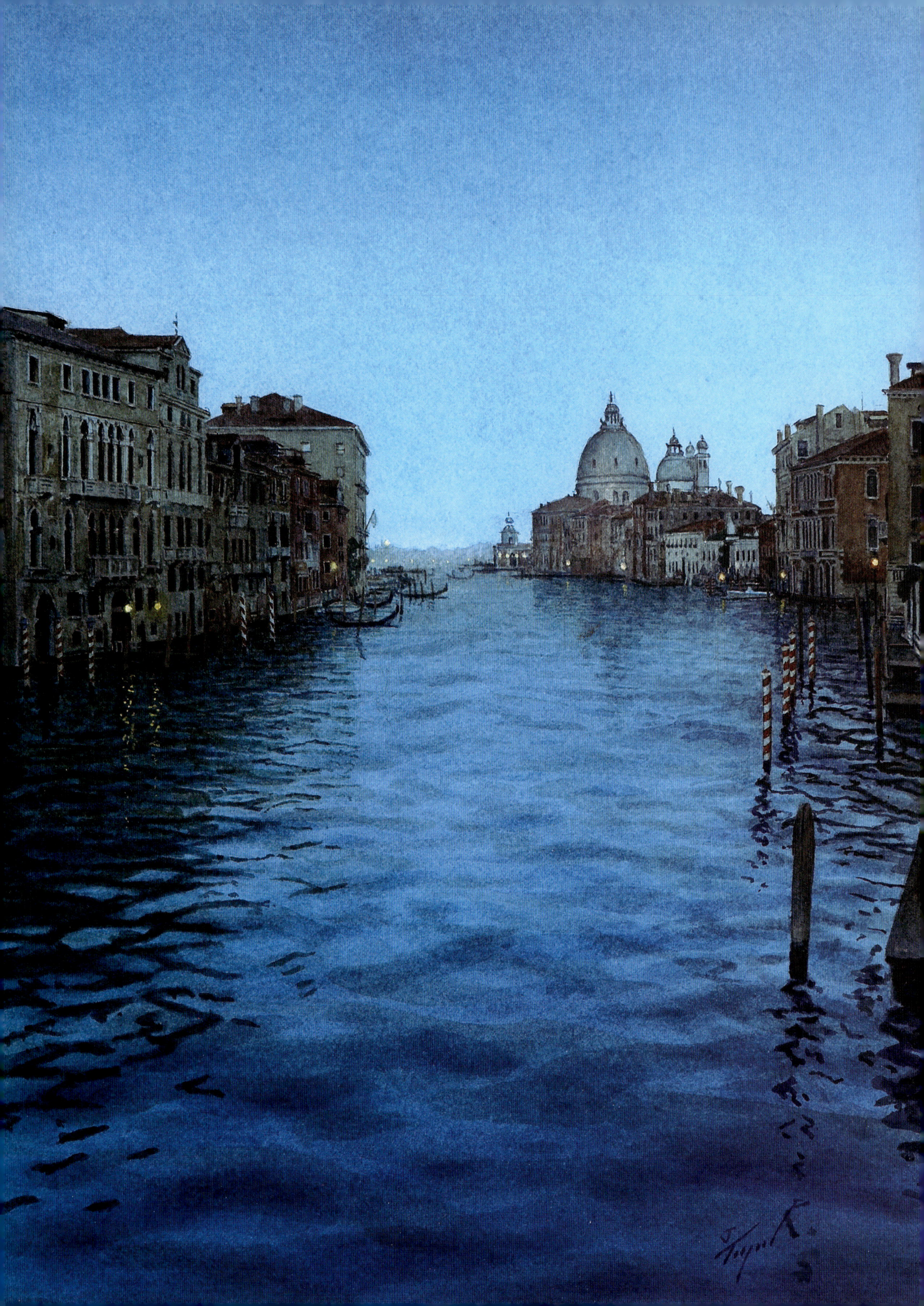

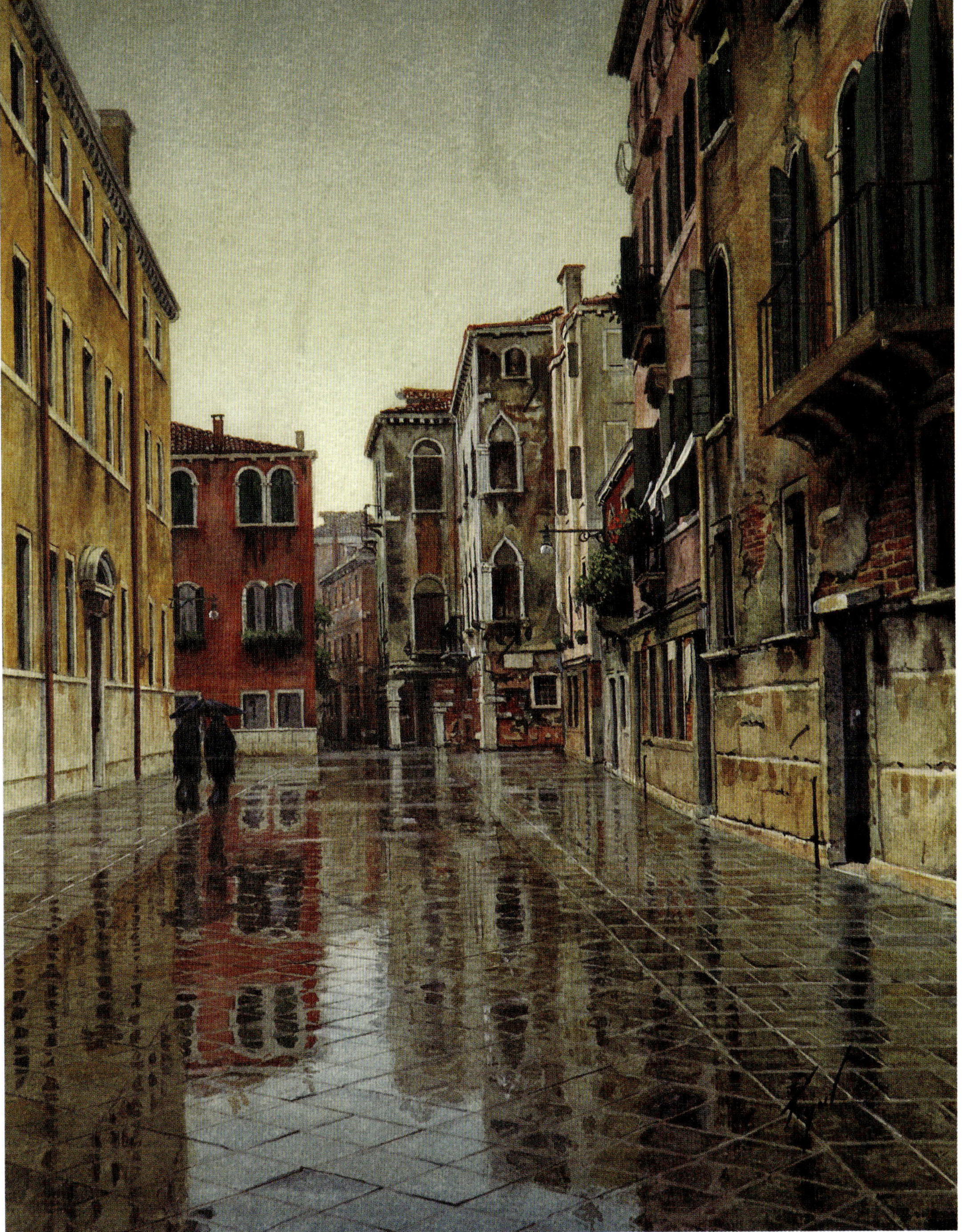

RIO TERÀ DEI CATECUMENI | JAMES TOOGOOD
Watercolor on paper, 14" × 11" (36cm × 28cm)

I visited this quiet Venetian neighborhood repeatedly trying to figure out how best to paint it. Bright golden sunshine did not inspire me here. I decided instead to portray it during a gentle rain, with its soft, silver light. Still, the use of Raw Sienna throughout gives an underlying warmth to the painting. The mood is tranquil, discreet, dreamlike.

NOCTURNE, GRAND CANAL | JAMES TOOGOOD
Watercolor on paper, 14" × 11" (36cm × 28cm)

This scene looks east from the Accademia Bridge, where you can see many famous Venetian structures including the Peggy Guggenheim Collection on the right and the Church of Madonna della Salute just beyond it. This painting explores delicate qualities of light dominated by a single unifying color with a series of graded washes. Masking was used for the "street" lights.

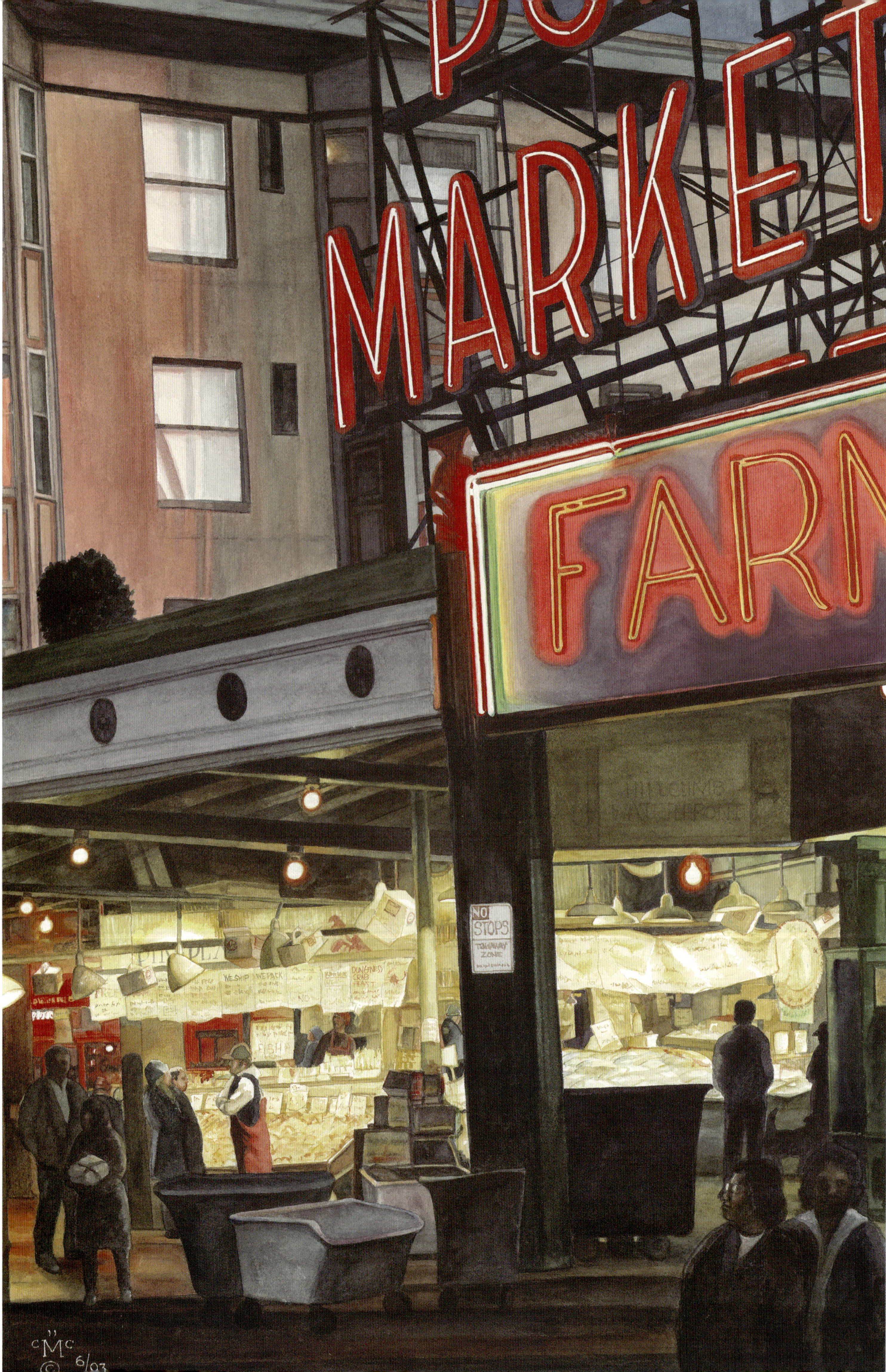
MARKET
NO STOPS
TOWAWAY ZONE

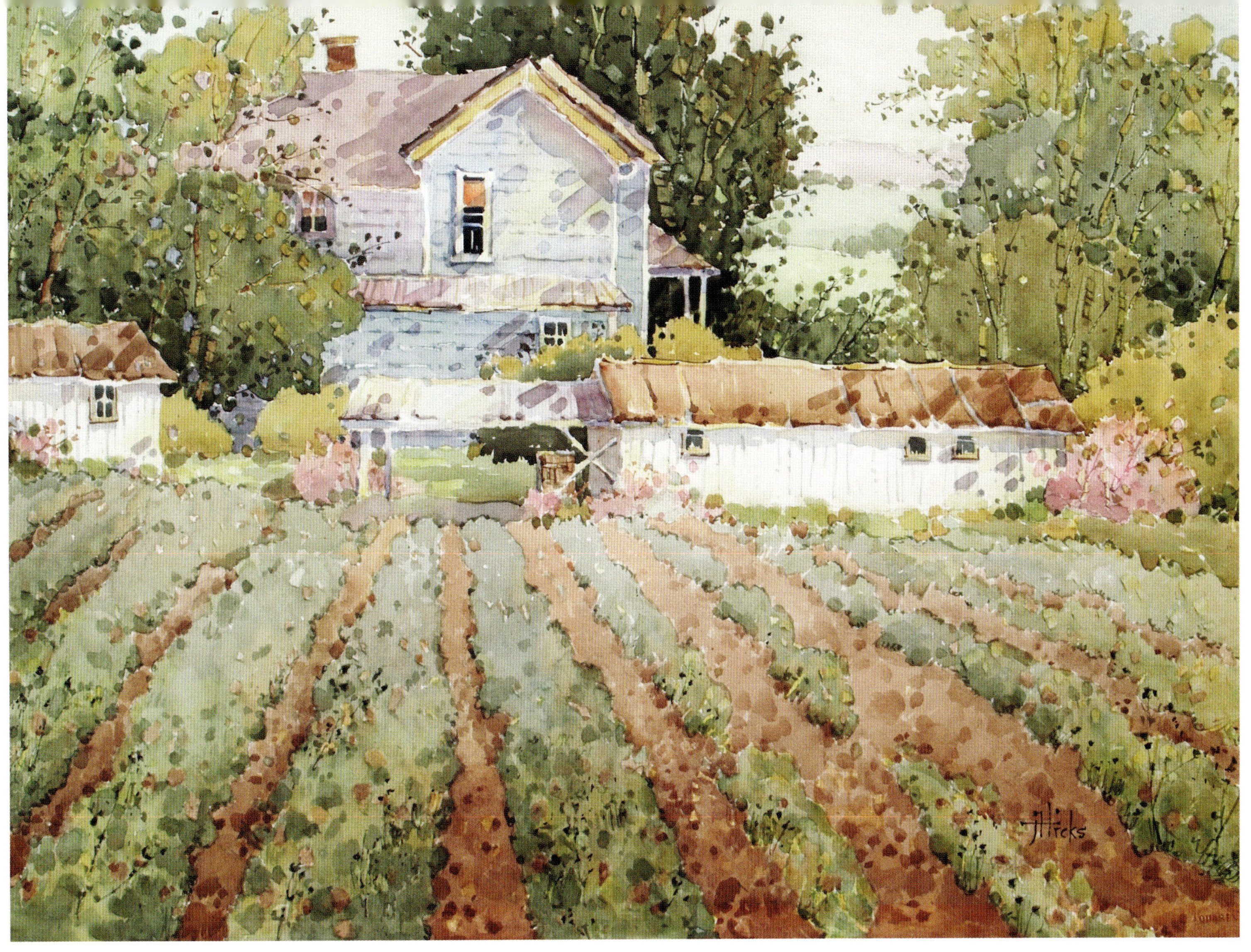

A FARMHOUSE I SAW IN VIRGINIA | JOYCE HICKS

Transparent watercolor on cold-pressed Arches, 22" × 30" (56cm × 76cm)

Original paintings of beautiful places are the underlying theme of my work, and traveling coast to coast is the source for my inspiration. While traveling the Virginia countryside, I recorded this scene with photographs, sketches and notes. My painting process involves becoming intimate with a scene by doing studies for composition, value and color. These steps allow me to begin a painting with confidence. Standing before an upright easel with brushes and palette knife in hand, I paint intuitively on dry paper bringing the whole painting to completion. I use a glazing technique as a final step. My purpose is not to describe a scene exactly but to express my personal response. I'm especially drawn to sunlight and how it transforms an ordinary scene into one capable of taking one's breath away.

WINTER MARKET | CLAUDIA MCKINSTRY

Transparent watercolor on cold-pressed Arches, 24½" × 38" (62cm × 97cm)

Seattle in the winter is a place of mist, rain and very early sunsets. The Pike Place Market, the heart of the city, is bustling with shoppers and tourists till closing time. The market is part of my heritage; we shopped here as I grew up and it was here that I first began selling my artwork as a teenager. This famous corner has not changed. My vision was to catch the moments after sunset, the closing down of the market, when the last rays of the sunset compete with the neon of the sign. Knowing the location helped, along with dozens of photographs. For a big statement, I started with oversized 555-lb. (1200gsm) paper, then began with the neon, the most challenging part. I worked with a limited palette of primaries and built up innumerable layers to give it a glow. Special care was taken to create transparent darks. Last-minute changes like the ladies in the foreground were scrubbed in to create the feeling of activity in the dusk.

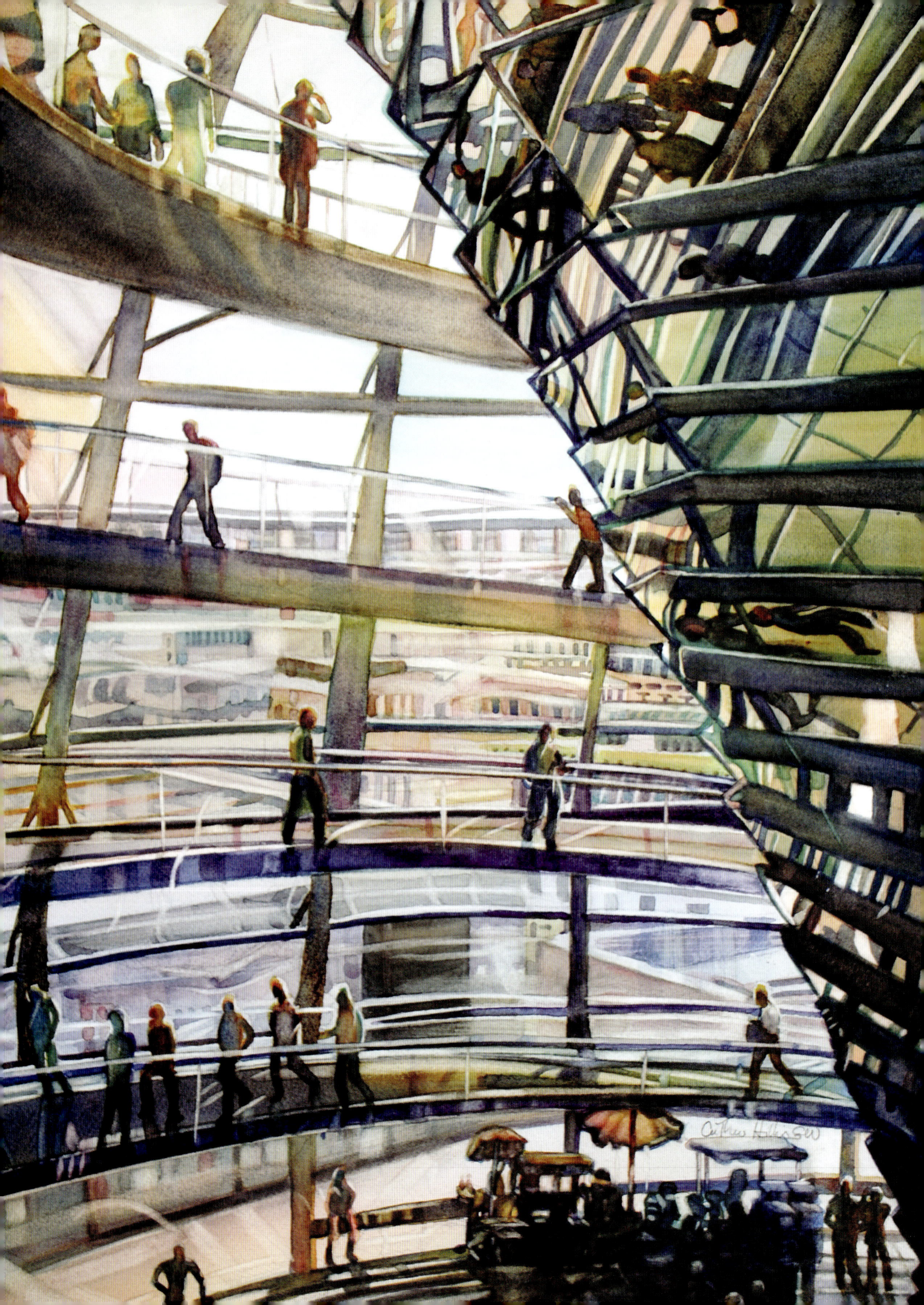

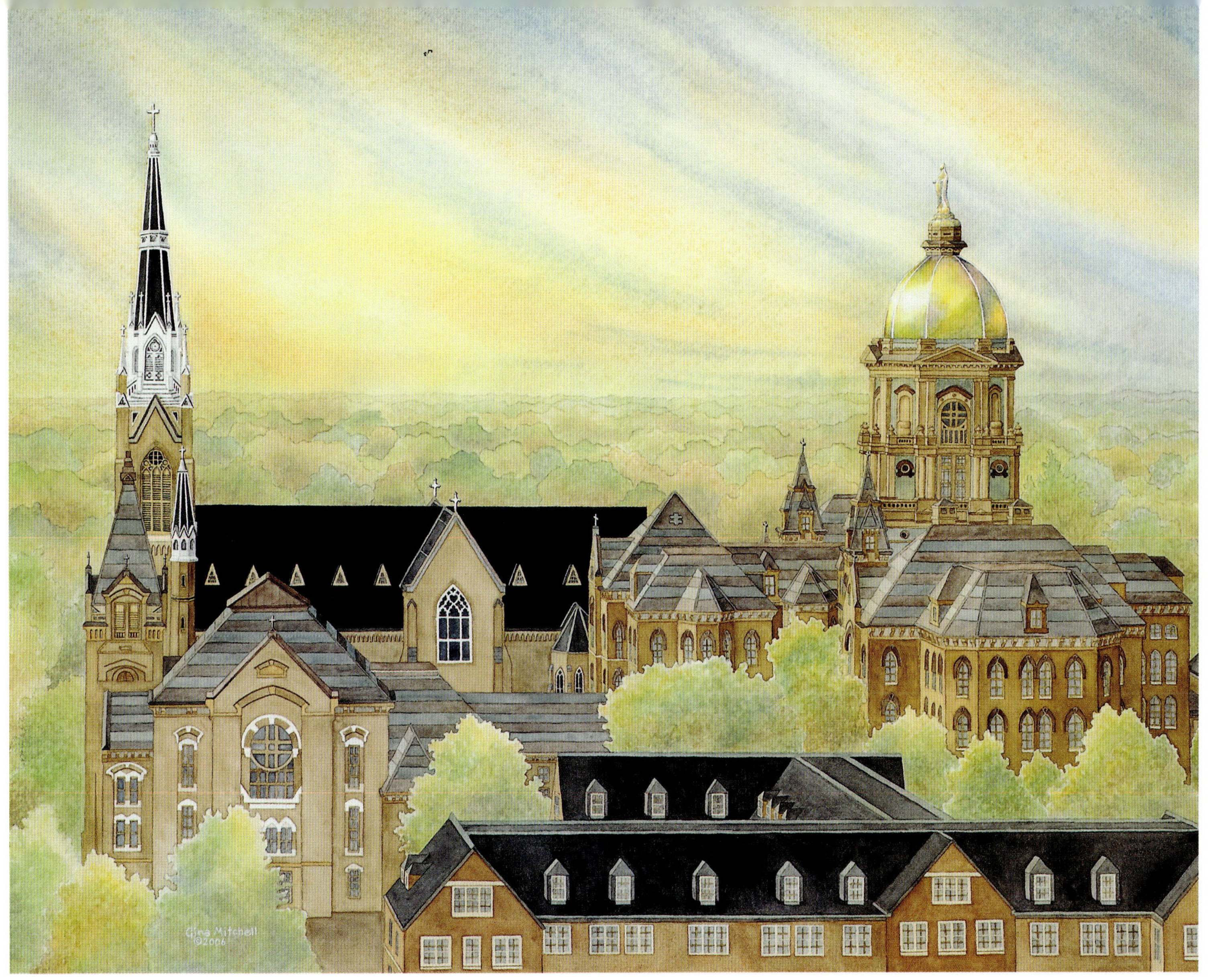

CAMPUS SUNSET | GINA MITCHELL

Transparent watercolor on 140-lb. (300gsm) cold-pressed Arches, 16" × 20" (41cm × 51cm)

> At the heart of my watercolors is a desire to combine creativity with detail to inspire unique and captivating illustrations.
>
> *Gina Mitchell*

I grew up just down the street from the beautiful University of Notre Dame in South Bend, Indiana, so it has been a part of my life. The building on the right is the main building, also referred to as the Golden Dome, and on the left is the Basilica of the Sacred Heart. Working from my photos, I sought to capture the character of the campus from an uncommon angle. A detailed pencil drawing was applied to the watercolor paper. After adding frisket to save white areas, I immersed the paper in water. Several washes of color were then applied to create a warm radiance that also gives a feeling of depth. When painting the dome, I used many shades of yellow, blue and red to create the golden glow.

ROUND 'N ROUND | CATHERINE HILLIS

Transparent watercolor on Artistico Fabriano, 19" × 15" (48cm × 38cm)

In my quest for artistic vision I like to relay commonplace drama. Though I usually paint detailed figures, I decided to lean towards abstraction here, as I wanted to illustrate the theatrical nature of the scene the architecture creates—the silhouettes of figures circling round and round, some isolated and others relating. I worked wet-into-wet, fusing warm into cool right onto the paper, paying close attention to the development of proper values.

> Pursue what you love, love what you pursue.
>
> *Catherine Hillis*

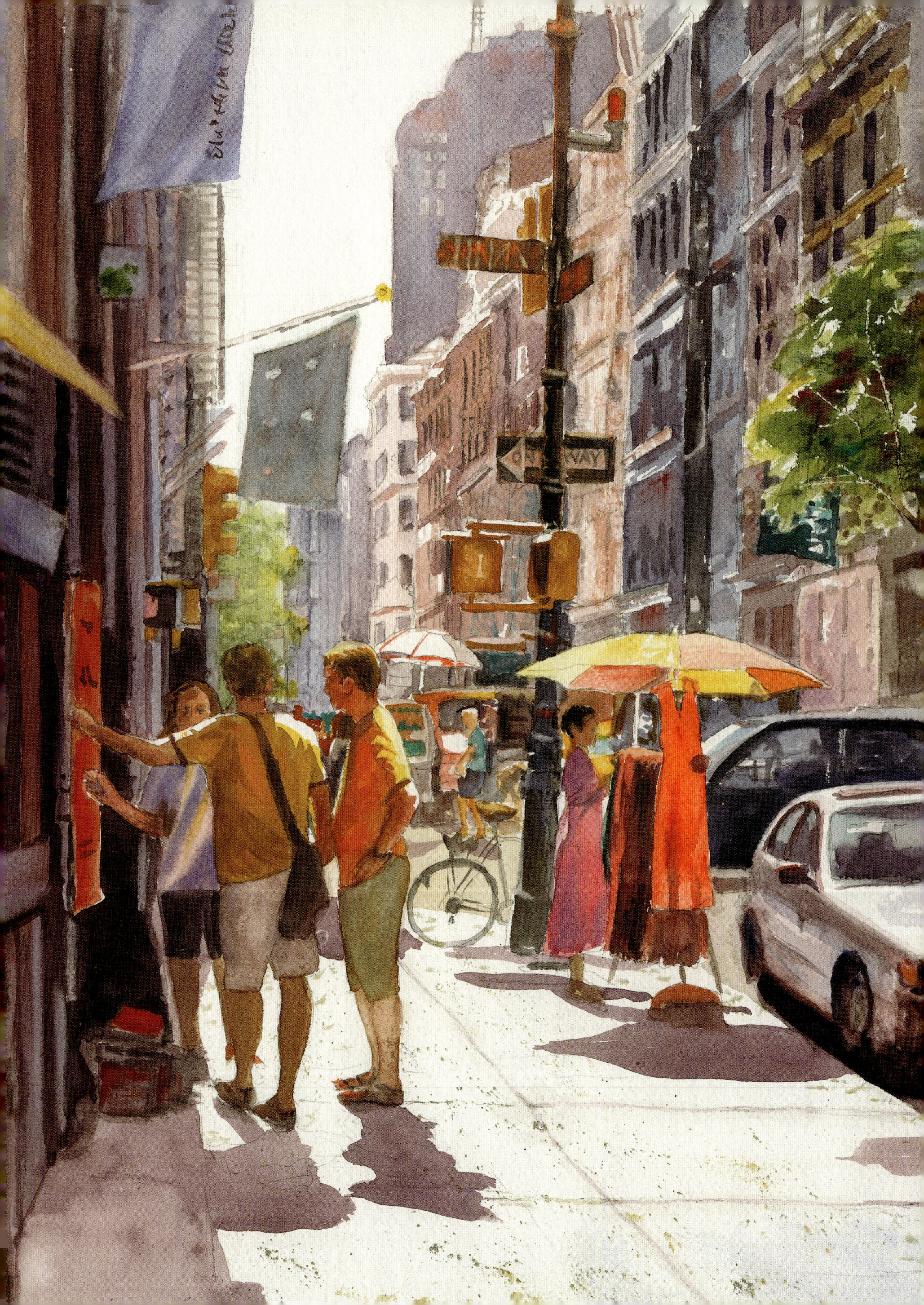

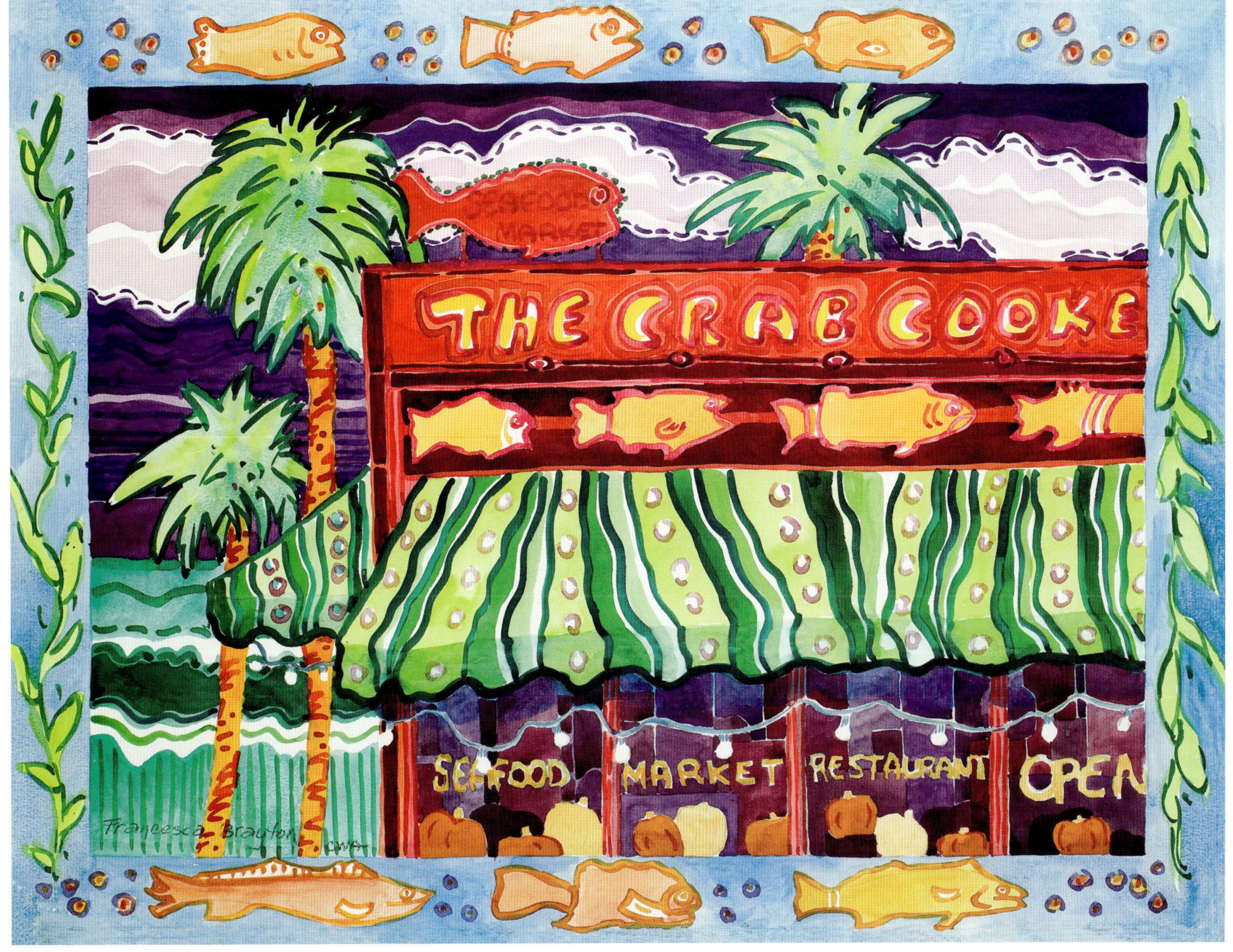

CRAB COOKER | FRANCESCA BRAYTON

Transparent watercolor on 140-lb. (300gsm) watercolor paper, 22" × 30" (56cm × 76cm)

I painted most of *Crab Cooker* on-site in Newport Beach, California, finishing it at home over the next few days. I first draw a loose pencil sketch, then work my way around the scene adding painted shapes, calligraphic lines and marks, like putting together a puzzle. I looked at my painting in a mat that day and the next to see if I needed to add something. I like a border to show elements related to the main scene as here with the fish, featured on the Crab Cooker menu. I enjoy showing the essence, liveliness and fun feel of a location with vibrant, fanciful color and line.

CHECKING THE BOARD | RUTH NEWQUIST

Transparent watercolor on paper, 19" × 14" (48cm × 36cm)

Light falling on objects draws me to a subject. On a trip to New York City, I took a photograph that was full of possibilities for creating a warm, sunlit day: an abundance of interesting shapes, varied light and shadow patterns, energetic people, and all the bright colors that describe the city I love. I make choices intuitively as I paint, and *Checking the Board* allowed me to use the wet-into-wet technique to its best advantage.

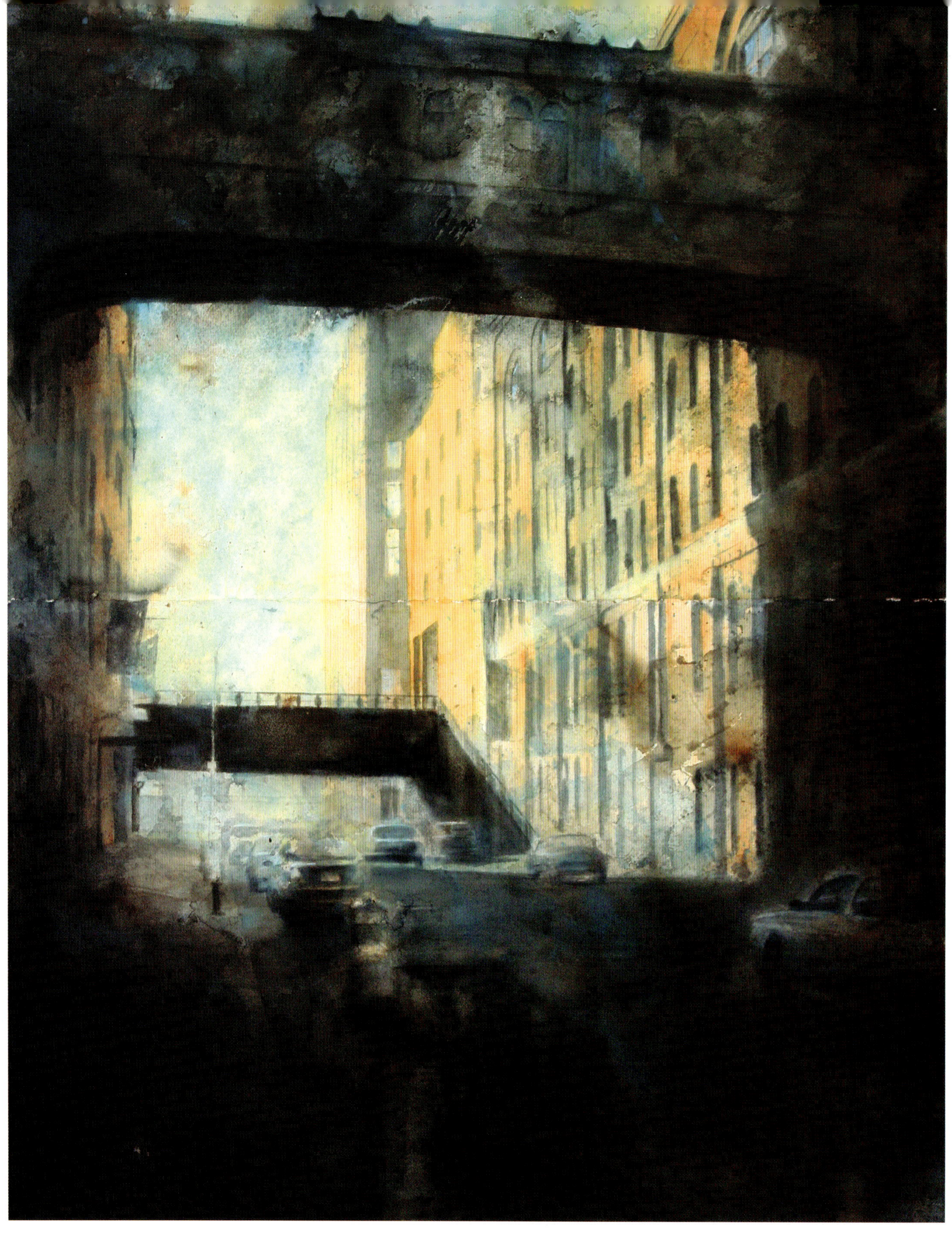

WEST 15TH STREET, TWO BRIDGES (DIPTYCH)
TIM SATERNOW
Watercolor on Arches single elephant rough paper
52" × 40" (132cm × 102cm)

I love seeing the distinct urban light playing across the buildings and streets of New York City, especially the warehouses, factories and long-forgotten areas. I paint the grime, age and rust of this city's vital industrial past that's quickly disappearing. It is the tension of opposites that excites me: cool and warm, light and dark, hard edges and soft edges—the drama of this city. These paintings explore the tension between carefully drawn linear perspective and a two-dimensional play on the surface of the paper through glazing, drips, watermarks and spatters. I weather the paper's surface like the patina of the old steel and concrete of the streets of New York City.

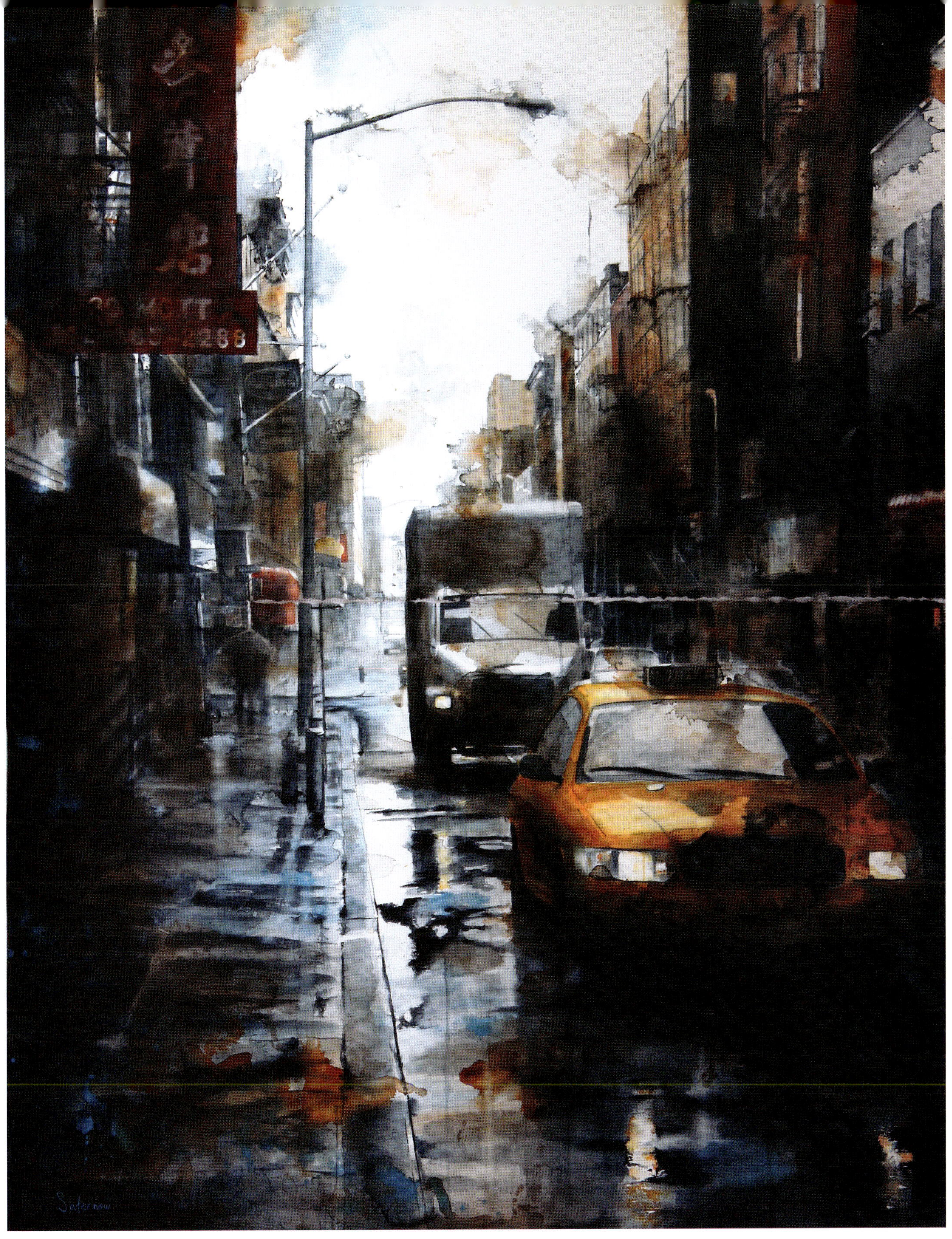

39 MOTT STREET, RAIN (DIPTYCH) | TIM SATERNOW
Watercolor on Arches single elephant rough paper, 52" × 40" (132cm × 102cm)

A painting is good not because it looks like something, but because it feels like something.

— *Jerry Stitt*

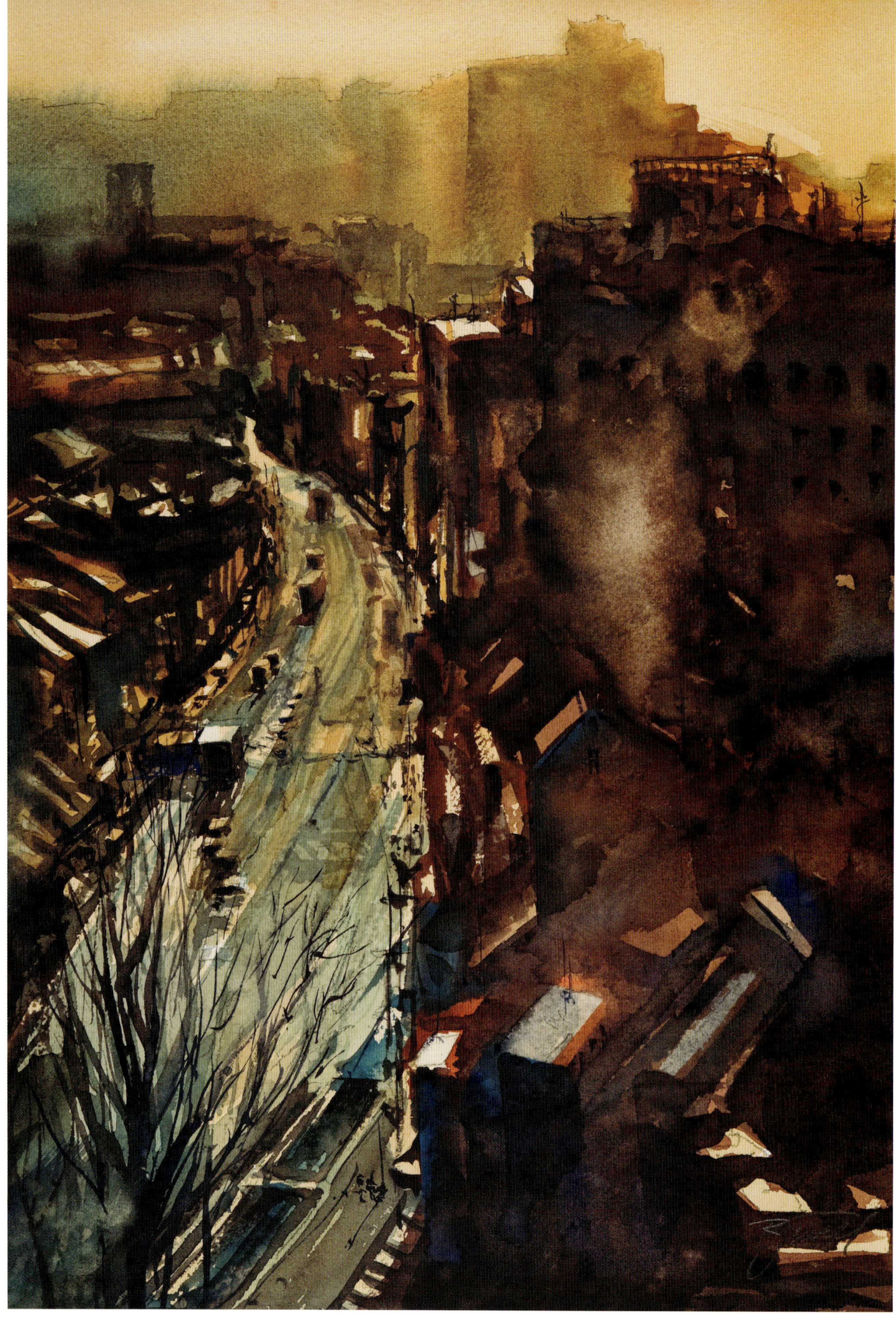

AMSTERDAM MORN
RUSSELL JEWELL
Transparent watercolor on
140-lb. (300gsm) rough Arches
15" × 11" (38cm × 28cm)

The image for my painting was caught with my camera as I clamored down an Amsterdam hotel stairwell headed for breakfast. Belgian waffles were in the air, and as I gazed out the window, the early morning light dissolved details and accentuated value contrasts. I had lately been exploring edge qualities in my work, and this scene provided a myriad of edges to explore, from the soft distances to the hard-edge foreground. Artistic vision is open ended. Couple an interesting scene with personal exploration and vision comes into focus.

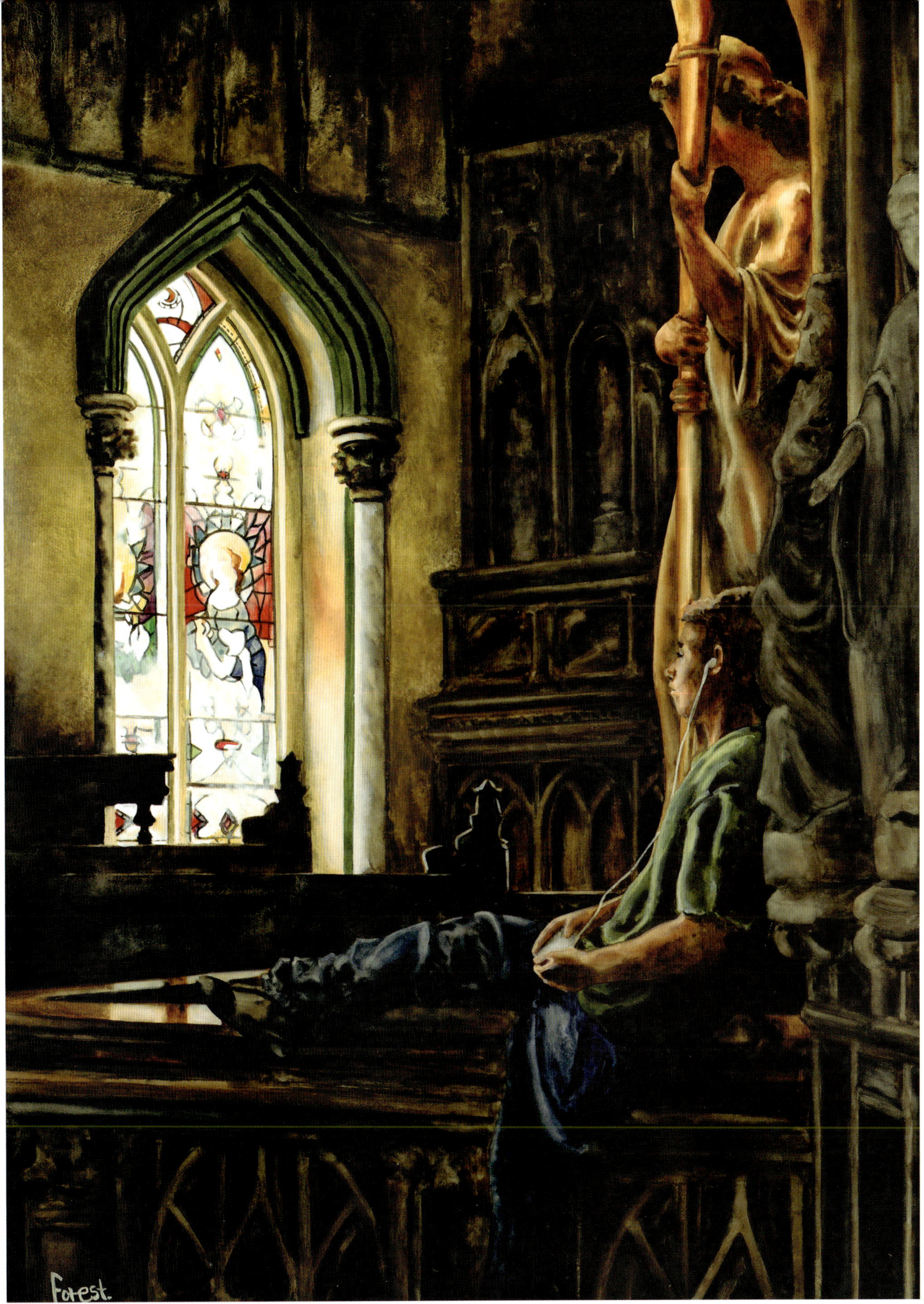

GENERATION | DIANE FOREST

Transparent and opaque watercolor on illustration board, 20" × 16" (51cm × 41cm)

Generation is a celebration of life, with respect for the past and hope for the future. Symbolic references abound. In the foreground, my son represents today's youth. The cool blues and greens characterize the present, hope and life. Leaving out light rays, surrounding the subject with warm colors and using contrasts helped to reinforce the dignity and timeless spirituality of this imaginary scene. With the use of a lot of water the surface became like a mirror. Once the pigments were introduced, I played with the elements until I obtained satisfying results.

Light colors create movement, dark colors suggest a pause. We all learn to read black letters on a white page—the "reading" of a painting is done in the same manner.

— Diane Forest

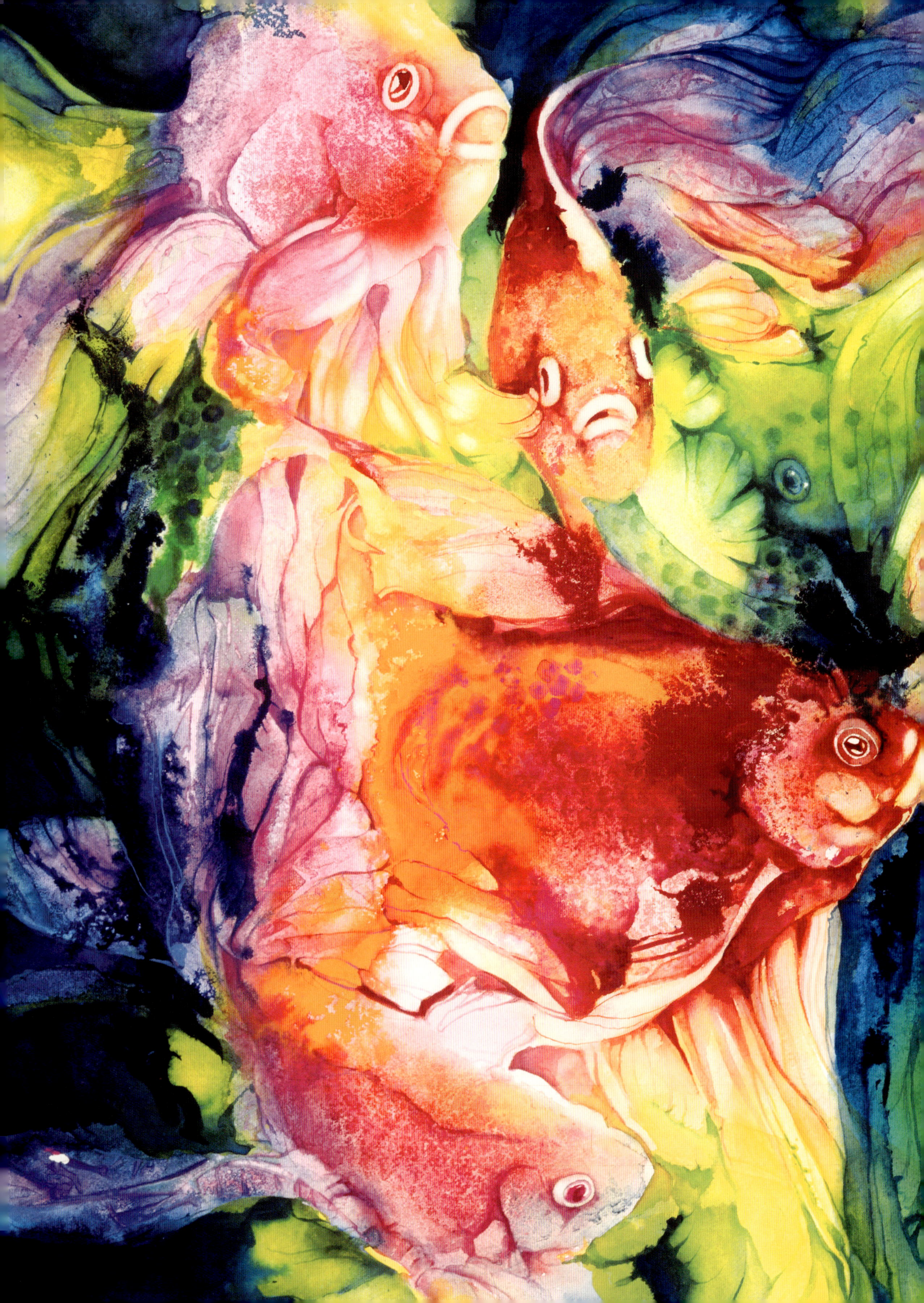

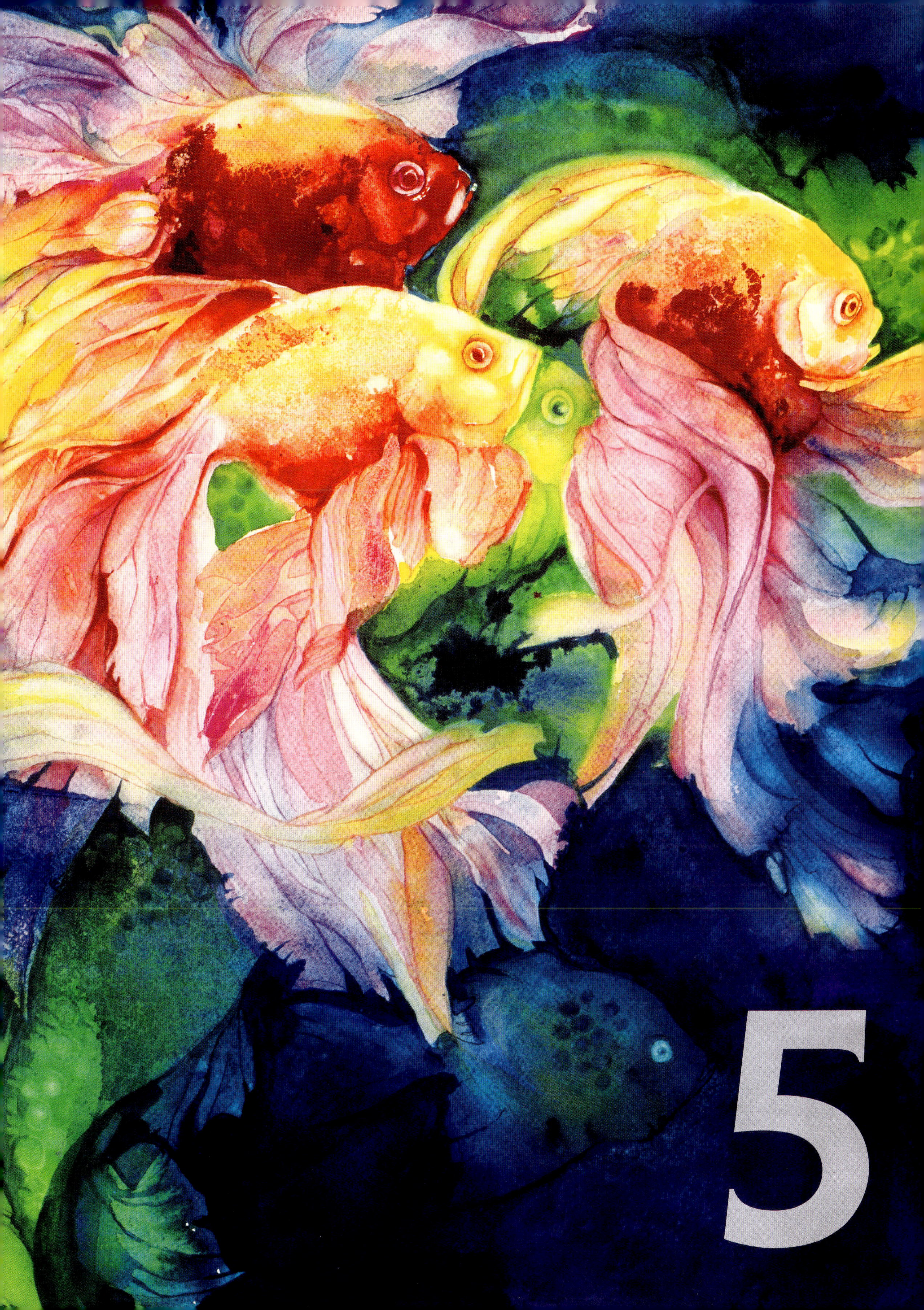
5

5 | THE ANIMAL WORLD

{ art on previous spread }

FISH TALES | ELIZABETH S. GROVES

Transparent watercolor on paper, 22" × 30" (56cm × 76cm)

Sometimes it is wonderfully freeing to adopt a loose, splashy approach. This painting is one of a series done strictly from imagination. I wet the paper and flung on beautiful, vibrant colors with gusto and without thought as to the results. After randomly applying texturing devices such as tissue paper, salt and Plexiglas, I let everything dry. Then I studied the result and determined that the flowing forms of blended colors could resemble fish, so I intentionally formed fish shapes to finish the painting.

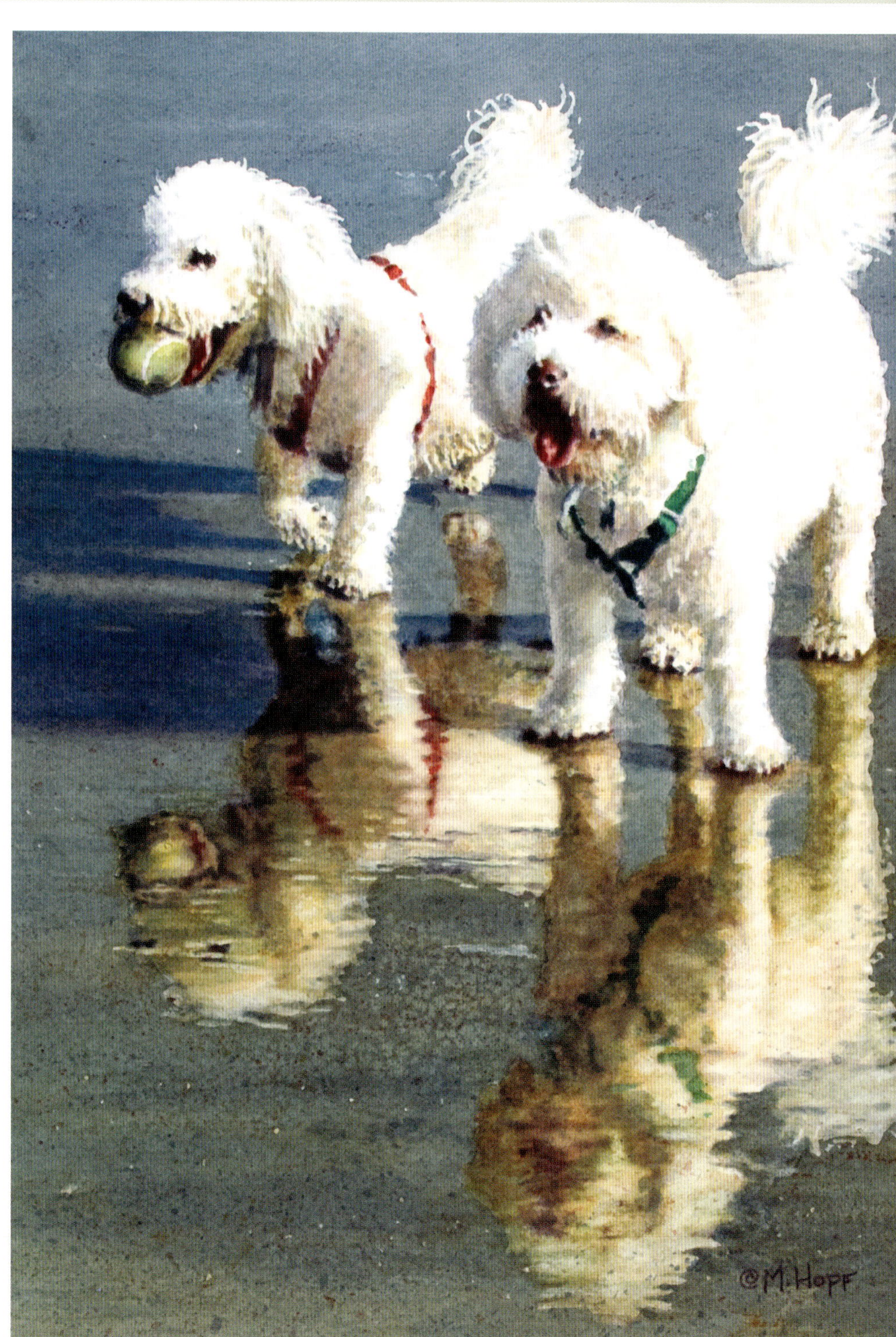

BEACH BUDDIES
MARY HOPF

Transparent watercolor on paper
16" × 12" (41cm × 30cm)

Walking my favorite beach with a friend and his dogs, I realized that with a little luck I might be able to show reflections and shadows in one picture. Just then Pepper found a tennis ball, ran around the back of his pal, and I had my shot! In the studio I adjusted a bit for composition, then masked the dogs and their reflections in order to play freely with the wet sand. I then glazed pure unmixed colors on the dogs in a layering process until I'd captured the nuance and my characters came to life.

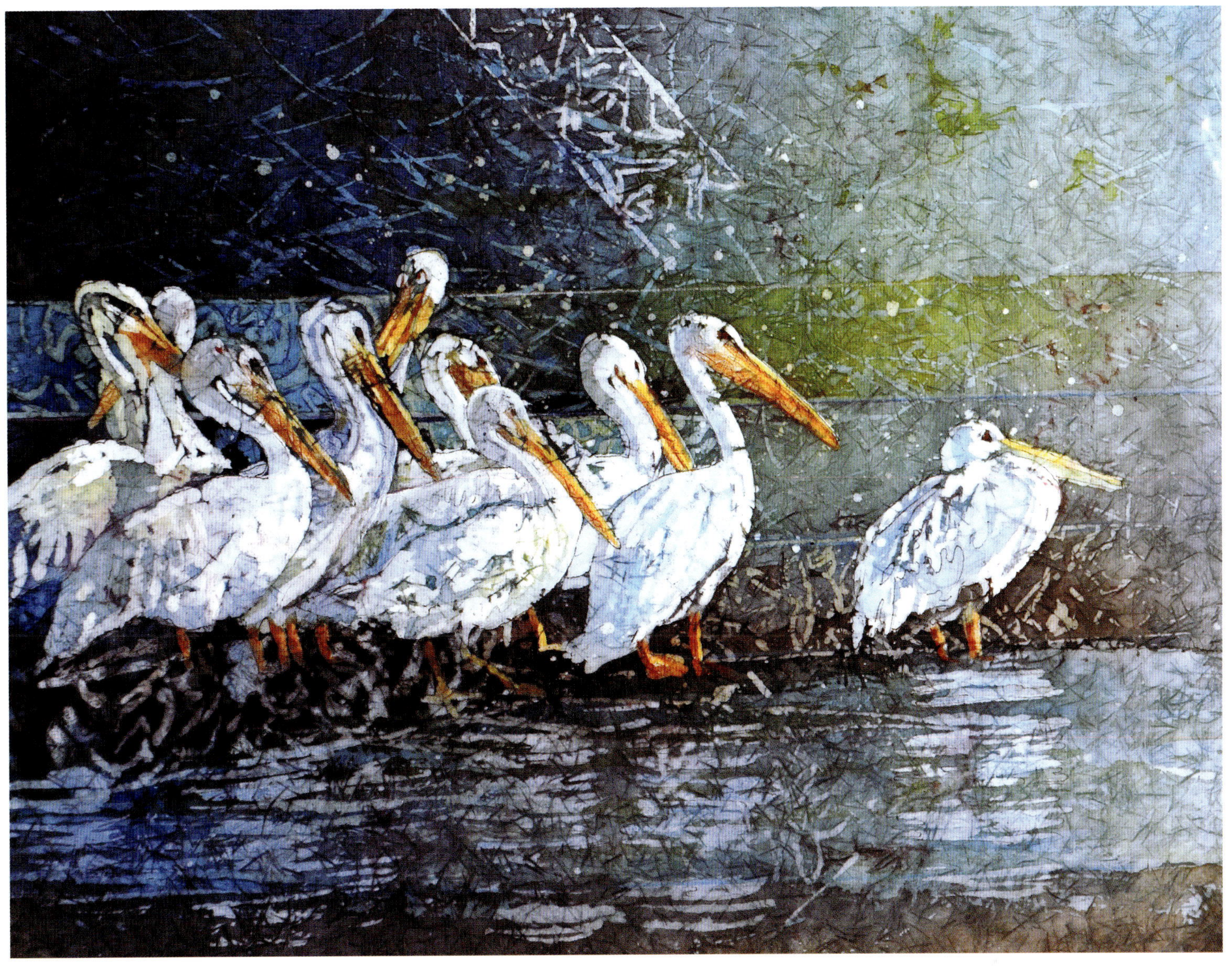

THE GATHERING | KATHIE GEORGE
Watercolor batik on rice paper, 20" × 26" (51cm × 66cm)

I began watercolor batik on rice paper over twenty years ago. Using the wax as a resist on beautifully textured rice paper, I first wax everything I want to remain white. Then I begin to layer color, light values first, saving a bit of each wash with wax. I work progressively darker, sometimes using unusual color to spice things up a bit. Eventually, the entire piece is covered with wax. At that point, I crumple it and wash over a final time, working the color into the cracked wax. Then it's ironed between newspapers to remove wax and voilà! It's like Christmas! What could be more fun?

Some of my worst painting starts have turned out to be my best, because once I think I've ruined the piece, I loosen up and that's when the real creativity begins.

Kathie George

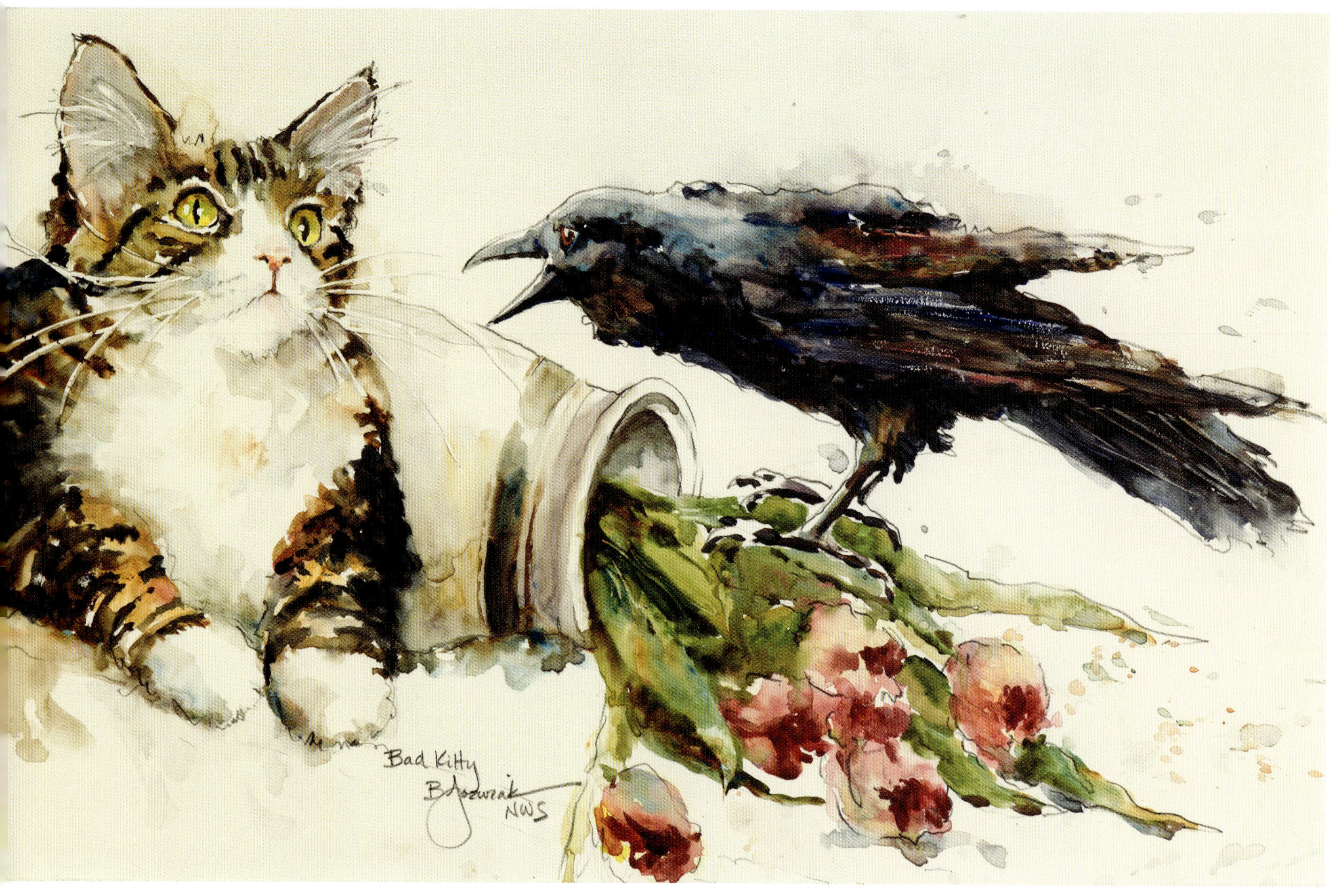

BAD KITTY | BEV JOZWIAK

Transparent watercolor with 9B pencil accents on 140-lb. (300gsm) hot-pressed Fabriano Artistico, 13½" × 21" (34cm × 53cm)

To be able to fulfill your artistic vision, you must first put in the hard work of learning to paint. Tenacity wins out over talent every time.

Bev Jozwiak

In my *Crow* series I use a combination of photographs and imagination. I study crows and their habits, but feel free to put them in all sorts of unusual situations. I paint on hot press paper because the slickness of hot press causes paint to sit on the surface of the paper, which allows me to create deep colorful blacks, and with lots of water let the paint run, splash and puddle. Crows are by nature curious, brash and bossy, and in my artistic vision I place them in situations that may not be entirely realistic, yet reflect their personality.

PROUD PETER | RUTH ARTHUR

Transparent watercolor on 140-lb. (300gsm) cold-pressed watercolor paper, 16" × 13" (41cm × 33cm)

When I paint or draw something I like, then it belongs to me forever!

Ruth Arthur

My paintings have become my favorite souvenirs; I try to preserve special moments that evoke the emotions and insights of my travels. As I have not had the luxury of painting on-site, I rely on my photographs for reference. *Proud Peter* is a wonderful reminder of our trip to Israel and that very first day looking across the Kidron valley toward the walled city of Jerusalem. The camel's haughty expression and colorful trappings caught the essence of the excitement, the wonderful air and even the smells of that beautiful morning and place. I used very basic watercolor techniques and had so much fun reproducing the hair texture and the colorful tassels.

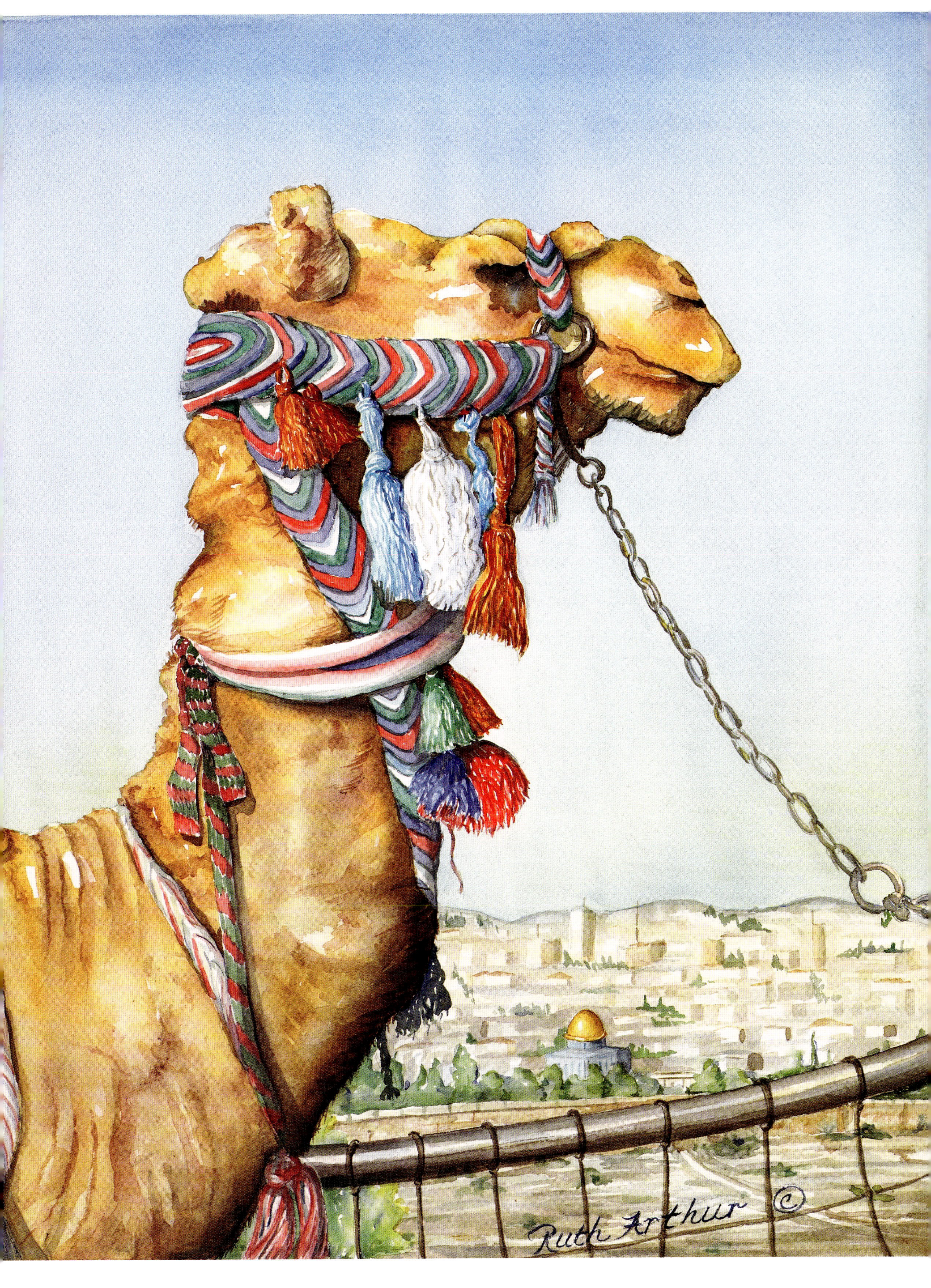
Ruth Arthur ©

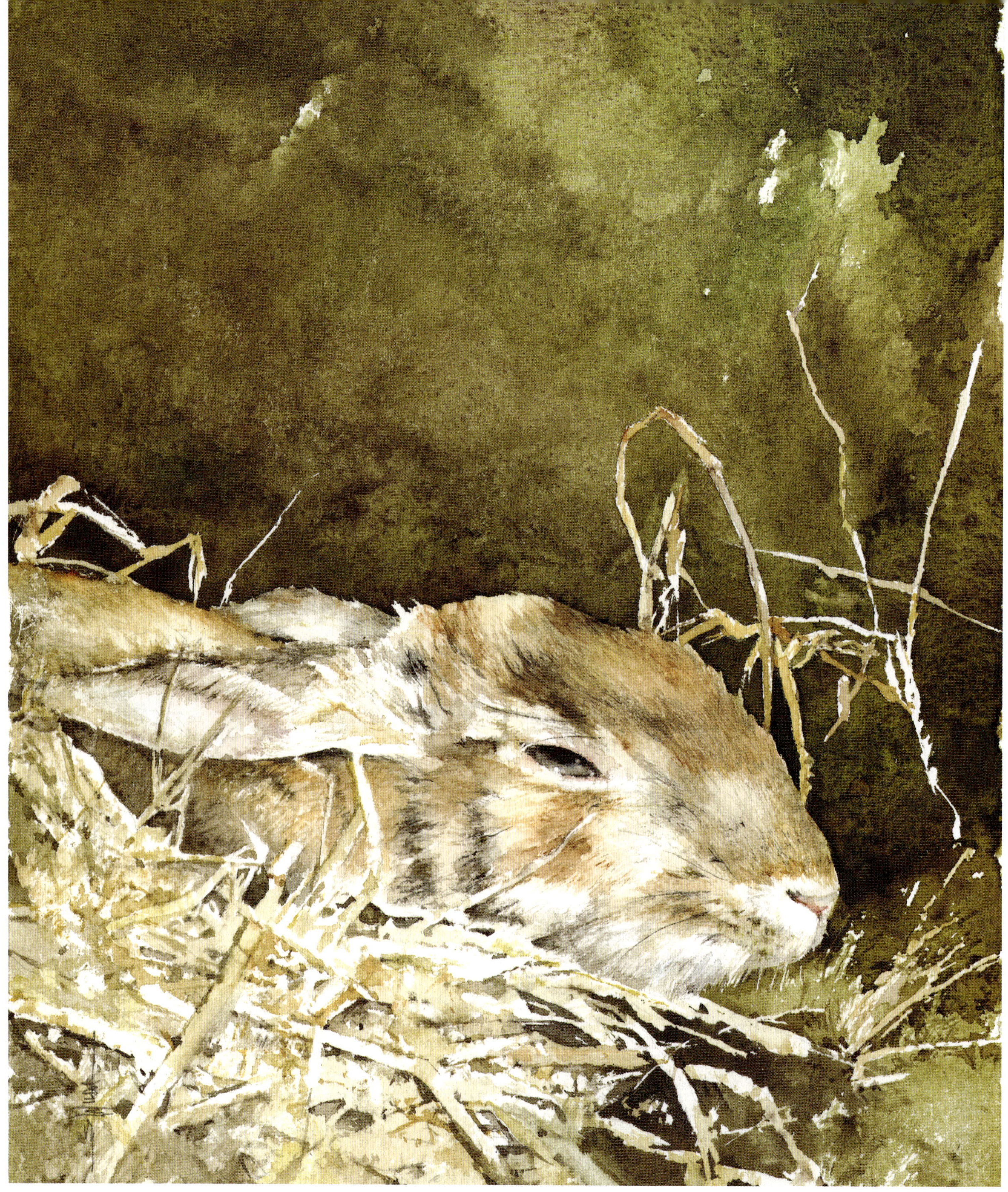

SANCTUARY | STEVE WILDA
Transparent watercolor on 300-lb. (640gsm) Arches, 10" × 8½" (25cm × 22cm)

The fleeting disposition of wildlife typically necessitates painting from photographs. Our eastern cottontail rabbit, with its numerous almond-shaped features, was caught during a gentle moment. Most often, my artwork focuses on weathered objects in disrepair, but occasionally the opposite spectrum of tranquil beauty will entice me. Masking fluid was used on the loosely painted grass, leaving the most definition in rendering for the main subject. Attention is centered on the animal's eye of wisdom, always aware of its surroundings.

An intense passion for your subject must be apparent before the first brushstroke or pencil line is drawn.

Steve Wilda

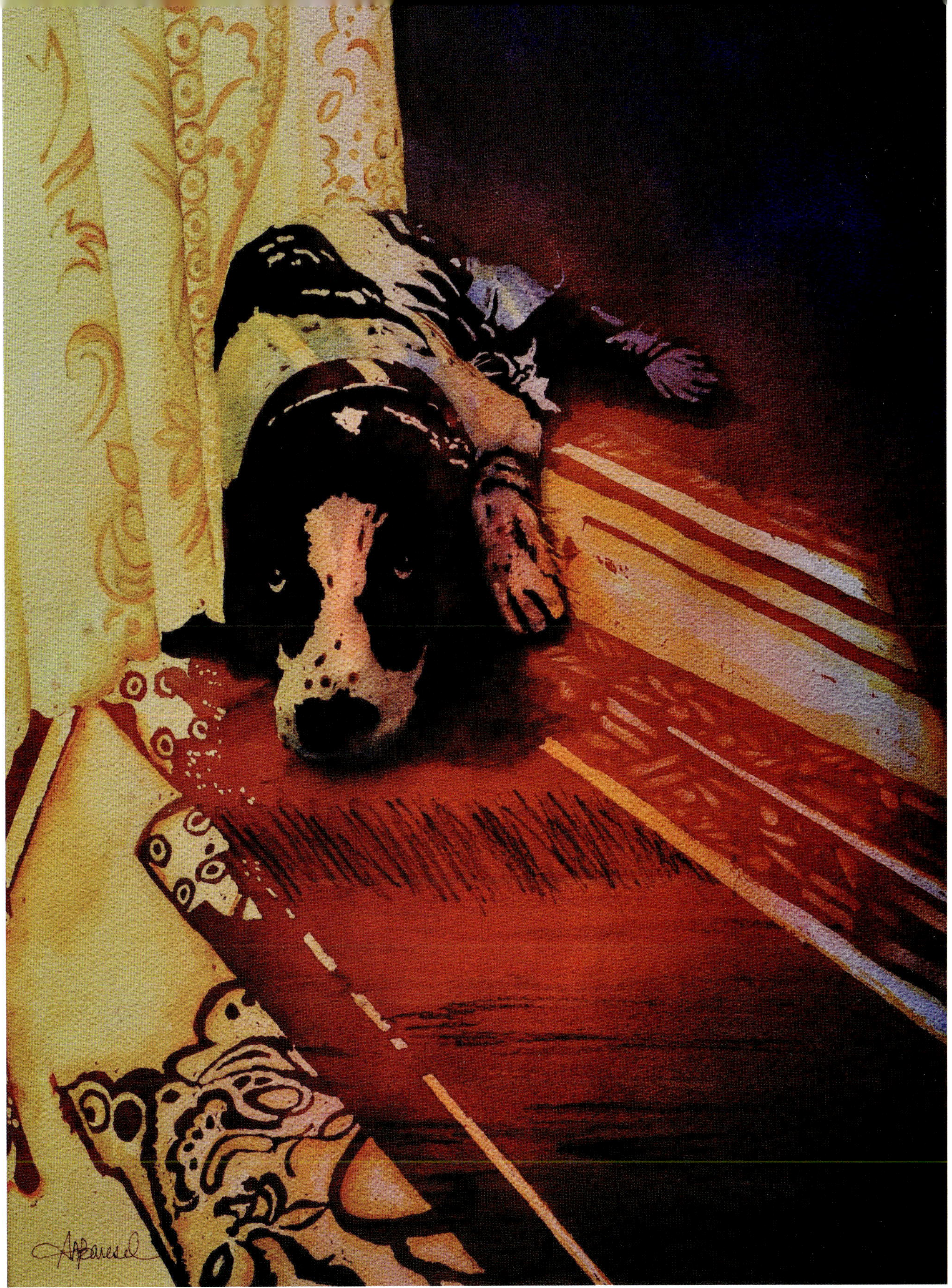

SERENDIPITY
SUSAN BARESEL
Transparent watercolor on 300-lb. (640gsm) Arches
24" × 18" (61cm × 46cm)

The oblique morning sunlight became my subject along with my sulking spaniel, who clearly resented artwork usurping his morning hike. I would not have seen this lucky juxtaposition if not for recent participation in a photography course—a fantastic exercise in composing light and value from which my watercolor work has profited enormously. I started the painting with an initial wash of Quinacridone Gold and a sketch using the photo I had snapped. I masked the sunlit areas and poured successive washes of Quinacridone Red and Cobalt Blue into the shadowed areas. Dense glazes built up the darkest areas. Final details included lifting soft highlights with a damp cloth, and wood details done with a rigger. Look down occasionally ... beautiful and unexpected things may be at your feet!

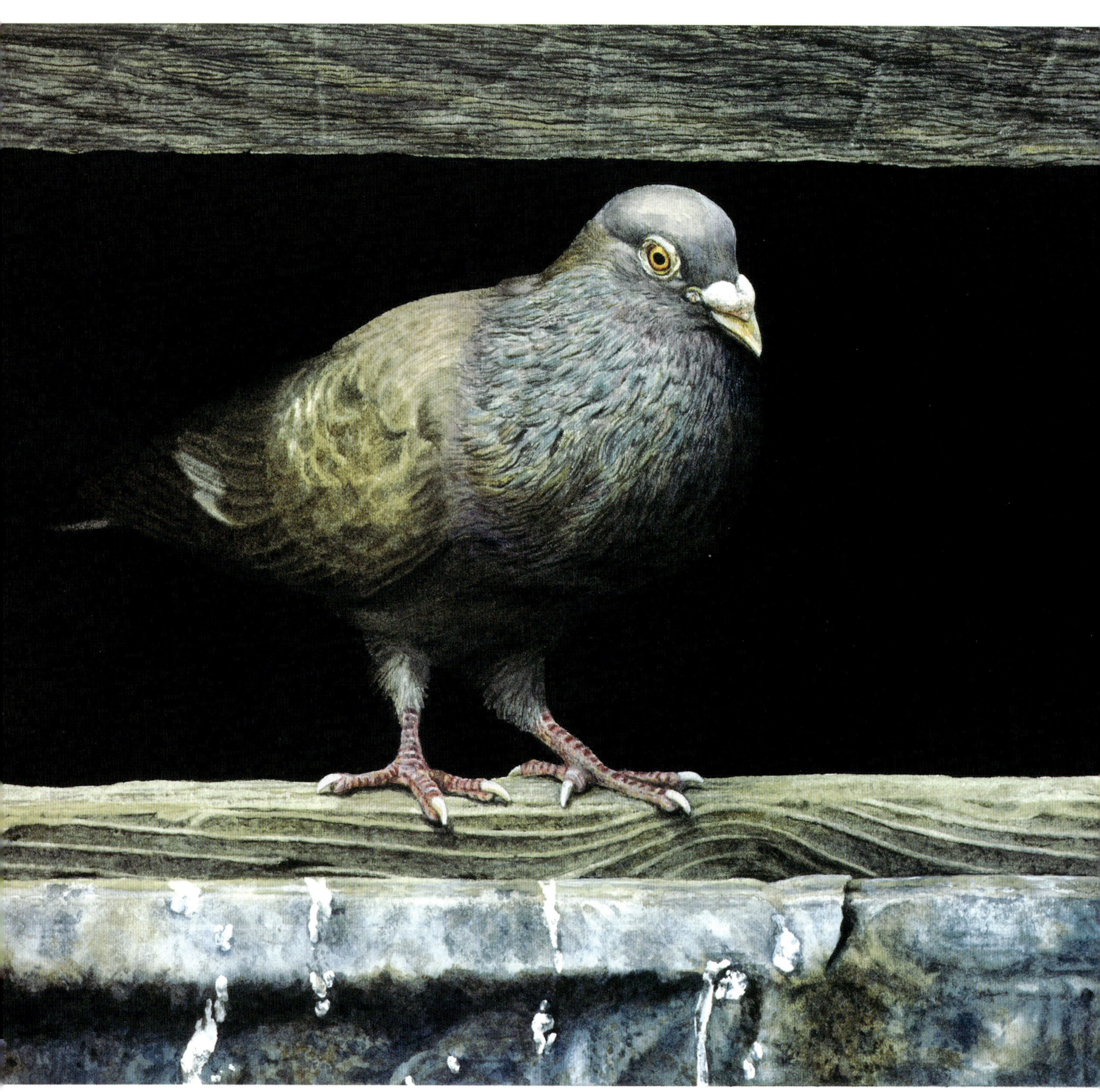

NORA'S COOP | SANDRA BLAIR

Transparent watercolor on 100 percent rag bristol board, 7" × 11" (18cm × 28cm)

Working from my own photographs, I use multiple glazes of transparent watercolor to build up rich color and depth of value, with an occasional touch of acrylic gesso for whiskers and fur accents. My up-close and personal format increases drama and showcases the unique beauty and power of each animal. It creates a sense of intimacy that few people will ever experience in the wild. My artistic vision is to entice people to slow down and observe with fresh eyes the world and the creatures that live among us. Until we truly see, we cannot fully understand the devastation that is occurring through loss of habitat and vanishing species.

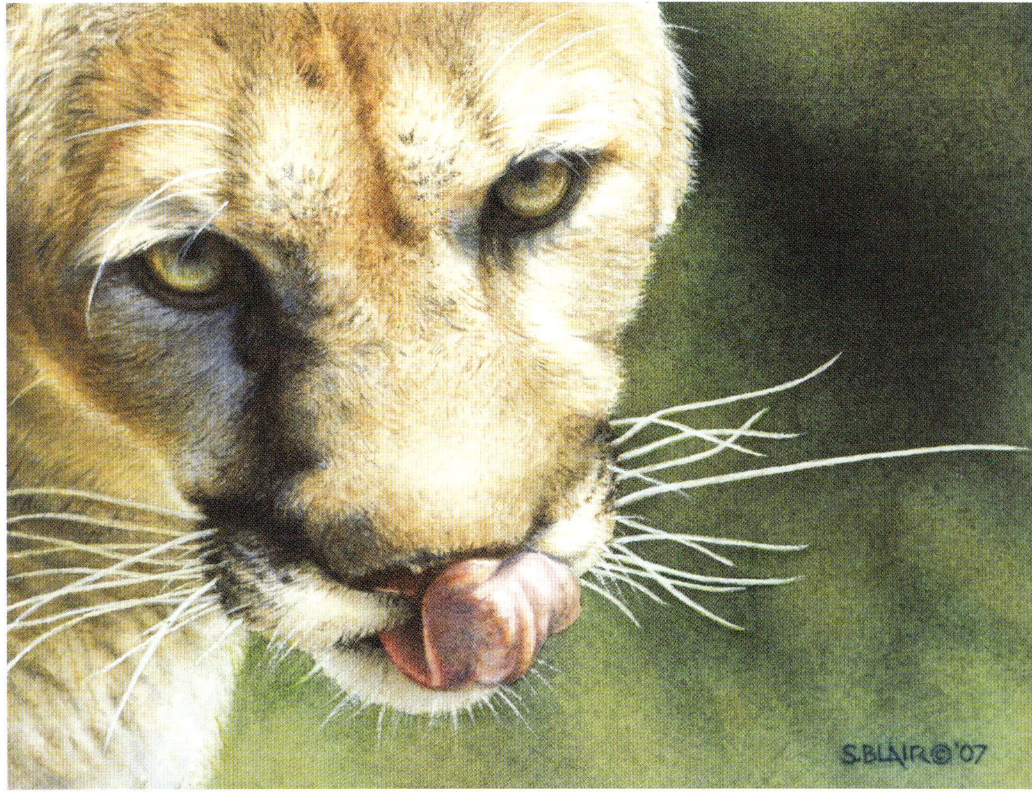

YUMMM | SANDRA BLAIR

Transparent watercolor with acrylic accents on 140-lb. (300gsm) cold-pressed Arches 4¼" × 6" (11cm × 15cm)

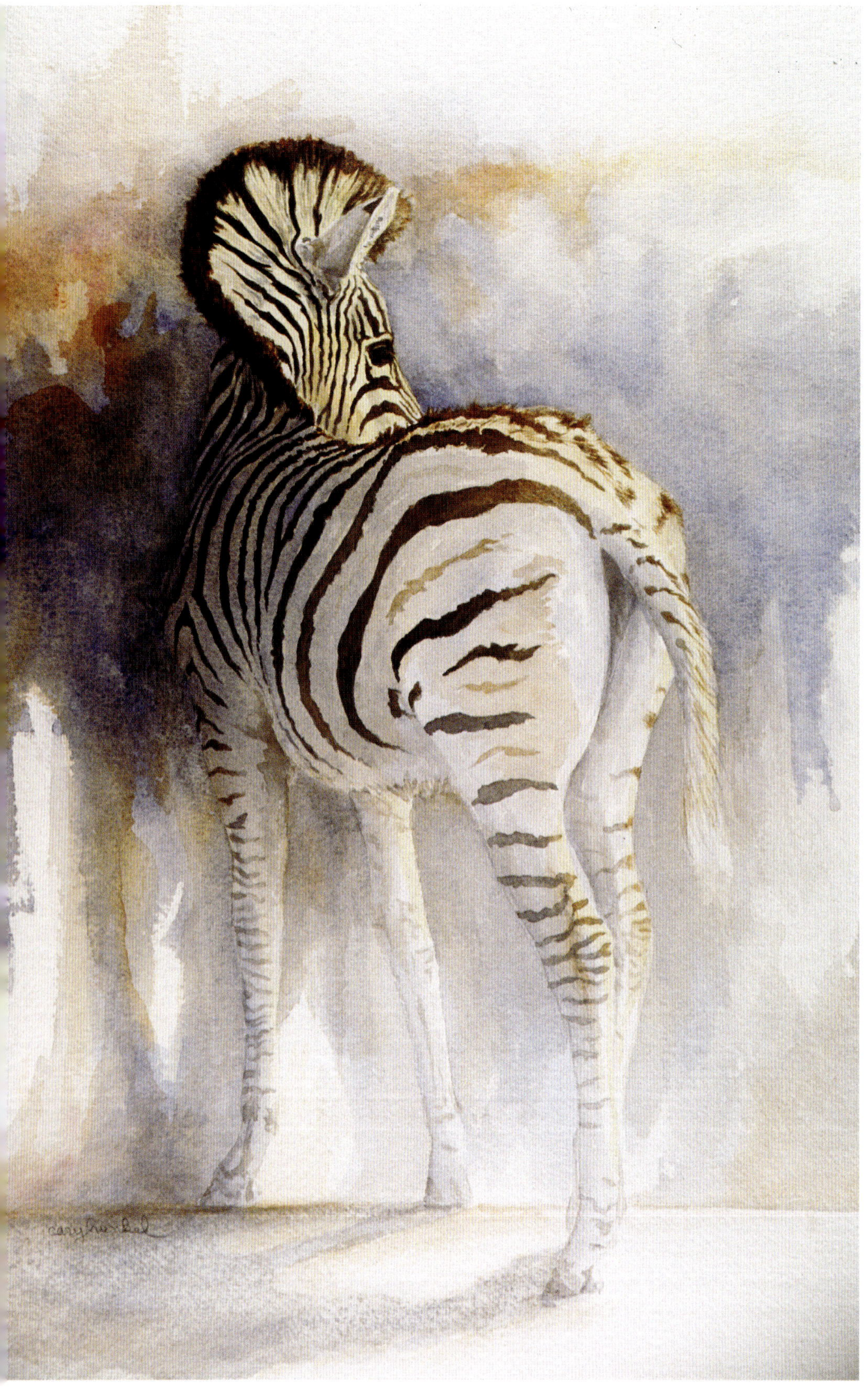

CONNECTION | CARY HUNKEL
Transparent watercolor on
300-lb. (640gsm) cold-pressed Arches
22" × 16" (56cm × 41cm)

The boldly patterned zebra is integrated into its environment through the use of lighting and value contrasts in both the figure and the ground. One of my goals is accurate representation, but I also want my work to appeal to viewers and to spark in them greater appreciation of my subjects. I do thumbnail sketches, paying special attention to the figure/ground relationship. I gradually develop my piece as a whole while adding deeper values and details, searching for its essence.

To capture a moment of time, to ignite the spark of life, to help connect us to our natural heritage—can this be done with art? Let me try!

Cary Hunkel

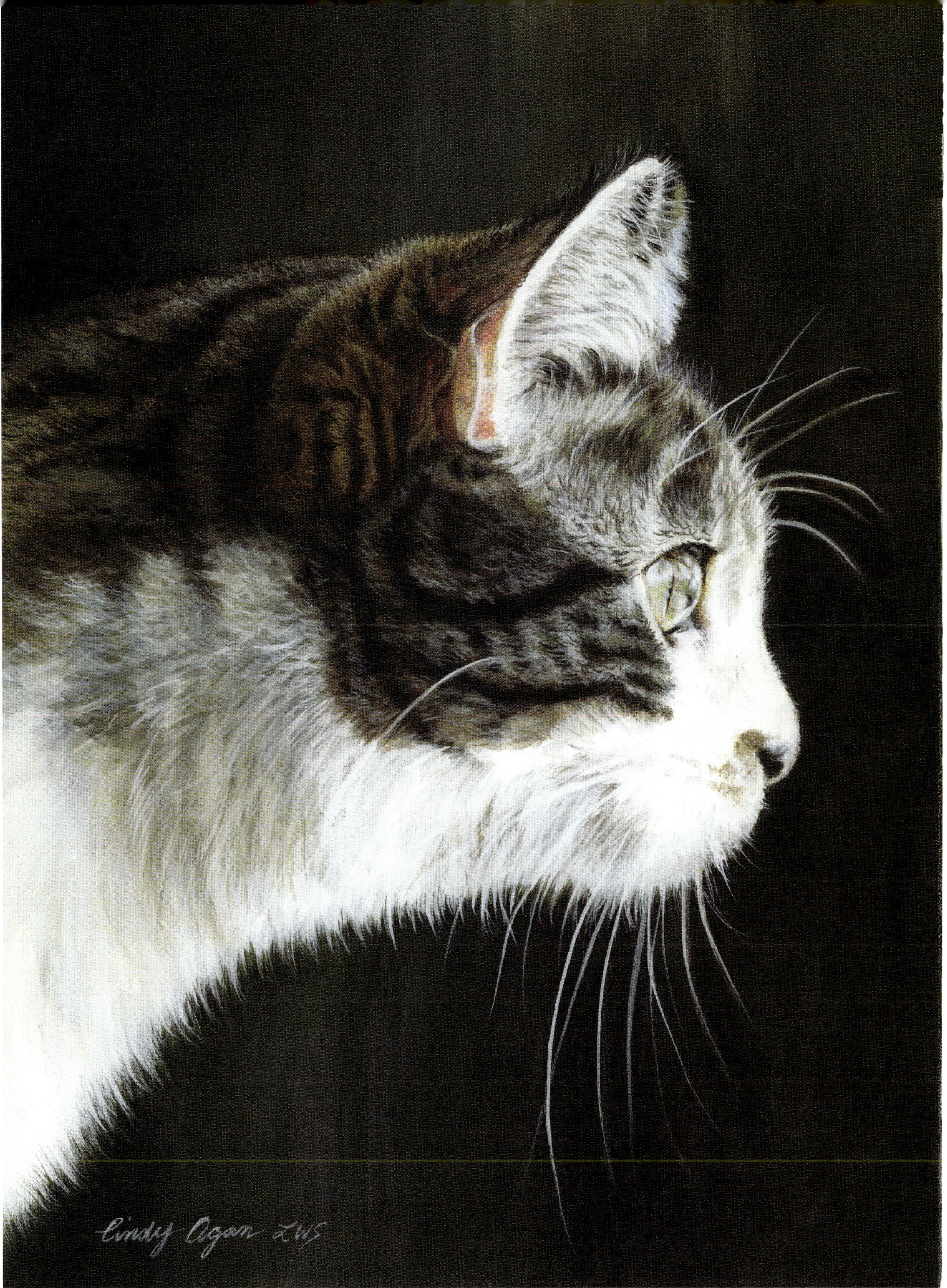

CAT IN PROFILE
CINDY AGAN
Watercolor with fluid acrylic on watercolor canvas
14¼" × 10½" (36cm × 27cm)

As I studied the composition and striking contrasts of my photo, I began to imagine this painting on watercolor canvas, a surface new to me and one I had longed to try. I began by glazing the underpainting in watercolor and drybrushing the details as I followed the growth pattern in the fur. The eye appears moist with carefully placed highlights. Fluid acrylic was gradually added and handled like watercolor. It seems my artistic vision is constantly changing. One great image can spark a creative flurry as one idea leads to the next. Maddening—and wonderful!

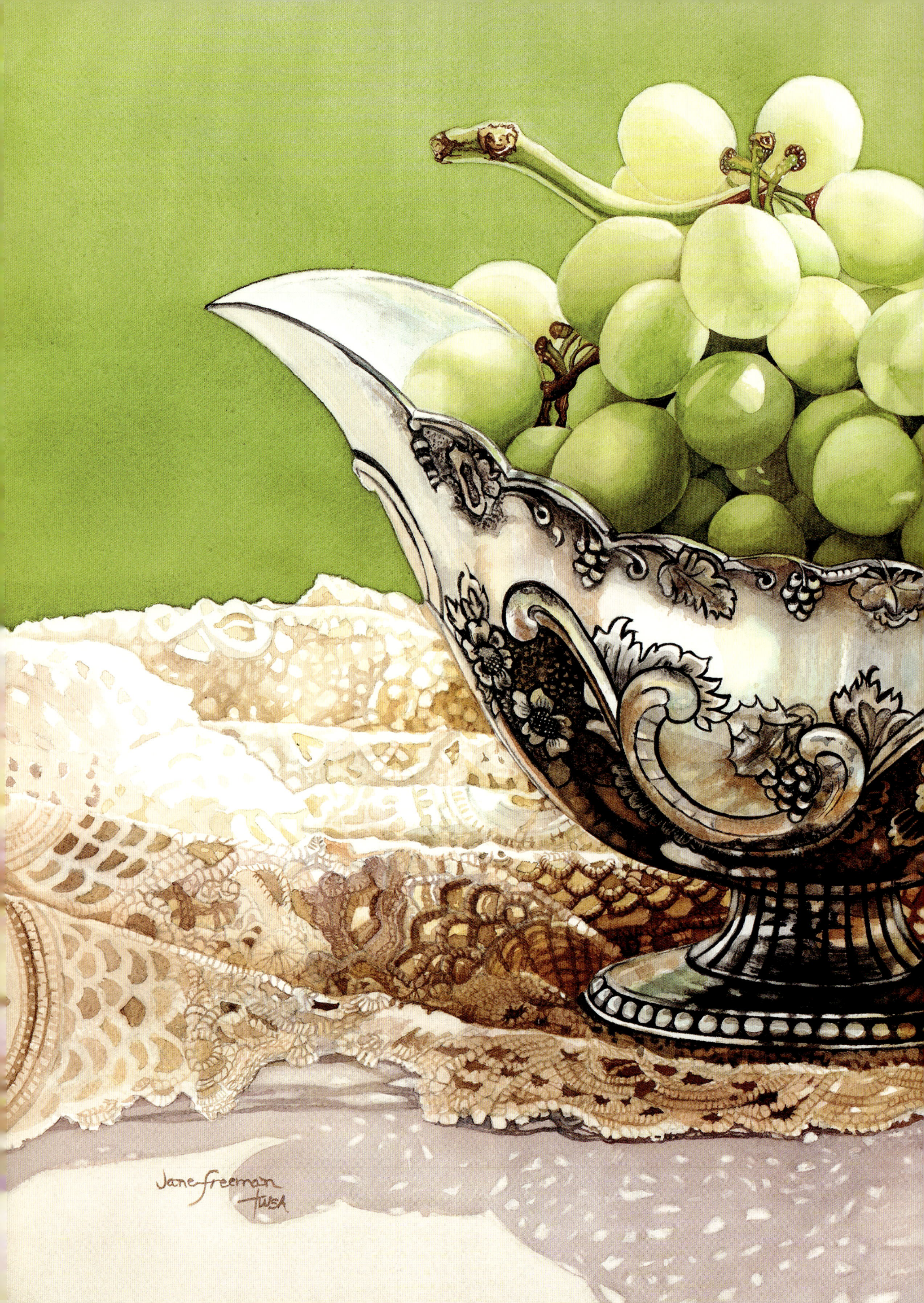
Jane Freeman
TWSA

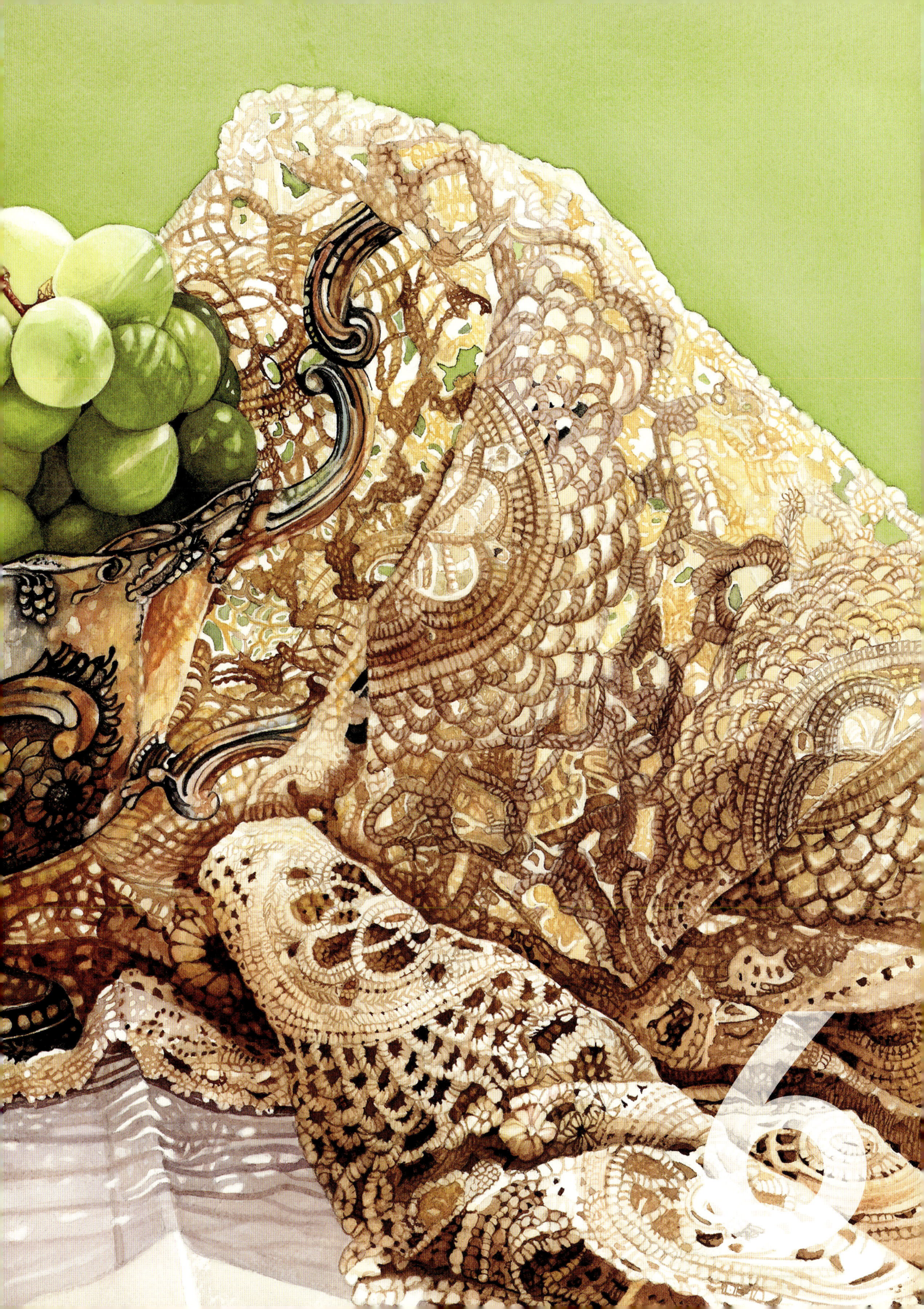
6

6 | STILL LIFE

If you paint the things you love, you are going to love what you paint.

— *Jane Freeman*

{ art on previous spread }

SAUCED GRAPES | JANE FREEMAN

Transparent watercolor on 300-lb. (640gsm) cold-pressed Arches
19" × 28" (48cm × 71cm)

This gravy boat and handmade tablecloth are heirlooms that I treasure. I am emotionally tied to them and that emotional connection begins my artistic vision in nearly every painting. I took many digital pictures as I worked with the folds in the cloth until they moved the eye into and around the composition. By using multiple glazes on the grapes and gravy boat, I was able to create a glow that sets them apart from the texture of the crocheted tablecloth.

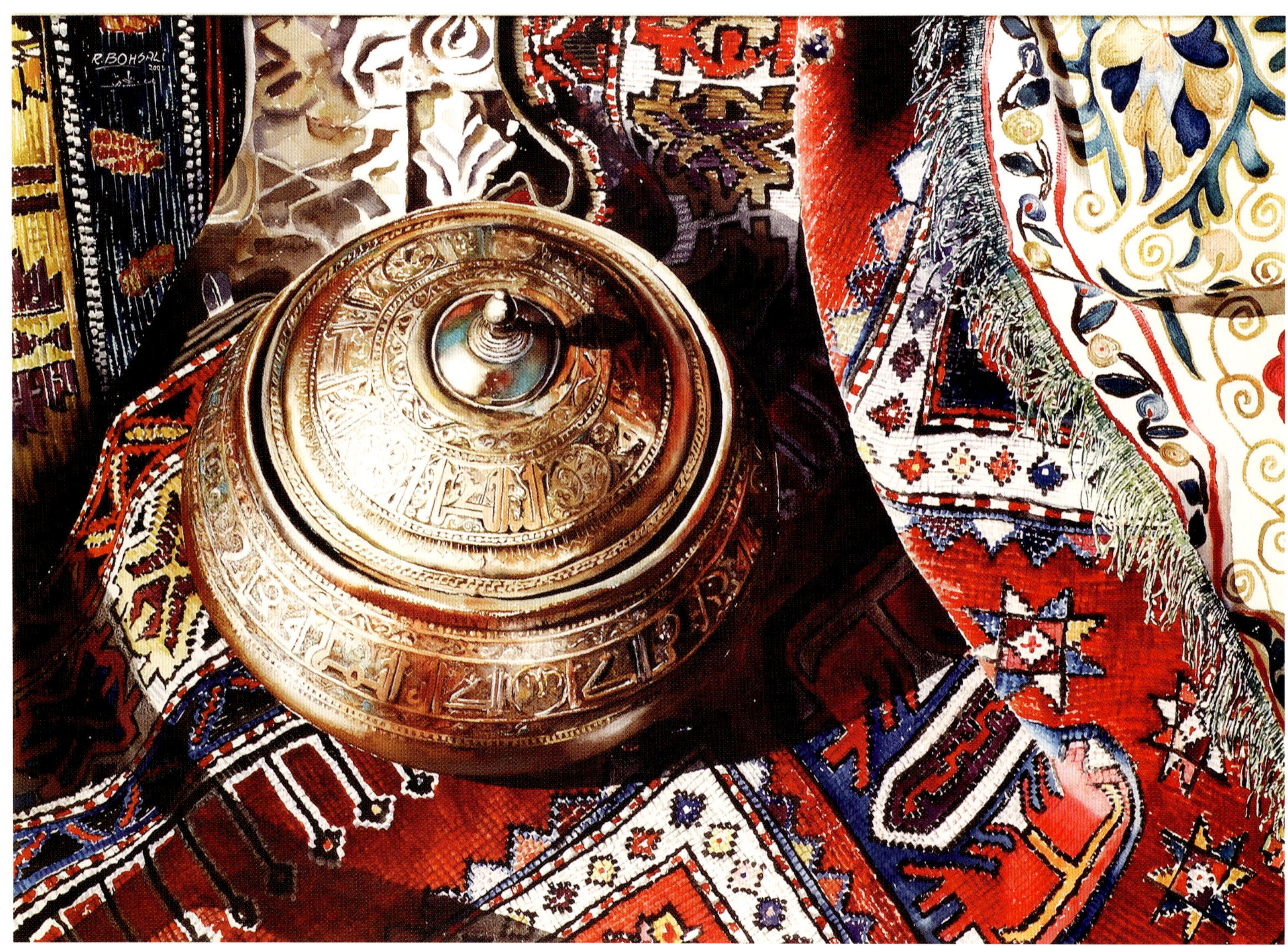

ORIENTAL CHARM | RACHED K. BOHSALI

Transparent watercolor on Arches Aquarelle (Perrigot) paper, 30" × 42" (76cm × 107cm)

I love contrasts, be it cold vs. warm, shiny vs. matt, soft vs. hard, light vs. dark, simple vs. complex.

— *Rached Bohsali*

While setting up the composition of this painting, I was listening to Rimsky-Korsakov's *Sheherazade*. This pure coincidence made me unconsciously create a simple still life from two Caucasian rugs, a Persian Suzani and an antique brass pot from Baghdad. A friend said that he sensed in it the spicy fragrances of the warm and exotic old souks of the East—*Oriental Charm*?

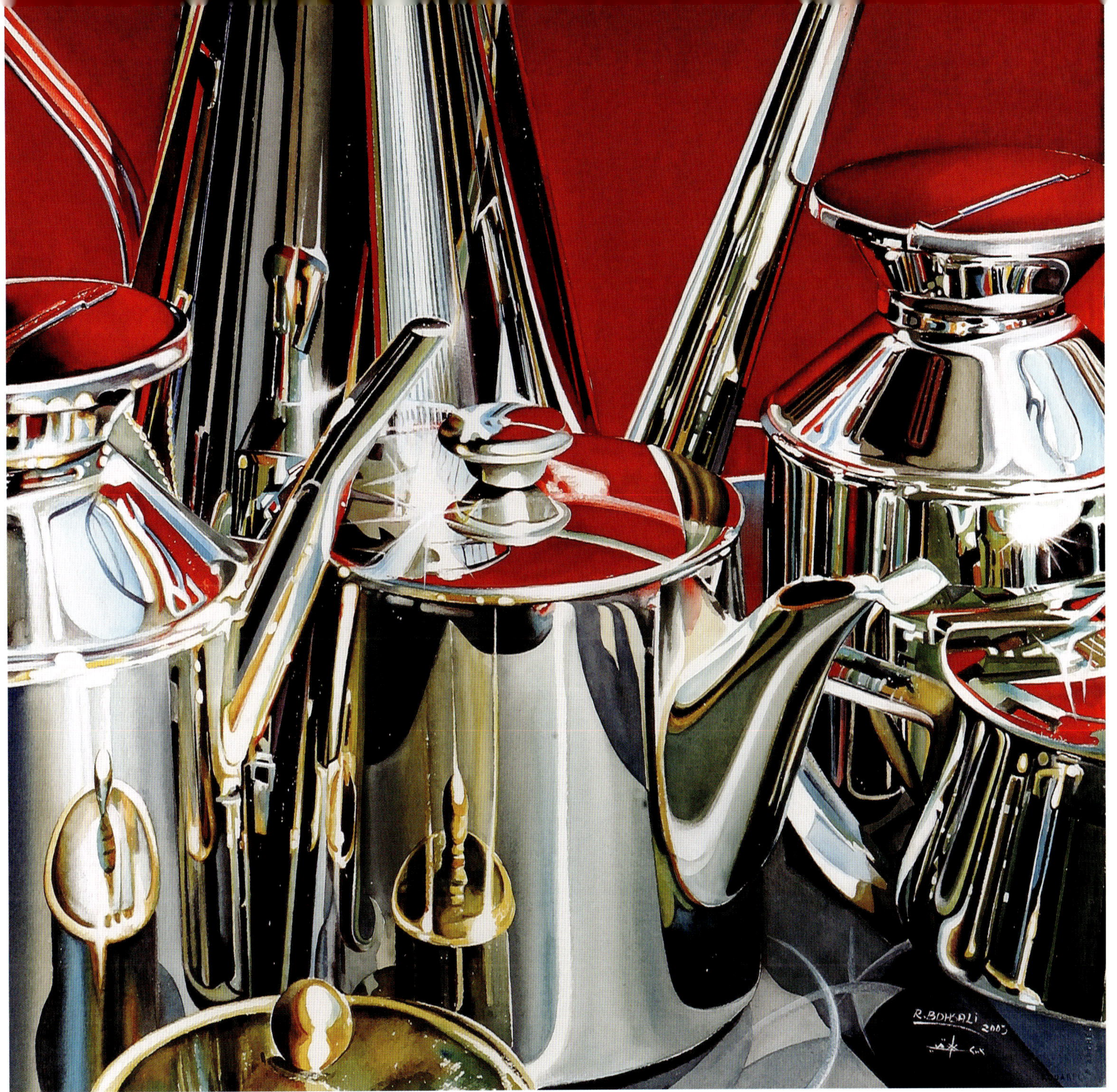

REFLECTIONS OF THE REFLECTED REFLECTIONS | RACHED K. BOHSALI
Transparent watercolor on Arches Aquarelle (Perrigot) paper, 30" × 30" (76cm × 76cm)

The shapes of the conical metallic surfaces are defined by their own stylized reflections ricocheting back and forth: reflections of reflections. This distorts and changes the reality as it also creates interesting dynamic abstraction. One could see a metaphor for the way truth is distorted through the rumor mill.

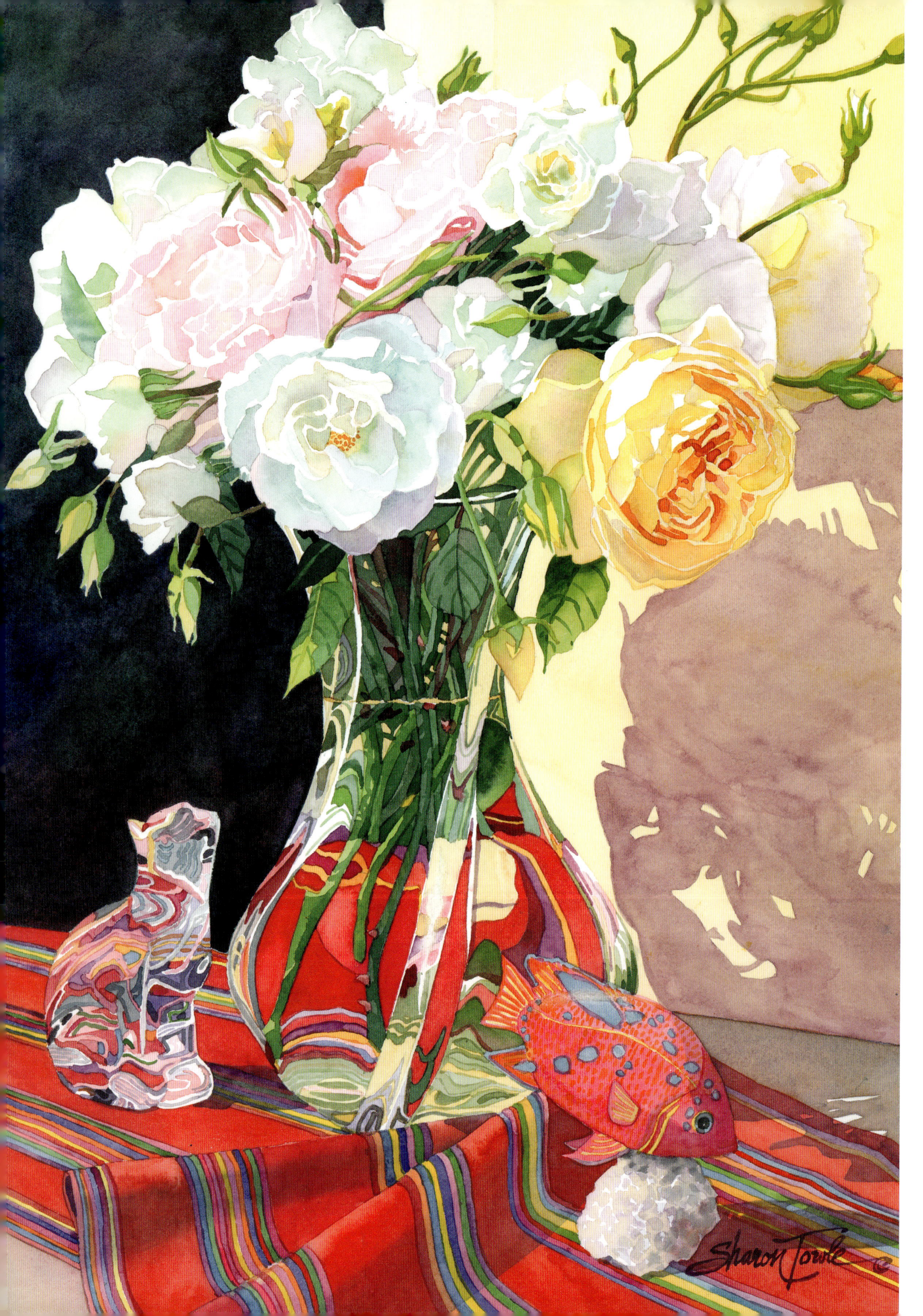
Sharon Towle ©

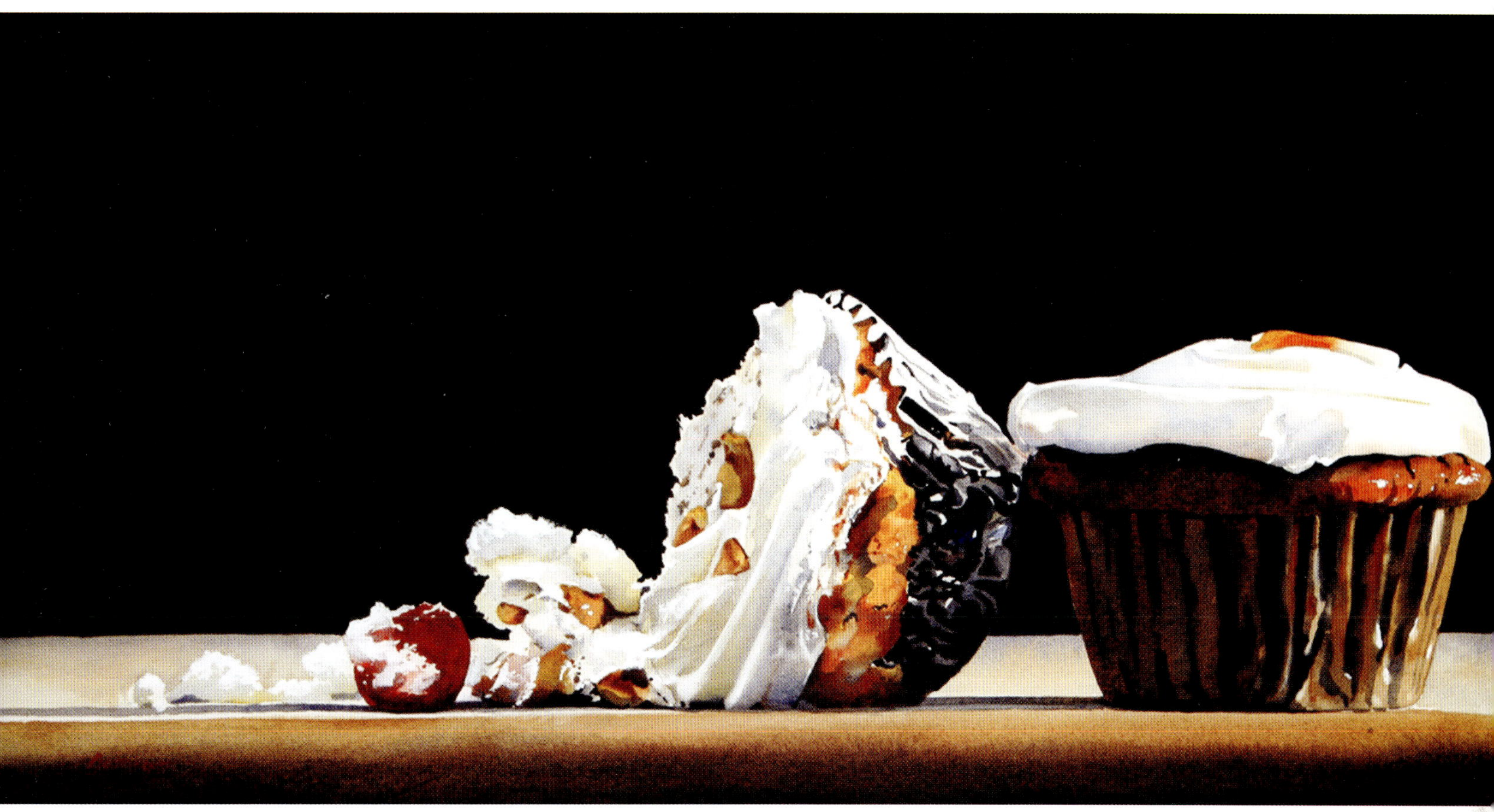

CUPCAKE FALLS | RIC DENTINGER

Watercolor with gouache on 300-lb. (640gsm) cold-pressed Arches, 20" × 34" (51cm × 86cm)

Artistic vision is to take an ordinary subject and present it in an extraordinary way.

Ric Dentinger

While traveling in New York I stopped at a bakery one day and marveled at the artistry of the pastries—in particular the cupcakes. While ordering cupcakes to go, I watched the baker drop a cupcake, as the cherry rolled off the top almost in slow motion. I thought: that would make a great painting. My objective in painting the cupcakes in my studio was to give the feeling of movement with the cherry rolling across the table. I painted an extremely dark background so the white of the frosting would really pop. On the frosting I used gouache for the creamy effect.

CURIOUS CAT | SHARON TOWLE

Transparent watercolor on 140-lb. (300gsm) cold-pressed Arches, 22" × 15" (56cm × 38cm)

I set up most of my still lifes on a patio table when it is sunny. My inspiration was the roses that had just bloomed in my garden. I photographed different combinations of objects, and it was clear that this was the one. My compositions have a fairly large, quiet resting place, a smaller area of medium busyness and a small area with lots of detail such as in the cat. As with this painting, my artistic vision in general is to create traditional paintings in a very contemporary manner, using bold, bright colors, a fairly flat picture plane and interesting shadows.

Use the lightest, brightest, most transparent paints you can buy. No dirt colors!

Sharon Towle

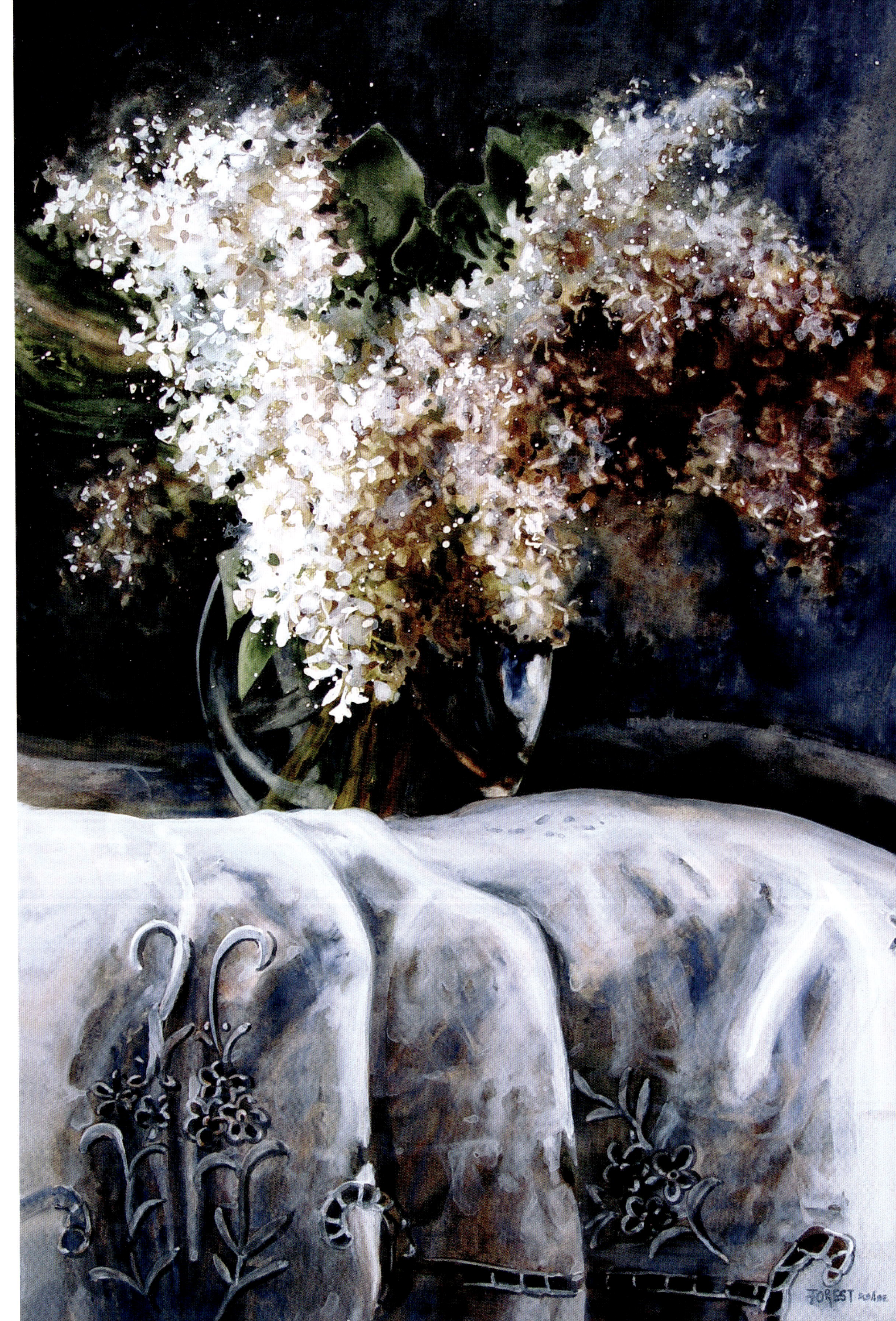
FOREST

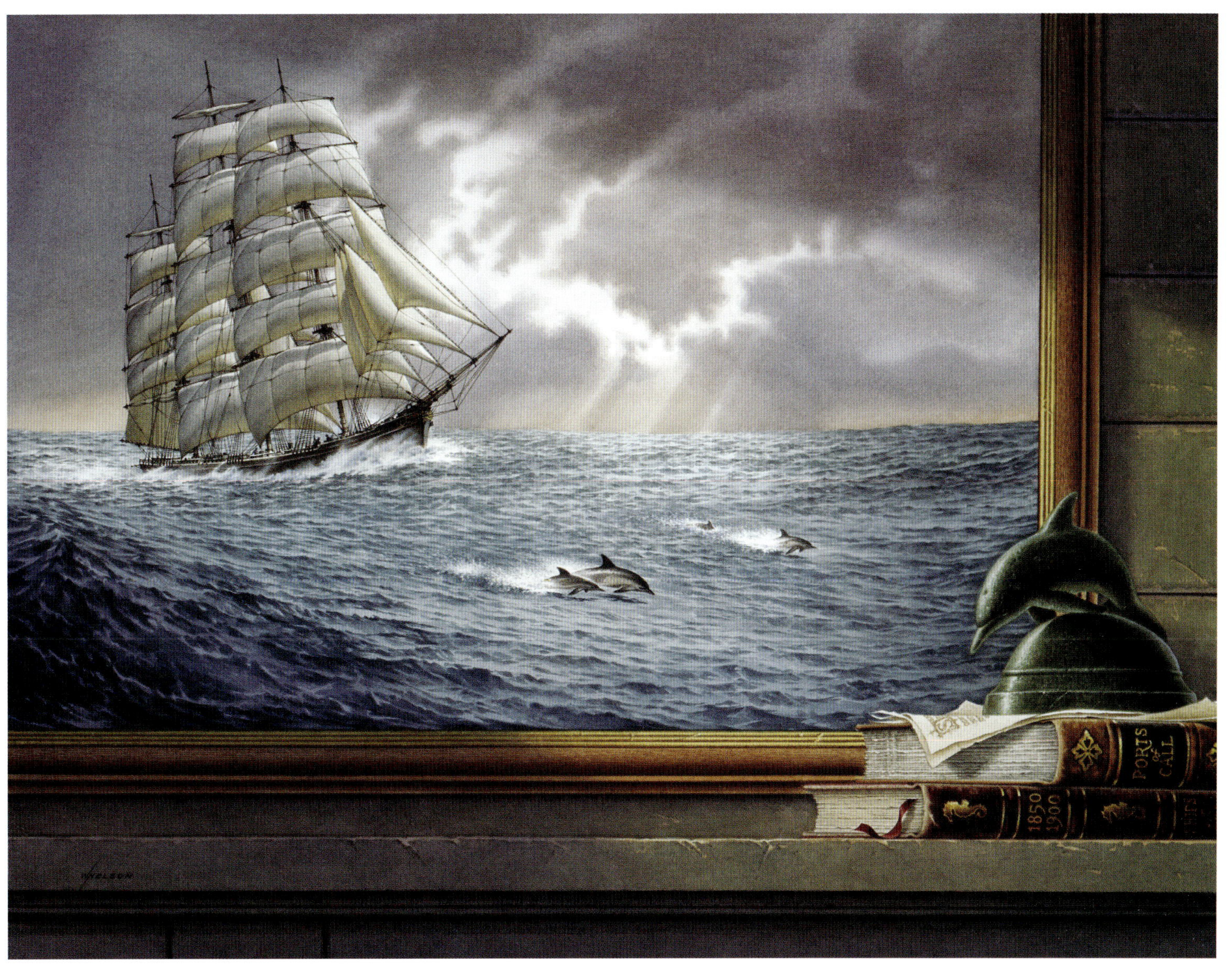

RACING THE WIND | WILL NELSON

Watercolor on 300-lb. (640gsm) cold-pressed Arches, 15" × 22" (38cm × 56cm)

This painting was primarily composed from on-site sketches of ships with rigging researched from detailed English model ship plans. The animals are drawn from various visual reference sources—both pictorial and video. The whites in the painting are solely from painting around the subjects using the white of the paper rather than risk disturbing the surface of the paper with masking methods. This format allows the painting of subject matter not always practical to sketch from life. Using the painting-in-a-painting composition also allows me to paint imaginary scenes and wildlife along with my first love in painting ... the still life.

EPHEMERAL WHITENESS | DIANE FOREST

Transparent and opaque watercolor on illustration board, 21" × 14" (53cm × 36cm)

I love to create an atmosphere in my paintings—even the illusion of fragrance. This still life symbolizes the arrival of spring when these ephemeral and fragile lilacs blossom and spread their perfume. The flowers are the main subject, allowing me to play with the pigments and manipulate the interactions between the heavy earthy and mineral inorganic pigments, and the lighter synthetic ones. In order to succeed with the introduction of white, without affecting the other colors, I used the floating color technique to produce the diaphanous result I wanted to achieve.

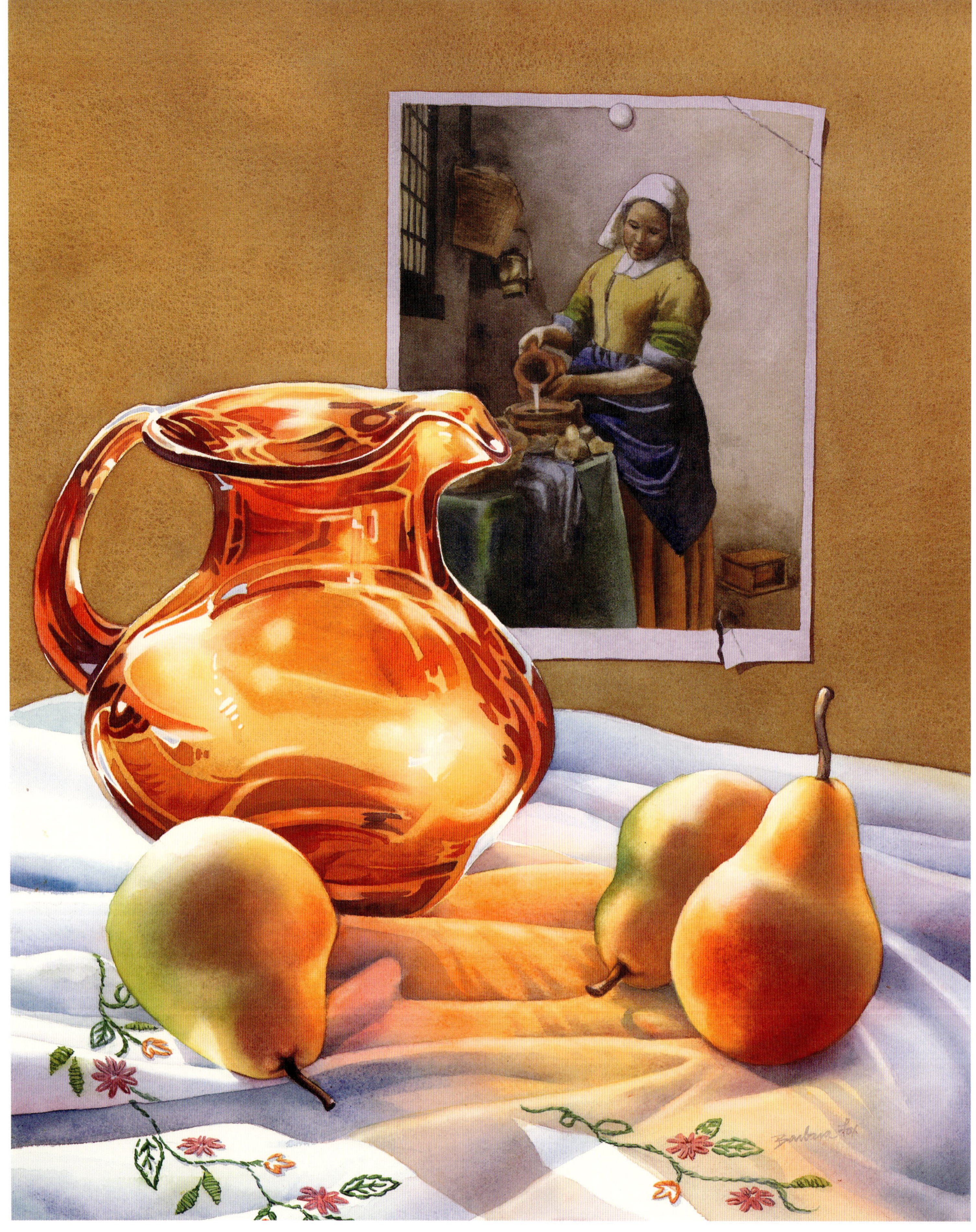

HARMONY | BARBARA FOX
Transparent watercolor on 300-lb. (640gsm) cold-pressed Arches, 18" × 15" (46cm × 38cm)

I consider the process of painting to be a prayer, a meditation and a journey.

— Barbara Fox

From the first inspiration to the finishing touches, I work from both photographs and life. I've begun integrating old photographs, patterns and other artists' work, within the still life, giving a bit of a trompe l'oeil effect. This adds another dimension and allows me to work on many different subjects in one painting. My artistic goal is to paint all of my subjects faithfully and beautifully, but present them in a new way, making the ordinary extraordinary.

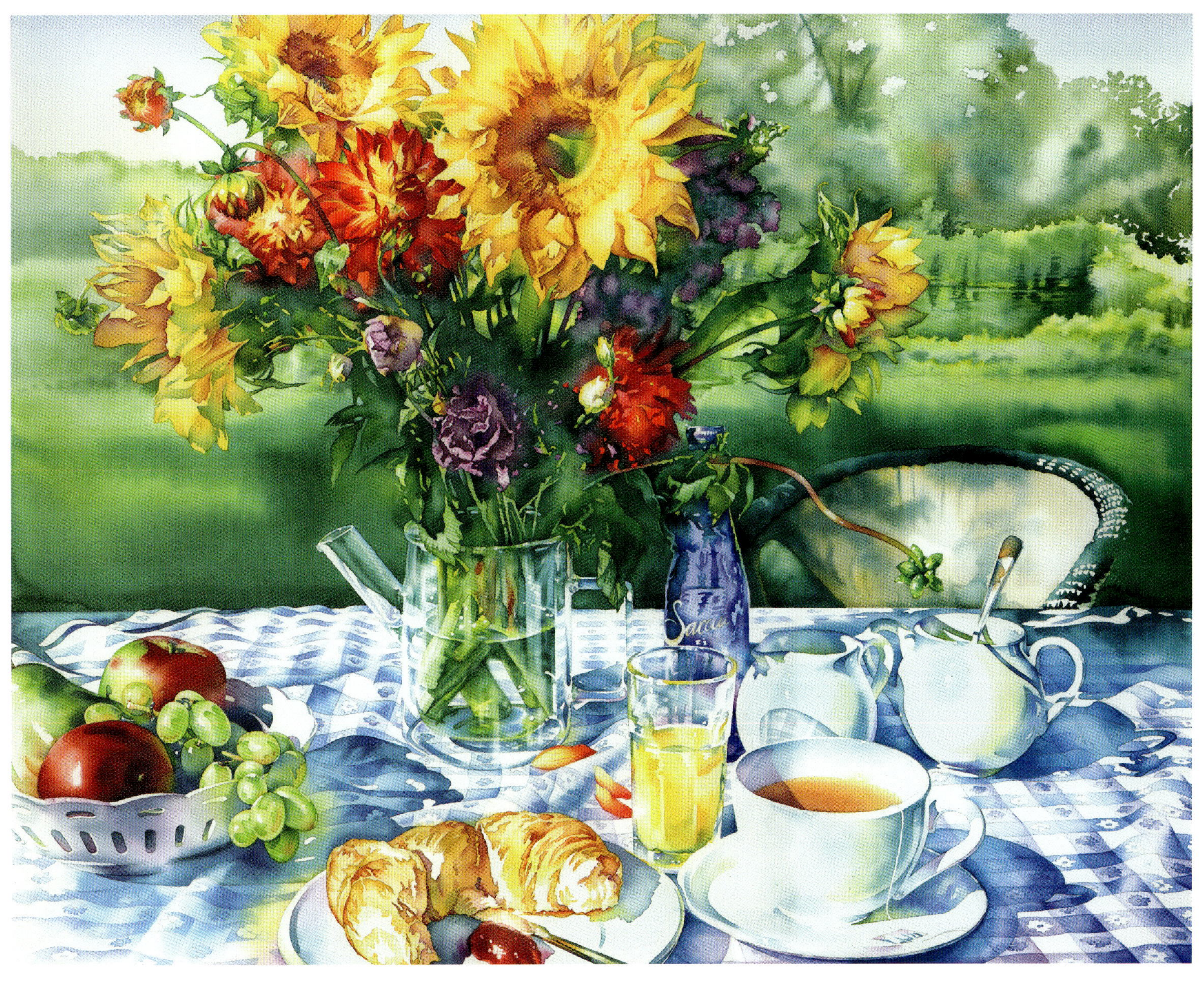

SARATOGA BRUNCH | CHERYL CHALMERS

Watercolor on cold-pressed Arches, 20" × 25" (51cm × 64cm)

On a brilliant summer day I visited the local farmers' market to pick a variety of flowers and fruit for inspiration. Near our backyard pond, I quickly set up my still life in direct sunlight. I spent a lot of time visualizing the composition, color and values. I am fascinated with sun on glass, so I placed a beautiful blue Saratoga water bottle into my scene. After masking out the flowers and table plane, I painted the background wet-into-wet. I then used luminous washes of transparent color to form the flowers and objects, adding as many layers of pigment as needed to build up the color values and define the subject. I wanted the viewer to share the intensity of color and light, to feel the heat of late summer and the joy of a picnic.

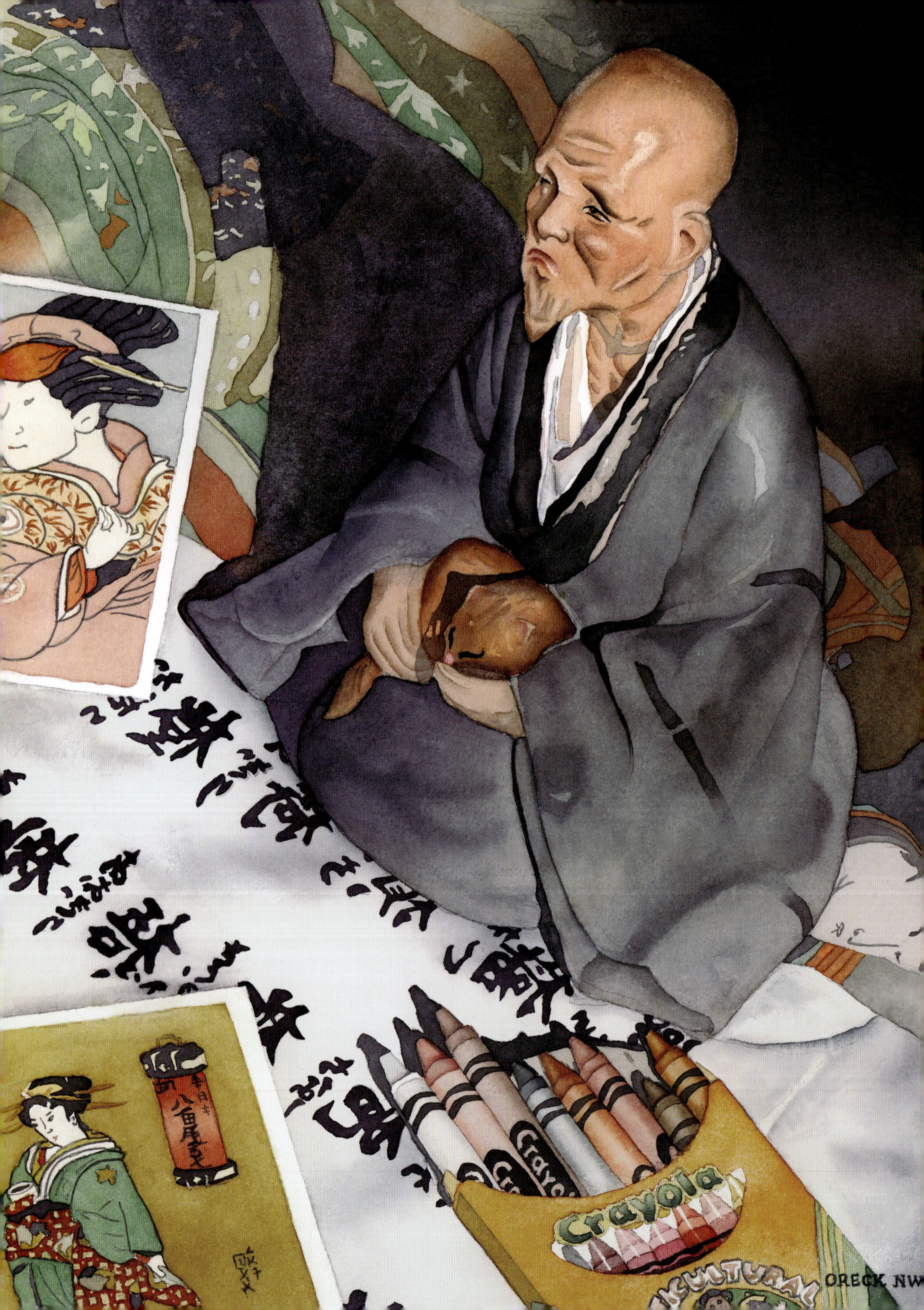
Crayola

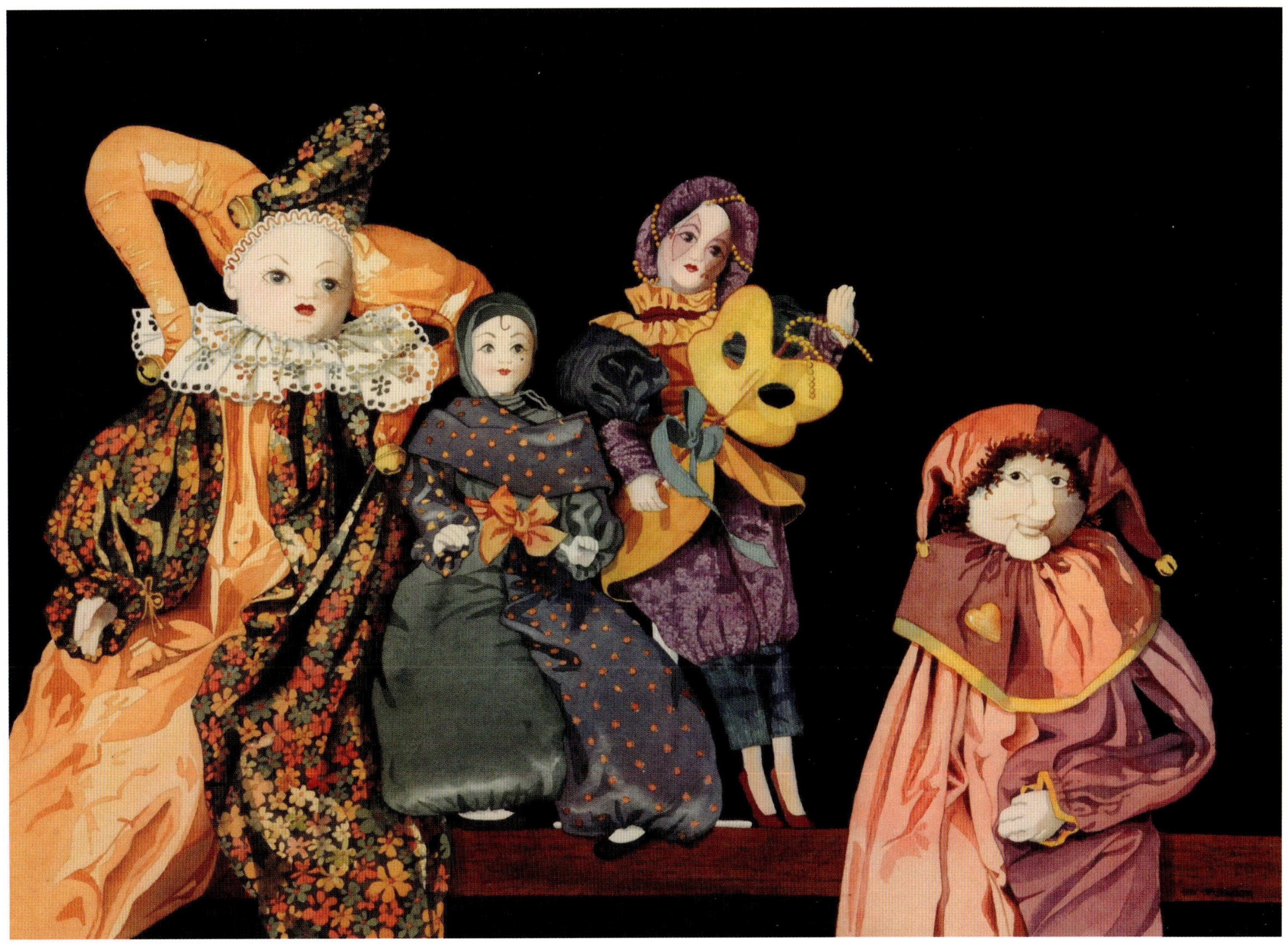

ODD MAN OUT | SIV SPURGEON

Transparent watercolor on 140-lb. (300gsm) cold-pressed Arches, 21" × 29" (53cm × 74cm)

Odd Man Out is based on my daughter's collection of clown dolls. The plain doll on the right inspired me to position him so that the more fanciful dolls on the left appear to push him out of the picture (a comment on this sad human tendency). The dolls were precariously propped on a shelf and photographed to hold the pose, but the actual dolls were used as reference for the multitude of fabric textures. A "thirsty brush" was used to remove color at the bottom of the puffy pants, and salt was used to create the look of crushed velvet. The rich background was a result of many strong washes of Viridian, Alizarin Crimson, Ultramarine Blue and Burnt Sienna.

GENERATIONS | KAAREN ORECK

Transparent watercolor on 300-lb. (640gsm) paper, 17" × 13½" (43cm × 34cm)

My fond connection to Japan started at an early age with love of the figurine featured in my painting. Returning from the Korean War, my father brought it back from Japan. Participating in four recent Japanese-American exhibits served to solidify that connection. Composing this still life, I moved objects around and photographed from various angles to find the one that best expressed my artistic vision. During this phase I ask myself questions about mood, color temperature, value pattern, and how I want to lead the viewer's eye through the painting. Honoring the subtle Japanese aesthetic, I painted *Generations* with glazes of the color triad of Alizarin Crimson, New Gamboge and Prussian Blue.

Paint what you know and the painting will then speak the rest.

— *Kaaren Oreck*

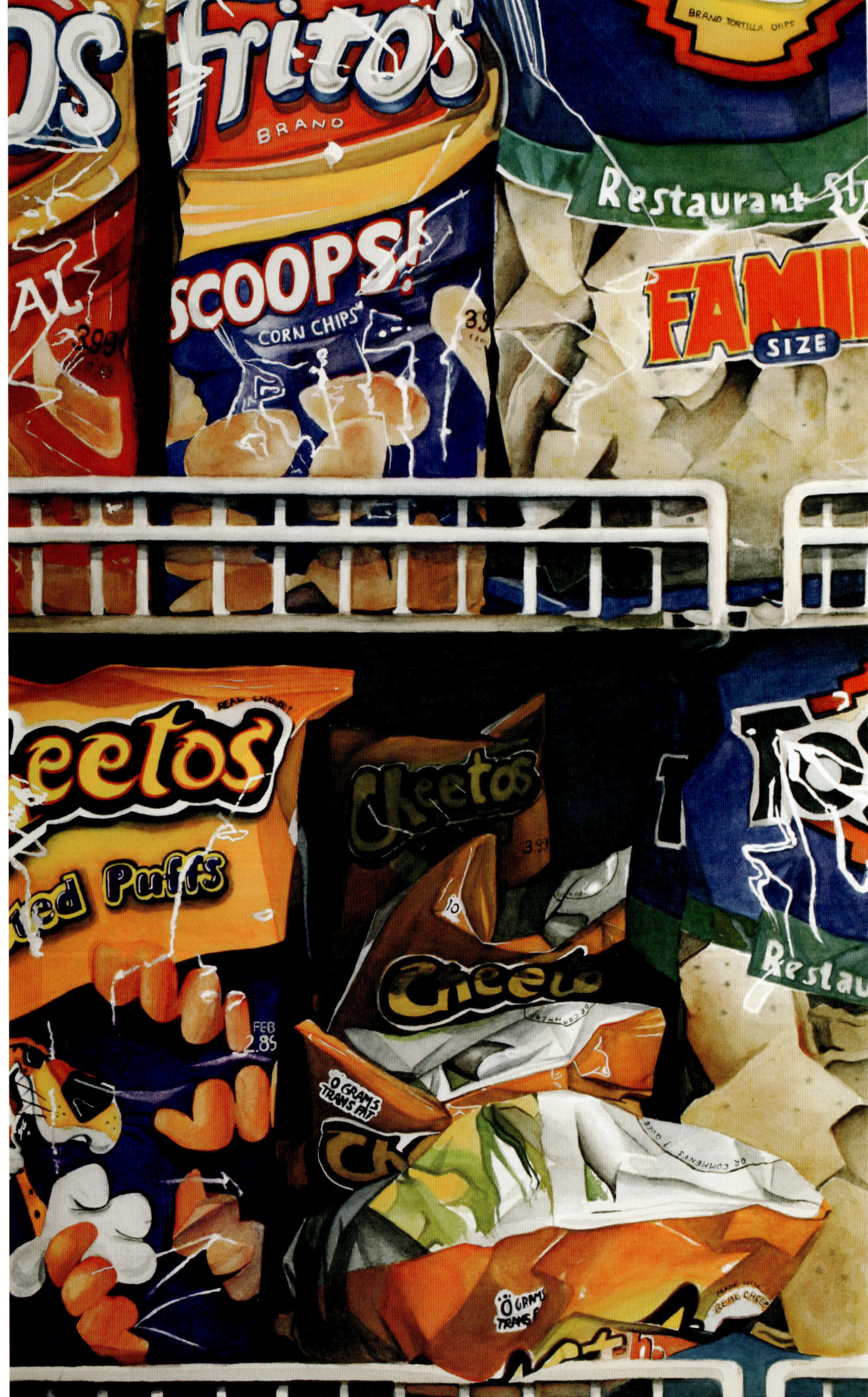
BRAND TORTILLA CHIPS
Fritos
BRAND
SCOOPS!
CORN CHIPS
Restaurant
SIZE
Puffs
Cheetos
FEB
2.85
0 GRAMS TRANS FAT
Cheetos
REAL CHEESE

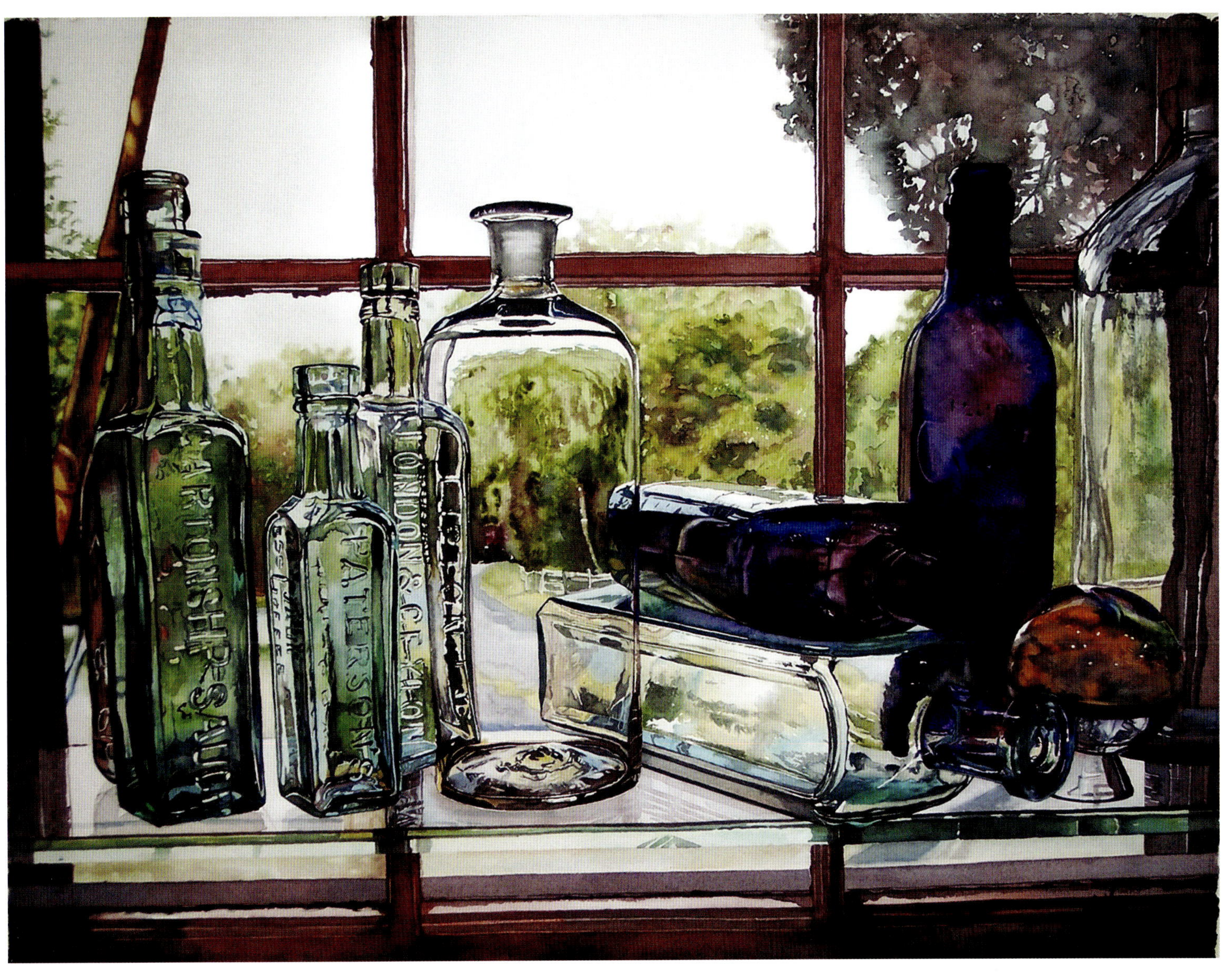

GRANARY GLASS | HEIDI LANG PARRINELLO

Transparent watercolor on 300-lb. (640gsm) cold-pressed Arches, 20" × 29" (51cm × 74cm)

There are whole worlds inside of glass if one looks closely. I have a long-standing fascination with glass and love to collect sea glass—those little shards of broken glass found on the beach. As I was painting this, I kept thinking: what beautiful sea glass this would make! Since there was so much going on in this painting, I chose to simplify my color palette for unity. After experimenting I narrowed it down to four, mixing colors as needed. This is also one of the rare pieces where I used masking fluid (sparingly) to help with the lettering on the bottles. It was very important not to get bogged down with the details too soon and to keep my washes broad until the very end. Then a small brush was essential in capturing the little nuances found inside the glass.

OH SILLY CHIPS | CINDY BERNHARD

Watercolor and gouache on 140-lb. (300gsm) cold-pressed Arches, 15" × 11" (38cm × 28cm)

I worked on this painting section by section, using a photo I took at a local grocery store in my town. I finished painting one bag of chips before I moved on to another. I was very careful and precise with the lettering so that the brands would be easily recognizable to the viewers.

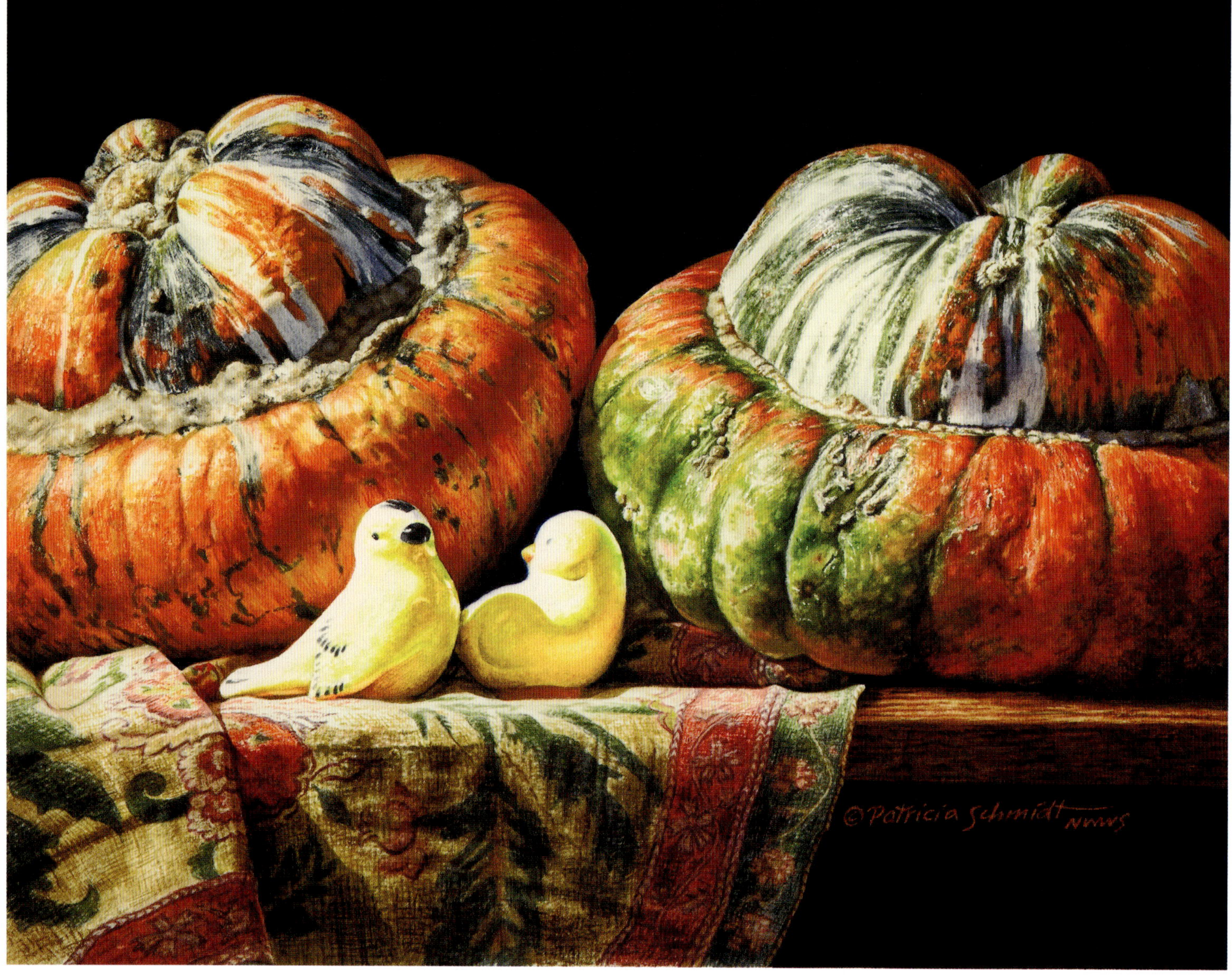

DUET | PATRICIA SCHMIDT
Transparent watercolor on 300-lb. (640gsm) cold-pressed Arches, 11" × 14" (28cm × 36cm)

The story of *Duet* developed during a photo shoot outside in the warm fall evening light. I wanted to paint the turban squash and this cloth because of the beautiful rich patterns. Magic happened when the two yellow birds joined the arrangement. The painting changed from my original idea of the turban squash to being about the yellow birds. What previous life did these birds live before my husband rescued them from an estate sale where they had lived in a kitchen? And now they are appearing in a book! Artistic vision is an evolving, creative process that rejoices in unexpected beauty.

Stay in touch with the artist within by asking *I wonder what would happen if?* and your paintings will flow out.

Patricia Schmidt

SHADOW DANCE | LINDA BAKER
Transparent watercolor on paper, 30" × 22" (76cm × 56cm)

Shadow Dance is from my signature *Clothes Pin* series. I was doing laundry one day when clothes pins were suddenly strewn across the floor. As I went to collect them, I realized what an amazing abstract design they were making. Needless to say, laundry day turned into art day as I started sketching and photographing. I loved their iconic symbolism and universal appeal. The tradition of women's work and our evolution has a significant message, but clothes pins can also be simply colorful entertainment as in *Shadow Dance* .

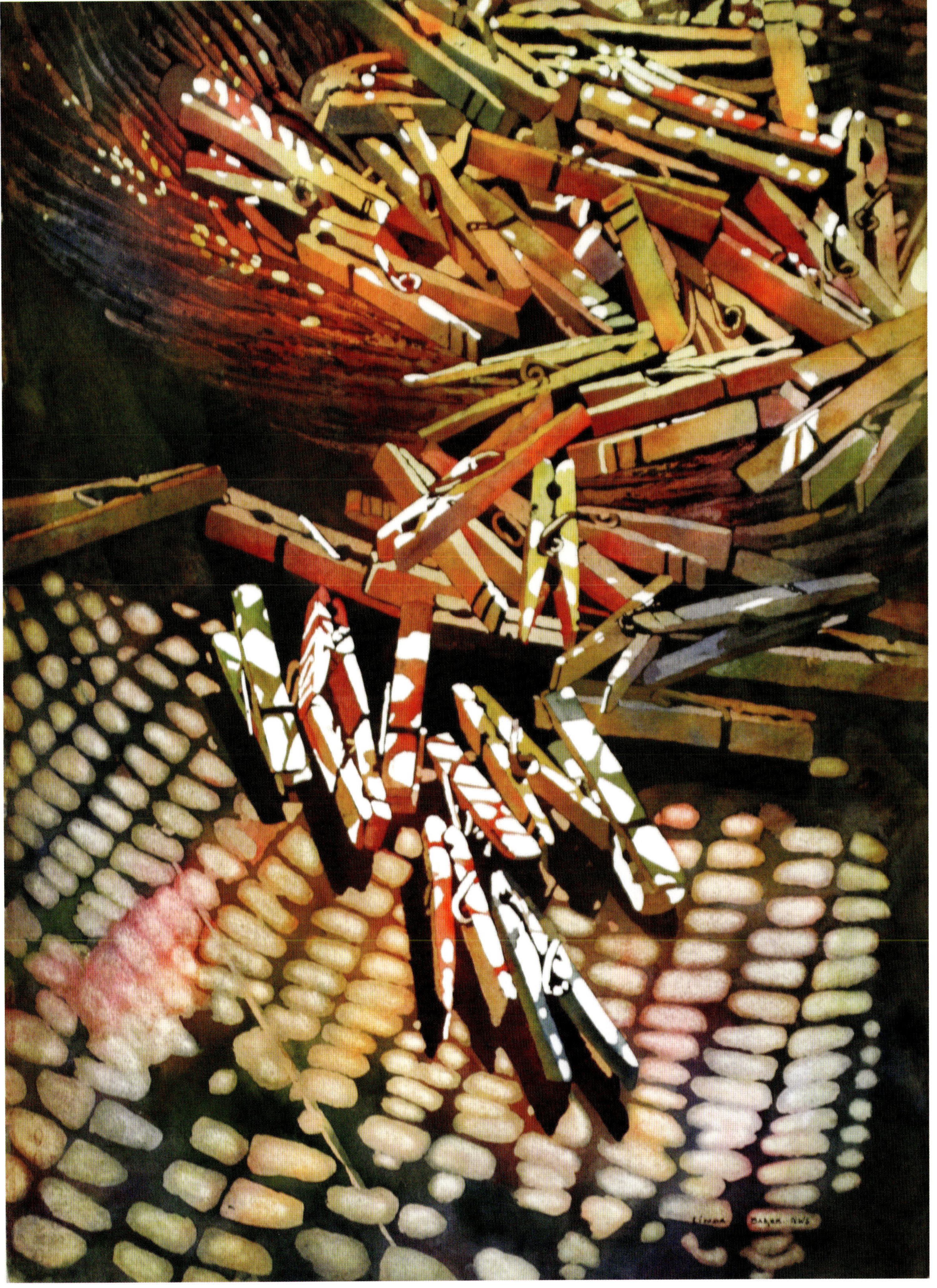

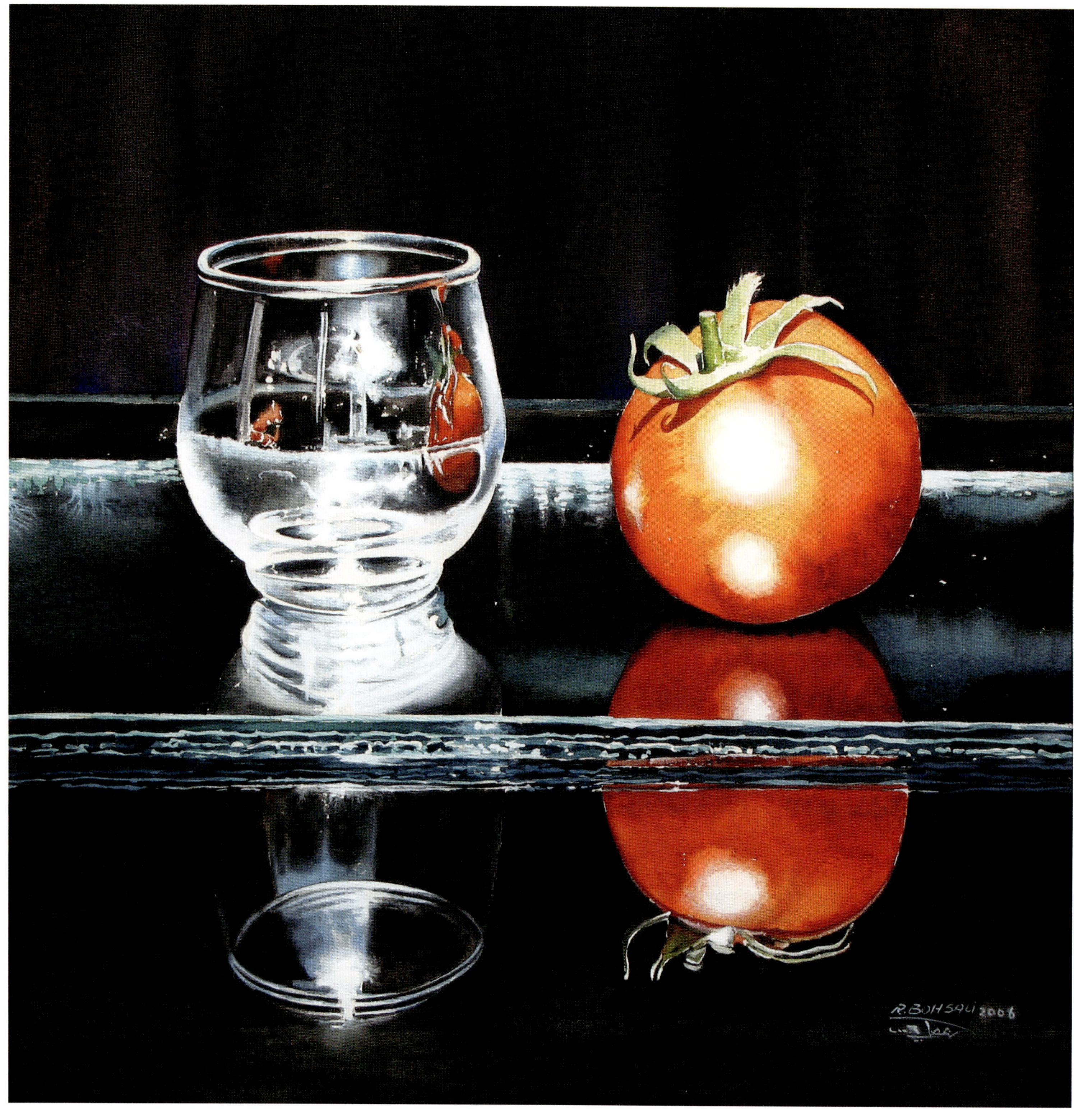

FIRE ON ICE | RACHED K. BOHSALI

Transparent watercolor with gouache on Arches Aquarelle (Perrigot) paper, 24" × 24" (61cm × 61cm)

The strong contrast of the warm red tomato and the chilling green glass surfaces on a black charcoal background suggested the name. Because fire and ice are quite unstable, I stabilized the composition with the simplicity of a square, a circle and two horizontal lines. Moreover, I love contrasts—perhaps due to my extremist Libran character.

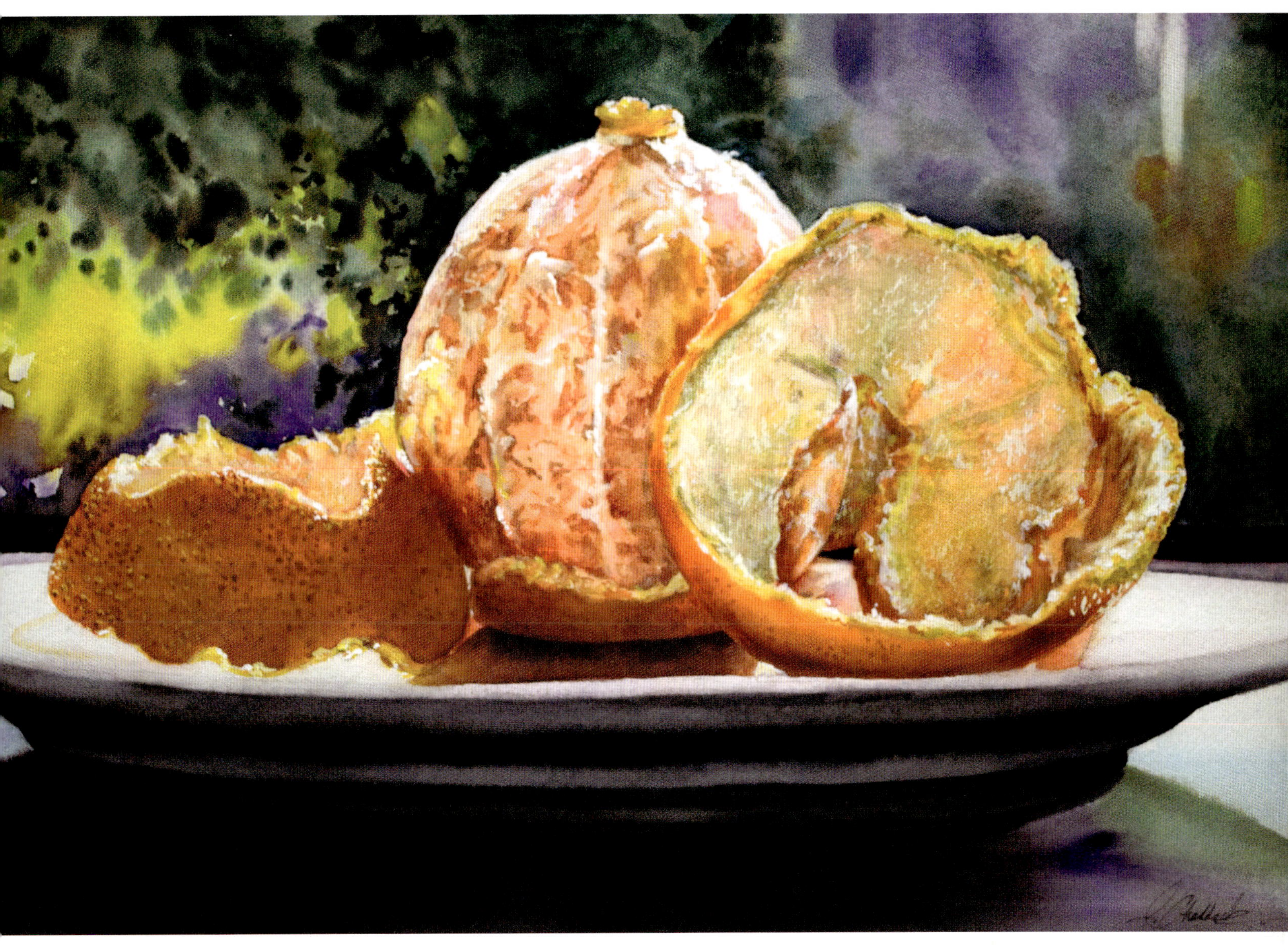

ORANGE APPEAL | A. CHADDOCK

Watercolor on 300-lb. (640gsm) cold-pressed watercolor paper, 15" × 22" (38cm × 56cm)

I placed the peeled orange in a window on a rainy day in Ireland. I tried to work around the whites on the flesh of the orange and then build on the darks. But in the end, I had to retrieve some of the lights by picking and scraping. The dimpled texture of the skin was done by dropping tiny dots into the local color, blotting them and letting it dry. (Local color is the general color that exists in a particular area.) That color is then lightened, darkened, warmed or cooled with the dots of color. I then use a tiny wet no. 2 brush and lift little lights next to the darker dots. The background was all painted wet-into-wet.

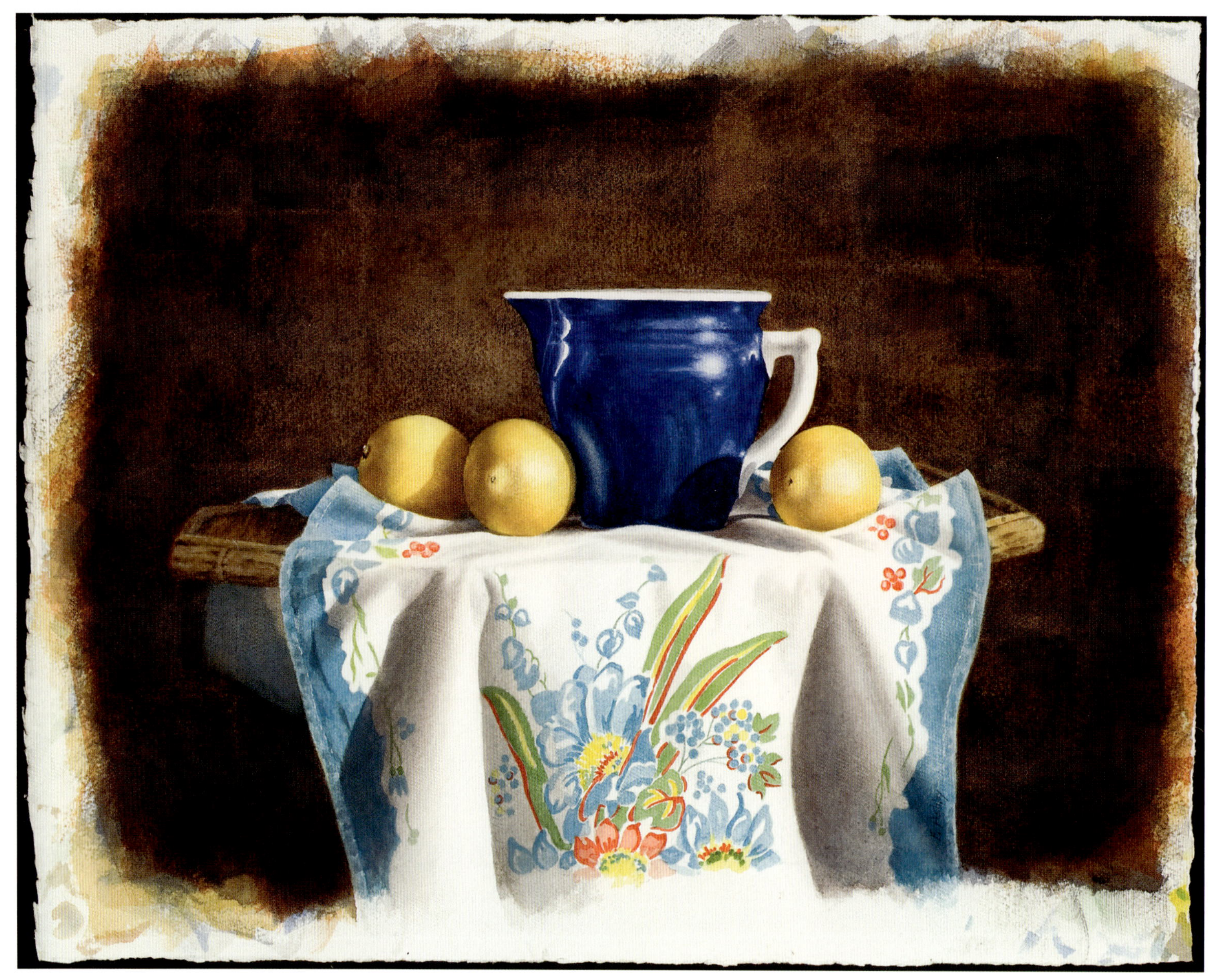

BLUE PITCHER WITH LEMONS | FRANCES ASHLEY
Transparent watercolor on 300-lb. (640gsm) Arches, 13" × 17" (33cm × 43cm)

Blue Pitcher with Lemons is from what I refer to as my *Vintage Linens* series. I am a collector of vintage linens, and enjoy using them in my still-life setups. I also like to include family pieces in my work as they add to the painting's personal meaning. I begin painting from life, but eventually use the photographs I have taken before beginning the painting. My style is quite time-consuming and fresh produce doesn't last forever! Although executed in transparent watercolor, I utilize heavy saturation of paint in some areas to obtain intense color, as in the blue of my grandmother's porcelain Czech pitcher.

PERSIMMONS WITH THE BLUES | SALLY BAKER
Watercolor on 140-lb. (300gsm) Arches, 22" × 16" (56cm × 41cm)

I always paint from the real objects in my still lifes but also use photo references. Each painting is a puzzle to be solved; I carefully plan the composition before I ever pick up a brush. I have explored Italian, Japanese and Hawaiian themes, but I am best known for my still-life series that focuses on Asian artifacts, kimonos and bamboo. As a child, my parents' best friends were Asian importers and we shared dinner with them once a week for the first eight or ten years of my life. I began at this young age to appreciate the Asian aesthetic and it has continued to permeate my style. My work is sharp-focused with emphasis on strong shadows and luscious colors. I feel that I am rescuing moments in time that otherwise would fade into obscurity.

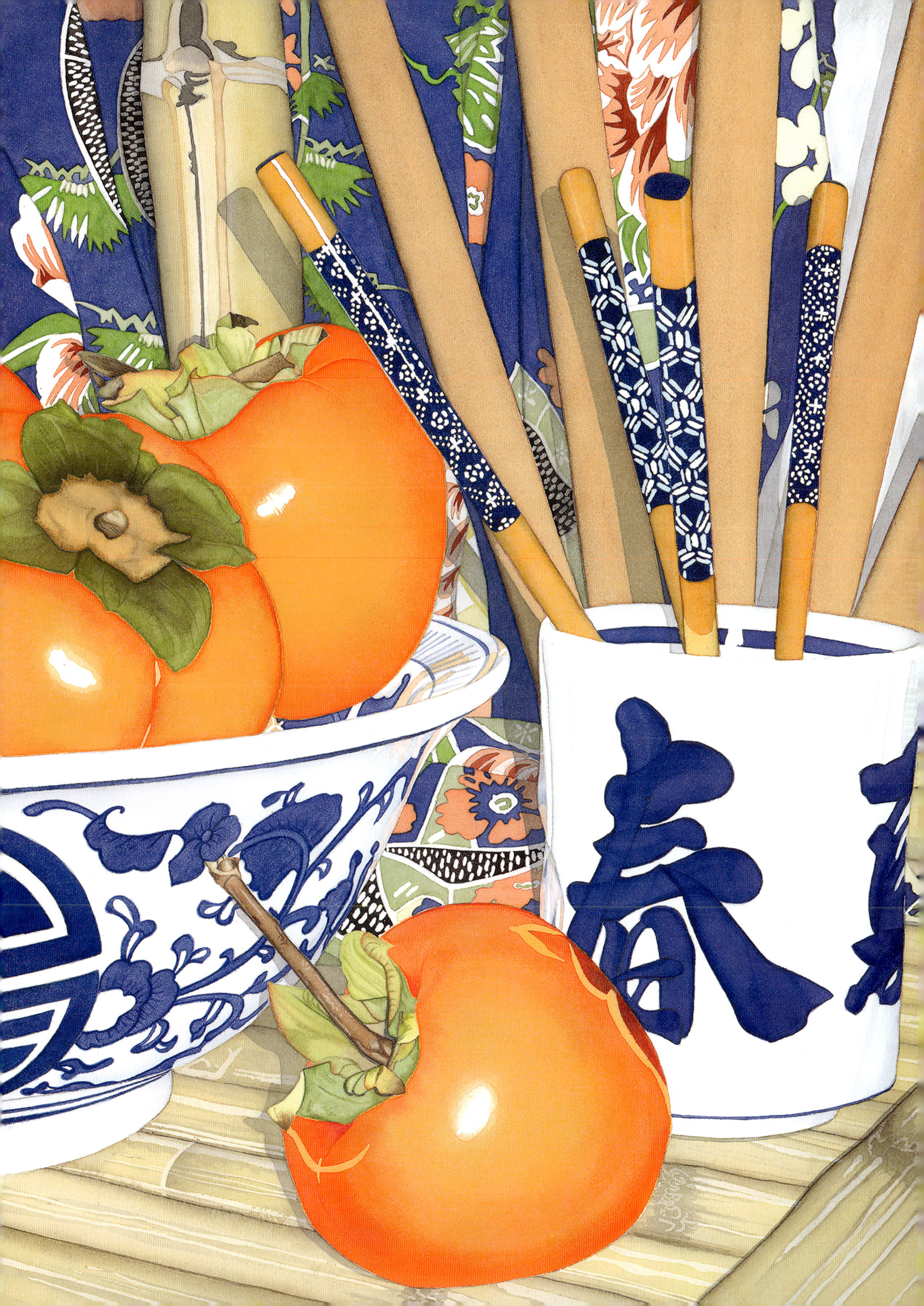
春

CONTRIBUTORS

CINDY AGAN, LWS
1201 Belmont Ave.
South Bend, IN 46615
574.233.7950
cindyaganart@hotmail.com
www.cindyaganart.com
p115 *Cat in Profile*

KATHLEEN ALEXANDER, WW, NWWS
P.O. Box 300
Pacifica, CA 94044
650.455.0998
studio@kathleenalexanderwatercolors.com
www.kathleenalexanderwatercolors.com
p25 *Sonoma Vines*
First Place in Watercolor, 1st Annual Autumn Arts Painting Challenge; Transparent Watercolor Society of America 34th International Exhibition; Ken Hetzel Memorial Award 2010

RUTH ARTHUR
5228 E. Hanbury St.
Long Beach, CA 90808
562.425.1609
ruthnbill@earthlink.net
p109 *Proud Peter*

FRANCES ASHLEY, SW, SWS, TWS
4806 Roundup Trail
Austin, TX 78745
512.444.4527
francesashley@hotmail.com
www.francesashley.com
p134 *Blue Pitcher with Lemons*
First Place, Waterloo Watercolor Group Annual Exhibit

LINDA BAKER, AWS, NWS, TWSA
138 Stonemaker Rd.
Mooresville, NC 28117
616.846.3453
lindabakerartist@gmail.com
p33 *Back in Five: Life Cycle* series
p131 *Shadow Dance*
Back in Five—Watercolor West Award; Published Best of Watermedia, Kennedy Publishers
Shadow Dance—American Watercolor Society Award; Adirondacks National Award

SALLY BAKER, WW
5990 Vine Hill School Rd.
Sebastopol, CA 95472
www.sallybaker.com
Graton Gallery, Graton, CA
p135 *Persimmons with the Blues*

DEENA S. BALL, PWCS, BWS
Pennsylvania Guild of Craftsmen—State Juried Member
18 Colfax Rd.
Wavertown, PA 19083
610.789.1003
deenaball@mac.com
www.deenasball.com
Hardcastle Gallery, Centreville, DE
p12 *Up the Hill*
First Place, Delaware Valley Art League Winter 2009; included in Pennsylvania Water Color Society; 30th International Tuned Exhibition

SUSAN BARESEL, NEWS
P.O. Box 891
Greenwood Lake, NY 10925
susanbareselart@rocketmail.com
www.susanbareselart.com
p111 *Serendipity*

CINDY BERNHARD
815.274.4833
cindyindylo@hotmail.com
www.cindybernhardart.com
p128 *Oh Silly Chips*

SANDRA BLAIR, SAA, AFC, BWS
Harrisburg, PA
sblairart@verizon.net
www.natureartists.com/sandra_blair.asp
Village Artisans Gallery, Boiling Springs, PA
p112 *Nora's Coop*
p113 *Yummm*

RACHED K. BOHSALI
Bohsali Bldg., Caracas, Raoucheh
Beirut, Lebanon 00961 3 903074
rachedb@cyberia.net.lb
rachedb2@hotmail.com
p21 *Self … Portrait*
p118 *Oriental Charm*
p119 *Reflections of the Reflected Reflections*
p132 *Fire on Ice*
Self … Portrait—Special Recognition, 8th Annual Realism Juried Online International Art Exhibition, Upstream People Gallery
Oriental Charm—Award of Excellence, 8th Annual Realism Juried Online International Art Exhibition, Upstream People Gallery
Reflections of the Reflected Reflections—Special Recognition, 8th Annual Realism Juried Online International Art Exhibition, Upstream People Gallery
Fire on Ice—Anchor Dip 1, Award of Excellence, 8th Annual Realism Juried Online International Art Exhibition, Upstream People Gallery

FRANCESCA BRAYTON, CWA, HWS
3961 Toland Circle
Los Alamitos, CA 90720
562.596.8909
francescabrayton@socail.rr.com
www.francescabrayton.com
p99 *Crab Cooker*

NAOMI CAMPBELL, TWSA, NWS, PSA
177 7th Ave., #3L
Brooklyn, NY 11215
Studio: 718.499.5891 Cell: 917.754.7349
naomicampbelltheartist@gmail.com
www.naomicampbelltheartist.com
p54 *Bluenote*
Transparent Watercolor Society of America Phil Austin Award

KARA CASTRO, CWA
Castro Fine Arts
P.O. Box 4081
Auburn, CA 95604
530.632.9592
castrofinearts@yahoo.com
www.castrofinearts.com
pp44–45 *Gideon's Pinwheel*

A. CHADDOCK, VWS, SW
National Arts Club
5 Hunting Ridge Rd.
Manakin-Sabot, VA 23103
Home: 804.784.7017 Cell: 804.512.0319
Work: 804.740.1400
forartssakegallery@comcast.net

www.forartssakegallery.com

p14 *Suncluster*

p133 *Orange Appeal*

Suncluster—Second Place, National Watercolor Society 110th Annual, 2006

MARGUERITE CHADWICK-JUNER
33 Earley St.
City Island, NY 10464
718.885.0933
m.juner@verizon.net
www.margueritechadwickjuner.com

p16 *Moment of Reflection XI*

CHERYL CHALMERS
5074 Rice Rd.
Trumansburg, NY 14886
Studio: 607.387.4133 Cell: 607.379.1606
cherchalmers@yahoo.com
www.cherylchalmers.com

p125 *Saratoga Brunch*

CHOW CHIN CHUAN
Malaysian Watercolor Society
No. 6, Jalan Titian U8/42, 40150 Bukit Jelutong
Shah Alam 40150, Selangor Malaysia
+6012-3529819
cccwatercolor@gmail.com

p42 *Flower Corridor 3*

p43 *At Home*

KATHY COLLINS, NWWS
Lake Forest Park, WA
kathy.collins2@comcast.net
www.kathycollinswatercolors.com
Kaewyn Gallery, Bothell, WA

p10 *At the Center*

SUSAN CROUCH, WSNC
631 Dogwood Rd.
Statesville, NC 28677
704.287.7697
susan@susancrouch.com
www.susancrouch.com

p29 *Pure Heart*

RIC DENTINGER, TWS , CWA, LWS
The Finesilver Building
816 Camaron, Ste. 1.06
San Antonio, TX 78212
210.260.2508
ric@ricdentinger.com
www.ricdentinger.com
The Hunt Gallery, San Antonio, TX 210.822.6527

p51 *Little Wing*

p121 *Cupcake Falls*

Little Wing—California Watercolor Association 2009 Richard Barrett Memorial Award

Cupcake Falls—Texas Watercolor Society 2009 Best of Show

OSCAR R. DIZON, AWS, TWSA
Society of Philippije American Artists
7 Windermere Dr.
Holbrook, NY 11741
613.472.2719
oscarrdizon@yahoo.com
www.oscarrdizon.com

p81 *Passage to the Park*

p86 *Late Summer at Zhouzhuang, 2006*

p88 *Bridge with "Gates"*

Late Summer at Zhouzhuang, 2006—Bronze Medal of Honor, American Watercolor Society, 2008; Mrs. John Newington Award for Excellence, Hudson Valley Art Association, 2008

Passage to the Park—Certificate of Merit, Salmagundi Club, 2009

Bridge with "Gates"—Exhibited at the Hudson Valley Art Association 78th Annual Exhibit, 2009

RICHARD H. DUTTON
Columbia Art League
Plain Air Artist Group, Columbia, MO
14650 N. Barnes School Rd.
Columbia, MO 65255
573.881.3198
rkdutton60@msn.com
www.duttonwatercolor.com
Sturdevant Gallery, Osage Beach, MO

p20 *Seasons 2*

SY ELLENS, NWS, WW, MOWS
326 W. Kalamazoo Ave., Ste. 321
Kalamazoo, MI 49007-3353
269.342.6326
syellens@sbcglobal.net
www.syellens.com
Synchronicity Gallery, Glen Arbor, MI

p13 *Serenity*

Finalist in *The Artist's Magazine* 25th Annual Art Competition

LYNN FERRIS, NWS, FWS
119 Hickory Hollow Rd.
Berkeley Springs, WV 25411
ferrislynn@yahoo.com
www.lynnferris.com

p64 *Harlequin*

DIANE FOREST, AIBAQ/M, SCA, IAF
4780 Place Bessette
Saint-Hubert, Quebec, J3Y-2P7, Canada
forest.diane@videotron.ca
www.dianeforest.artacademie.com
Galerie Le Balcon d'Art
866.466.8920
www.balcondart.com
infio@balcondart.com

p103 *Generation*

p122 *Ephemeral Whiteness*

Generation—First Prize, Public Vote, Academie Internationale des Beaux-Arts du Quebec; First Prize, Celebration of the 350th Anniversary of City of Lonqueuil

Ephemeral Whiteness—First Prize, Public Vote, Academie Internationale des Beaux-Arts du Quebec

NANCY FORTUNATO, TWSA/S, WW, ASMA
249 N. Marion St.
Palatine, IL 60074
847.359.5033
www.watercolorart.net

pp72–73 *London's Gem*

BARBARA FOX
7590 Maples Rd.
Little Valley, NY 14755
716.699.4145
bfoxart@yahoo.com
www.barbarafoxwatercolors.com

p50 *Anchored*

p124 *Harmony*

JANE FREEMAN
P.O. Box 1451
Bemidji, MN 56619
jane@janefreeman.com
www.janefreeman.com
pp116–117 *Sauced Grapes*

DIANE (ARISTARCO) FUJIMOTO
20 Farm Rd.
Los Altos, CA 94024
650.380.4505
diane@dianefujimotocom
www.dianefujimoto.com
p17 *Going for Grapeness*

HENRY FUKUHARA, 1913–2010, NWS, WW
c/o Grace Niwa
659 Cliffwood Ave.
Brea, CA 92821
ygniwa@aol.com
Anderson Gallery, Sunset Beach, CA
p90 *Rowland Heights Barn*
Lifetime Achievement Award, NWS
Lifetime membership, WW

CARLA GAUTHIER, CSPWC, WAS-H
2007 Walnut Green Dr.
Houston, TX 77062
281.384.2473
carla.gauthier@yahoo.com
www.carlagauthier.com
Carteret Contemporary Art
www.twogalleries.net
p74 *North, South, East and West*
p75 *Late Afternoon, Brugge*

KATHIE GEORGE, OWS, FWS
126 Blue Gate Circle
Kettering, OH 45429
www.kathiegeorge.com
Dovetail Gallery, Egg Harbor, WS
p107 *The Gathering*

STUART GIVOT
1548 Maple St.
Redwood City, CA 94063
artiststu@yahoo.com
p89 *Lumber Scow*

KEN GOLDMAN, NWS, SDWS, PSA
3939 La Salle St.
San Diego, CA 92110
goldmanfineart@cot.net
www.goldmanfineart.com
p68 *Live Rehearsal*

ELIZABETH S. GROVES
2430 Alamo Glen Dr.
Alamo, CA 94507
tgr6146000@global.net
pp104–105 *Fish Tales*

JANICE WALKER HALL, UWS
3017 E. Willow Creek Dr.
Sandy, Utah 84093
801.942.2069
walkerarts3017@yahoo.com
www.janicewalkerhall.com
p56 *Croquet: Straight Shot*
Award of Merit UWS 2009
Honorable Mention WFWS, 2010

SCOTT HARTLEY
5334 Nollar Rd.
Ann Arbor, MI 48105
734.355.2992
scotthartley@copper.net
www.scotthartleywatercolors.com
p84 *Ladder and Shadows*

VERNA HENDRICKS, NWS, UWS
10365 S. 2505 E.
Sandy, UT 84092
801.631.7145
watercolors_2000@comcast.net
www.vernahendrickswatercolorartist.com
p41 *Rustic Beauty*

JOYCE HICKS, AWS, SWS, TWS
jhicks@jhicksfineart.com
www.jhicksfineart.com
p95 *A Farmhouse I Saw in Virginia*

TERRI HILL, AAW
1944 De La Pena Ave.
Santa Clara, CA 95050
408.248.2354
terrihill@designerhill.com
pp30–31 *Pedal Power*

CATHERINE HILLIS, VWS, PWS, BWS, SW, PVW
P.O. Box 41
Round Hill, VA 20142
703.431.6877
chhillis@aol.com
www.catherinehillis.com
p96 *Round 'n Round*

MARY HOPF
3414 South Polo Dr.
Aptos, CA 95003
831.685.1205
maryhopf@cruzers.com
www.maryhopf.com
p106 *Beach Buddies*

LYNN HOSEGOOD
4475 Pleasant View Dr.
Williamsburg, VA 23188
757.564.3098
lynn@lynnhosegoodstudio.com
www.lynnhosegoodstudio.com
p83 *Bridge of Sighs*

ANNE HUDEC, SFCA
Victoria BC Canada
250.598.6851
ah@annehudec.com
www.annehudec.com
Federation Gallery, Granville Island, Vancouver, BC
p69 *Empathy*

CARY HUNKEL, SAA
caryhunkel@gmail.com
p114 *Connection*

DANA FOX JENKINS, NFWS
154 Norwood Ave.
Buffalo, NY 14222
danafoxjenkins@gmail.com
p61 *The Jarvis Girls*

RUSSELL JEWELL, ED.D., NWS, TWSA
116 Deer Creek Ct.
Easley, SC 29642
864.855.1251
jewellart@charter.net
www.russelljewell.com
Dobbins Gallery, Charleston, SC
p102 *Amsterdam Morn*
Exhibited at Transparent Watercolor Society of America, 2010

BEV JOZWIAK, NWS, WW, TWA
paintingjoz@hotmail.com
www.bevjozwiak.com
p108 *Bad Kitty*

JEAN KALIN, TWSA, MOWS, ISAP
20650 Hwy. 371
Platte City, MO 64079
816.992.3744
jeankalin@unitedwb.coop
www.mowsart.com
p67 *Siesta at Three*
$500 Daniel Smith Award, 2008 Transparent Watercolor Society of America, Annual Juried Exhibition

GEORGE F. KOCAR, NOIS, OWS
24213 Lake Rd.
Bay Village, OH 44140
440.871.8325
gkocar@aol.com
www.gkocar.com
p65 *Pablo's Nightwatch*

ANNE VAN BLARCOM KUROWSKI, PWCS, NJWCS, SPS
3929 Appleton Way
Wilmington, NC 28412
910.397.9111
annevank@ec.rr.com
www.vanblarcom.com
p59 *Bosun's Mate*

ANDREW KUSMIN, NWS, AAA, NEWS
10 Massasoit Ave. (P.O. Box 2319)
Mahomet, MA 02345
andrew@kusminarts.com
www.kusminarts.com
p34 *Door to Door*
p35 *Cardiac Arrest*
Door to Door—Gold medal, NEWS

FRANK LALUMIA, AWS, NWS, TWSA
31855 Old Sopris Rd.
Trinidad, CO 81082
719.845.1385
frank@lalumia.com
www.lalumia.com
Greenberg Fine Art, Santa Fe, NM
pp8–9 *Snow in the Foothills*
Rockies West National Exhibition, 2010, Grand Junction, CO

FEALING LIN, NWS, WW, MOWS
1720 Ramiro Rd.
San Marino, CA 91108
626.799.7022
fealinglin@hotmail.com
www.fealingwatercolor.com
p52 *Lobster Fisherman*
p53 *Farmer George*

GEOFFREY MCCORMACK, NWS, AWS, WSO
Eugene, OR
541.463.8475
mcsurf@mac.com
www.mcsurf.com
p22 *Three River* series: *The Rogue*

LAURIN MCCRACKEN, AWS, NWS, TWSA
215 N. Deer Creek W.
Leland, MS 38756
817.773.2163
laurinmc@aol.com
www.lauringallery.com
Southside Gallery, Oxford, MS
p91 *Rooftops New York*

MICHAEL ALLEN MCGUIRE, NMWS
1007 Calle Margarita
Santa Fe, NM 87507
505.471.5733
vistaman@earthlink.net
Arlene Siegel Gallery, Santa Fe, NM
pp2–3 *The Hens Are in the Hen House*

GERALDINE MCKEOWN, NWS, PWCS, BWS
227 Gallaher Rd.
Elkton, MD 21921
410.398.5447
gerrym@mckeownart.com
www.mckeownart.com
McBride Gallery, Annapolis, MD
p40 *Entwined*

TRISH MCKINNEY
9735 Bellefontaine Rd.
New Carlisle, OH 45344
937.470.3974
trishmc514@aol.com
www.trishmckinney.com
Town & Country Fine Art Center
p18 *Water Fireworks*
Best of Show, Western Ohio Watercolor Society

CLAUDIA MCKINSTRY
claudiamckinstry@earthlink.net
www.claudiamckinstry.com
Bainbridge Arts and Crafts
p94 *Winter Market*
Daniel Smith Faces and Places Contest

JENNY MEDVED, FWS
jennymedved@yahoo.com
www.jennymedved.com
p48 *What'll Ya Have*
Katherine Butler Gallery National Juried Show, 2010 Finalist

DAVID MILTON, NWS, WW, AAA
31682 Fairview Rd.
Laguna Beach, CA 92651
949.415.0155
dmiltonart@cox.net
www.davidmiltonstudio.com
p36 *Chief Hotel Court*

GINA MITCHELL
55980 Raintree Dr.
Osceola, IN 46561
574.674.5377
imagineonly@comcast.net
www.universitywatercolors.com
p97 *Campus Sunset*
Bea Zimmerman Memorial Award

JUDY MORRIS, AWS, NWS, TWSA
2404 E. Main St.
Medford, OR 97504
541.779.5306
judy@judymorris-art.com
www.judymorris-art.com
Hanson Howard Gallery, Ashland, OR
p66 *Pigeons in the Piazza*
San Diego Watercolor Society's 29th International Exhibition, Linda Doll Seminar Group Cash Award

GLORIA AINSWORTH MOUT, AFCA
FCA, Rockport Center for the Arts, White Rock & South Surrey Art Society
#208-15342 20th Ave.
Surrey, BC V4A 2A3
Canada
gjmout60@shaw.ca
www.myartclub.com
Federation of Canadian Artists, Vancouver, BC
p37 *Red Wheel: Reflections* series

TORGESEN MURDOCK, NWS, IWS, AWS
7385 N. Crestview Rd.
Pocatello, ID 83201
Home: 208.232.1778 Cell: 208.221.1778
torgesenmurdock@yahoo.com
www.torgesenmurdock.com
Zantman Galleries in Carmel and Palm Desert, CA

p27 *Strewn Jewels*

Best of Show, Idaho Watercolor Society

LAEL H. NELSON
600 Lake Shore Dr.
Scroggins, TX 75480
lael75480@yahoo.com

p55 *Rail Yard Flapper Fantasy*

WILL NELSON, AAA, IWS, WRVAG
603 Kingsford Dr.
Meridian, ID 83642
208.884.3227
will@wnelson.com
www.wnelson.com
Kirsten Galleries, Seattle, WA

p123 *Racing the Wind*

RUTH NEWQUIST, NWS, AAA, SALMAGUNDI CLUB
6 Phyllis Ln.
Newtown, CT 06470
ruthnewquist@gmail.com
www.ruthnewquist.com
State of the Art Gallery, Gloucester, MA

p98 *Checking the Board*

Kent Art Association Medal of Honor & Solo Show

TED NUTTALL, AWS, NWS, TWSA
4225 N. 36th St., Unit 34
Phoenix, AZ 85018
602.253.1605
ted@tednuttall.com
www.tednuttall.com
Jane Sauer Gallery, Santa Fe, NM

pp57 *Cosi' Comincia il Giorno*

p46 *Light and Shadow*

p47 *Whispering Smith*

p71 *Sisters*

Cosi' Comincia il Giorno—Best of Show, Western Federation Watercolor Society's 34th Annual Juried Exhibition

Nell Storer Memorial Award, American Watercolor Society, 142nd Annual Exhibition

SANDY O'CONNOR, HVAA
P.O. Box 63
Cotuit, MA 02635
508.420.3223
sandy@redhillstudio.com
www.redhillstudio.com

p19 *Back to the Sea*

First Place and Best in Show, All New England Juried Exhibition, Cape Cod Art Association

KAAREN ORECK, NWS
6215 S. Highlands Ave.
Madison, WI 53705
608.231.6702
kaaren.b.oreck@gmail.com
www.kaarenoreck.com

p126 *Generations*

HEIDI LANG PARRINELLO, NJWCS
www.heidilangparrinello.com

p129 *Granary Glass*

DONALD W. PATTERSON, AWS, NWS
441 Cardinal Court N.
New Hope, PA 18938
215.598.8991
donpatterson1@verizon.net
www.travisgallery.com

p11 *Dusk*

SANDRINE PELISSIER, AFCA
sandrine@sandrinepelissier.com
www.sandrinepelissier.com

p49 *Auto Portrait #4*

ANN PEMBER, RMNW, CLWAC, NAWA
Water Edge Studio
14 Water Edge Rd.
Keeseville, NY 12944
518.834.7440
ann@annpember.com
www.annpember.com
Southern Vermont Art Center

p82 *Museo Majestuoso*

JUAN PEÑA
720 Hi Pines Ranch Rd.
Colfax, CA 95713
530.887.0312
juan@paintingsbyjuanpena.com
www.paintingsbyjuanpena.com
Knowlton Gallery, Lodi, CA

p38 *Let the Sunshine In*

Paint America 2010

KRIS PRESLAN, TWSA, NWS, AWS
P.O. Box 1511
Lake Oswego, OR 97035
503.636.9677
krispreslan@mac.com
www.preslanart.com
Valley Art, Forest Grove, OR

p32 *The Old Indian*

SHARON RAJNUS
541.723.4371
www.rajnusart.com

p24 *Cascading Snows*

MICHAEL REARDON, NWS, CWA, WW
5433 Boyd Ave.
Oakland, CA 94618
510.655.7030
www.reardonwatercolors.com

p85 *Fountain, Sonoma Plaza*

JOHN SALMINEN, AWS-DF, NWS, TWSA
6021 Arnold Rd.
Duluth, MN 55803
218.721.3319
www.johnsalminen.com

p76 *Grant Lanterns*

p77 *Cable Car*

Cable Car—Zhujiajiao Shanghai International Biennial Award

TIM SATERNOW
New York, NY
tim.saternow@gmail.com
www.timsaternow.com
George Billis Gallery, New York, NY

p100 *West 15th Street, Two Bridges* (diptych)

p101 *39 Mott Street, Rain* (diptych)

RONALD A. SCHLOYER, AWS, PWS, PWCS
119 4th St.
Hanover, PA 17331
717.476.1230
schloyer@embarqmail.com
www.hanoverareaarts.com/19
Hanover Art Guild

p70 *Mat-terial Girls*

PATRICIA SCHMIDT, NWS, WSO, CPSA
1038 NE 76th Ave.
Portland, OR 97213
patty@patriciaschmidtart.com
www.patriciaschmidtart.com
Portland Art Museum Rental Sales Gallery

p28 *Siletz Bay Hydrangea*

p130 *Duet*

LYNN SLADE
Pioneer, CA
lynn@lsladeart.com
www.lsladeart.com
Studio 7 Fine Arts, Pleasanton, CA

p26 *Bale Patterns*

Second Place, *Watercolor Artist* Magazine's Watermedia Showcase Competition, 2009

DEAN W. SLADEK
302 Whitetail Dr.
Chagrin Falls, OH 44022
440.338.5141
gdsladek@windstream.net

p63 *Washing in the Ganges*

SIV SPURGEON, NWS, PWCS, PWS
600 N. Swarthmore Ave.
Swarthmore, PA 19081
610.544.1829
mail@sivspurgeon.com
www.sivspurgeon.com

p127 *Odd Man Out*

The Charles Knox Smith Founder's Prize

Frank Nofer Award for Representational, Transparent Watercolor

BRENDA SWENSON, NWWS, WW
514 El Centro St.
South Pasadena, CA 91030
626.441.6562
brenda@swensonsart.net
www.swensonsart.net
Schroeder Studio Gallery, 112 E. Maple, Orange, CA 714.633.0653

p78 *Mission Colors*

p79 *Rust Covered Memories*

ZHOU TIANYA, CAA, NWS
D1-901 ShanHuJu
488 CuiYin Road
LuoHu, Shenzhen
Guangdong 518019
China
0086.136.8244.2735
ztianya@126.com
Hong Kong HanXiangYuan Gallery

p62 *The Light from the Heaven*

Jack Richeson & Co. Purchase Award, 89th Annual Juried Exhibition of National Watercolor Society, 2009

JAMES TOOGOOD, AWS, NWS
920 Park Dr.
Cherry Hill, NJ 08002
856.429.5461
jtoogood@verizon.net

p6 *Rio di San Barnaba (Ca' Rezzonico)*

p87 *A Side Canal, Venice*

p92 *Nocturne, Grand Canal*

p93 *Rio Terà dei Catecumeni*

SHARON TOWLE
2417 John St.
Manhattan Beach, CA 90266
310.546.1864
sharontowle@ix.netcom.com
www.sharontowle.com

p120 *Curious Cat*

ROSA INÉS VERA
118 Via Finita St.
San Antonio, TX 78229
210.451.8041
rositavera@aol.com
www.rosavera.com

p58 *What She Missed*

Gold Medal, Mid-Atlantic Regional Watercolor Show, Baltimore Watercolor Society

MYRNA S. WACKNOV, NWS, CWA
675 Matsonia Dr.
Foster City, CA 94404
650.574.3192
myrnawack@prodigy.net
www.myrnawacknov.com
www.myrnawacknov.blogspot.com
Gallery Concord, Concord, CA

p60 *Reflections on Turning 65*

CFS Medal, American Watercolor Society

Semifinalist, 2009 Portrait Competition, National Portrait Gallery of the Smithsonian, Washington D.C.

SOON Y. WARREN, NWS, AWS, TWS
4062 Hildring Dr. W
Fort Worth, TX 76109
817.923.1586
soonywarren@gmail.com
www.soonwarren.com
Southwest Gallery, Dallas, TX

p39 *Circle of Wheel*

STEVE WILDA
Allied Artists of America (NYC, NY), Connecticut Academy of Fine Arts (Mystic, CT), Academic Artists Association (Springfield, MA)
53 Rocky Hill Rd.
Hadley, MA 01035
413.584.8482
swilda@acad.umass.edu
www.stevewilda.com

p110 *Sanctuary*

LAURA WILK, CWS
New Haven Paint and Clay Club
8 Gray's Farm Rd.
Weston, CT 06883
203.454.3859
wilklaura@gmail.com
www.laurawilk.com
Dragonfly Gallery, Martha's Vineyard

p15 *Purple-Hearted Peonies*

SCAN Award 2009, Society of Creative Arts of Newtown

CHRISTOPHER WYNN, VWS, BWS, WSA
10110 Hearthrock Ct.
Richmond, VA 23233
804.747.3446
christopherwynnart@yahoo.com
www.wynncreative.com

p80 *The Secret of Alleys*

DALE ZIEGLER, PWS, BWS, PWCS
660 Willow Valley Square, M-305
Lancaster, PA 17602
717.464.6887
fayendale2@yahoo.com

p23 *Nectar for Breakfast*, The collection of Nancy and Kendig Bare

INDEX

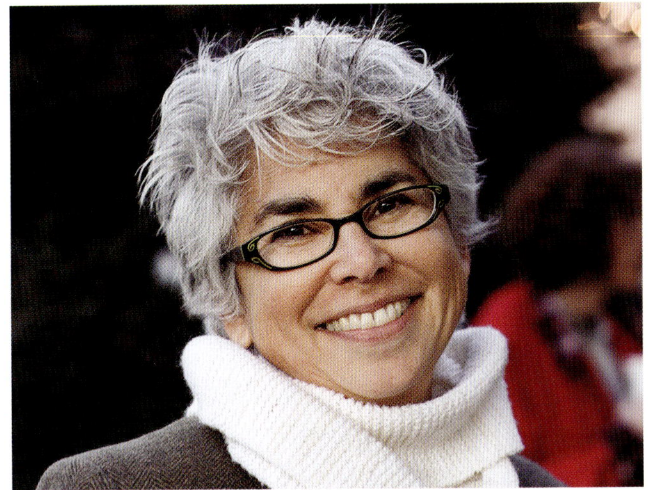

ABOUT THE AUTHOR

Rachel Rubin Wolf is a freelance editor and artist. She had edited and written many fine art books for North Light Books, including *Watercolor Secrets*; the *Splash: The Best of Watercolor* series; the *Strokes of Genius: Best of Drawing* series; *The Best of Wildlife Art* (editions 1 and 2); *The Best of Portrait Painting*; *Best of Flower Painting 2*; *The Acrylic Painter's Book of Styles and Techniques*; *Painting Ships, Shores and the Sea*; and *Painting the Many Moods of Light*. She also has acquired numerous fine art book projects for North Light Books and has contributed to magazines such as *Fine Art Connoisseur* and *Wildlife Art*.

ACKNOWLEDGMENTS

Much gratitude and credit goes to the editors, designers and staff at North Light Books who have done the detailed work needed to make this into a beautiful finished book, including Jamie Markle, Pam Wissman, Mark Griffin, Joie de Bostock and Marylyn Alexander. Special thanks to production editor Sarah Laichas and designer Wendy Dunning.

My gratitude, again, goes to all of the artists in this book who, with much generosity, shared with us their work and their thoughts. I am appreciative of the time (and money) spent in getting the properly formatted digital photos to us. And I thank you for your celebration of life that gives you your artistic vision.

 Published by North Light Books, an imprint of F+W Media, Inc., 4700 East Galbraith Road, Cincinnati, Ohio, 45236. (800) 289-0963. First Edition.

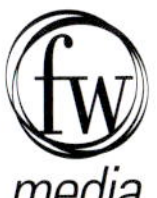

Other fine North Light Books are available from your favorite bookstore, art supply store or online supplier. Visit our website at www.fwmedia.com.

15 14 13 12 11 5 4 3 2

DISTRIBUTED IN CANADA BY FRASER DIRECT
100 Armstrong Avenue
Georgetown, ON, Canada L7G 5S4
Tel: (905) 877-4411

DISTRIBUTED IN THE U.K. AND EUROPE BY F&W INTERNATIONAL MEDIA
Brunel House, Newton Abbot, Devon, TQ12 4PU, England
Tel: (+44) 1626 323200, Fax: (+44) 1626 323319
Email: enquiries@fwmedia.com

DISTRIBUTED IN AUSTRALIA BY CAPRICORN LINK
P.O. Box 704, S. Windsor NSW, 2756 Australia
Tel: (02) 4577-3555

Edited by Sarah Laichas
Designed by Wendy Dunning
Production coordinated by Mark Griffin

Photo of Rachel Rubin Wolf by Don Lambert

Metric Conversion Chart

To convert	*to*	*multiply by*
Inches	Centimeters	2.54
Centimeters	Inches	0.4
Feet	Centimeters	30.5
Centimeters	Feet	0.03
Yards	Meters	0.9
Meters	Yards	1.1